FAITH AND PHILOSOPHY

FAITH
and
PHILOSOPHY

Philosophical Studies in Religion and Ethics

Edited by

ALVIN PLANTINGA

ASSOCIATE PROFESSOR OF PHILOSOPHY
WAYNE STATE UNIVERSITY

WILLIAM B. EERDMANS PUBLISHING COMPANY
GRAND RAPIDS, MICHIGAN

Foreword

THIS COLLECTION OF ESSAYS IS ISSUED BY HIS STUDENTS, FRIENDS, AND colleagues in honor of W. Harry Jellema, whose retirement this summer at the age of 70 closes a period of exceptional service to Calvin College, the Reformed community, and the cause of Christian philosophy.

What is here presented is no account of that service, but something issued in grateful recognition of it. What is offered is not a discourse on the esteem in which Professor Jellema is generally held, but a simple token of that esteem. The volume is not the payment of a debt, but the frank acknowledgment of a continuing indebtedness. It is hoped that what it offers will prove interesting and instructive to those who read it, but what it centrally intends is to celebrate the character and achievements of a man whom the essays scarcely mention but for whose scrutiny and satisfaction they were prepared, and to whom they are now respectifully and cordially presented.

William Harry Jellema, to whom these essays are dedicated, was born on March 10, 1893, in Chicago, Illinois, the son of Dirk and Gertrude (Dobben) Jellema. He was baptized in the First Roseland Christian Reformed Church and was enrolled at the age of 5 in the Roseland Christian School. In 1906, soon after his graduation from the four upper grades of the Van Vlissingen Public School, his family settled in Holland, Michigan, and in September of that year he entered the Calvin Preparatory School in Grand Rapids, where he pursued the four-year classical curriculum. Graduating in 1910, he immediately entered upon the three-year course of studies provided by the John Calvin Junior College. Finishing in 1914, after spending the academic year 1911-1912 teaching grades 6 and 7 in the Holland Christian School, he took the senior year of college work at the University of Michigan, from which he graduated with an A.B. degree in June 1915.

v

Having been introduced to philosophy by Professor Broene at Calvin and by Professor Wenley at Michigan, Harry Jellema entered the Graduate School of the University in September 1915 in order to pursue the subject which by now had captured his interest. Attaining his A.M. in June 1916, he enrolled as a candidate for the Ph.D. degree at the beginning of the following term. A year later, in the summer of 1917, Professor Wenley invited him to accept an Instructorship for the year 1917-18 involving responsibility for courses in the Introduction to Philosophy and in the Philosophy of Religion. The invitation was accepted, but the work was cut short by a call to the colors. Enlisting in the Officers' Training Course, first in the Medical Supply Service and then in the Field Artillery Corps where the prospect of front-line service seemed brighter, Jellema spent the spring, summer, and fall of 1918 in Camp Custer and Camp Taylor. The signing of the Armistice in November 1918 put an end to this military service, and from January 1919 to September of that year, while awaiting the reopening of school, Jellema found temporary employment in industry.

Resuming his studies at the University of Michigan in September 1919, he pursued philosophy under Wenley, Lloyd, Sellars, Vibbert, and Parker, and began the preparation of a dissertation on Josiah Royce. He had not gotten very far into his dissertation when, in the summer of 1920, he was invited to assume the chair of philosophy at Calvin College. After consultation with his mentors at Michigan, and in consideration of his love for Calvin and of the prospects opening up for the development of his emerging college, he accepted the appointment and began teaching at Calvin in September 1920. Being the only man in the department, Professor Broene having shifted to Psychology and Education, Jellema had to teach the whole range of courses and to work on his dissertation as well. He completed the latter during the summer of 1922, and was awarded the Ph.D. degree in Philosophy by the University of Michigan in October 1922.

It was at this auspicious juncture that he was married to Frances Peters, whom he had first come to know as a student of his in the 7th grade of the Holland Christian School, who had also been his student at Calvin College, who eventually bore him six children, and who, after being his faithful and affectionate wife for nearly forty years, died of the effects of a heart seizure in 1961.

Having previously applied to the Calvin authorities for a leave of absence for post-doctoral studies, Dr. Jellema and his bride left for Europe in November 1922. The winter semester was spent in Berlin, where Dr. Jellema attended lectures by Troeltsch, Dessoir, Harnack,

Wilamowitz, Mayer, Spranger, and others. Returning home after visiting various European centers, Jellema taught a summer course in Anglo-American Idealism at the University of Michigan, and in September 1923 resumed his teaching duties at Calvin.

For the next twelve years — until 1935 — Professor Jellema devoted himself to Calvin College. In the councils of the faculty, during this long decade, his voice was gladly heard, and in the classroom his teaching was eagerly absorbed. It is no denigration of the very considerable men who were his colleagues at this time to say that it was Jellema who exerted the dominant influence upon the school. His judgment, his graciousness, his scholarship, and his rare skillfulness in analysis and communication made him eminent in a faculty generally distinguished for excellence. During these years a continual stream of students were conducted by him into a deeper understanding of the Christian faith, and many of them were inspired to continue their studies and to pass into the ranks of the professional philosophers.

Professor Jellema was induced in 1935 to leave Calvin College and to accept a position in the department of philosophy at the University of Indiana. He became head of this department in 1939, and here, from 1940 to 1947, he was editor of the Powell Lecture Series on Philosophy. During this time he also spent a semester at Harvard University as Visiting Professor.

In 1947, after twelve years at Indiana, he was recalled to Calvin to join an expanding faculty and a growing college ministering to large classes of returning veterans. His return that year was greeted by the entire community, and the sixteen years of service that he has ably rendered since have enhanced the reputation and influence of the school which, even in his absence, never ceased to be the object of his affection and concern.

During the academic year 1961-1962 Professor Jellema was guest professor of philosophy at Haverford College. Now he will lay down his duties at Calvin. But he will not be idle. He has been asked by the new Grand Valley State College to help it get going in the right direction by assuming direction of its department of philosophy. This he has consented to do, and all his friends wish him well in this new undertaking.

To summarize the contributions of a man who has taught for forty-three years and has been intimately associated with one college for thirty-one of these is no easy matter, and I shall not make the attempt. Let it merely be said that Professor Jellema has placed an indelible stamp on Calvin College and upon the many students who, since leaving his classroom, have entered graduate school and from there have gone out to spread his influence on many campuses throughout the land.

Although Professor Jellema is not a prolific writer and has not published nearly as much as one could wish, he nevertheless lives and will live in his students. In this he resembles Socrates. Indeed, there is hardly anyone in the history of philosophy with whom he can better be compared than with the sage of Athens. Like Socrates, Professor Jellema is no system builder; but he is a teacher par excellence. He is an acute and stimulating thinker who, aware of the critical function of philosophy, knows how to ask the crucial questions. And he is a lover of the truth who, aware of the pedagogic function of philosophy, knows how to elicit mature and viable answers. He does not peddle ideas, nor does he merely commend them; he makes them alive and irresistible. He never indoctrinates, but he truly educates; and in the process he discloses truths that his students can appropriate as recognizably their own.

Most characteristic of him, however, is his firm stance within evangelical Christianity and his settled commitment to the Truth that is in Jesus Christ the Lord. Philosophy is for him a venture that takes place within the Kingdom, and the best philosopher is for him a trained and humble servant of the Gospel. Both philosophy and the philosopher, in his view, are there to deepen understanding and to delineate the perspectives of faith. The history of philosophy is for him the progressive articulation of competing faiths seeking appropriate understandings. These total diverging perspectives he deeply knows through a combination of disciplined scholarship and vital empathy, but it is only for one of them — the Christian — that he radically chooses, and into which he insinuates his students. He does this in ways appropriate to the philosopher, but he does it with power, enabling the student to understand from the inside both the thought-systems that as a Christian he is rejecting and the Christianity that as a thinker he is professing. It is for this that he is justly celebrated, not only as a teacher but as a Christian teacher, not only as a philosopher but as a Christian philosopher.

— HENRY STOB

Preface

THE FIRST TWO ESSAYS IN THIS COLLECTION ARE CONCERNED, BROAD-
ly, with aspects of the traditional question of the connection between
faith and reason, or between religion and philosophy. In "Faith and
Philosophy," Nicholas Wolterstorff points out that a philosophy is
usually (though not always) an elaboration and defense of a very
broad perspective or unified set of beliefs. A religious faith likewise
involves such a unified set of beliefs. Hence, philosophy and faith
stand in a complex and many-faceted relation permitting of various
degrees and kinds of conflict and accord. For almost any well-de-
veloped philosophy there are religious faiths with which it conflicts;
and for almost any religious faith there is a philosophy with which
it conflicts.

"Traditional Reason and Modern Reason" by Francis Parker contrasts the conception of reason dominant in the philosophical tradition with a widespread modern and contemporary estimate of the
function and limits of reason. Professor Parker concludes that this
modern view of reason is incoherent.

The next two essays concern certain questions about the nature
of God. Professor DeBoer, in "First Steps in Mysticism," begins by
outlining and contrasting the Platonic and Christian views of the
nature of the infinite and its relation to creatures. He then examines
and explains in detail the distinction between the finite and the
infinite as it occurs in the classic texts of mystical religion, the
Upanishads.

"Necessary Being," by Alvin Plantinga, is concerned with the
sense in which God can be said to be the *necessary being*. Arguing
that the proposition *God exists* is neither analytic nor logically necessary, Plantinga suggests that the assertion *God is the necessary being*

may be understood as the claim that some proposition referring to God is the *final* answer in a certain series of questions and answers.

The last five essays discuss, again broadly, certain questions concerning philosophcal ethics and its relations to Christianity. In "The Ethics of Jonathan Edwards," Henry Stob begins by giving a brief account of Edwards' general philosophy and its sources. Professor Stob then explains the ethical views of the great Puritan philosopher, paying particular attention to his unusual views regarding the relevance of the doctrine of the Trinity to ethics.

"For a Renewal of an Old Departure in Ethics," by Henry Veatch, points out that according to much contemporary ethical theory, ethics (as opposed to meta-ethics) is not the philosopher's proper concern. Professor Veatch then maintains that this contemporary dogma rests upon a pair of doctrines: relativism, and the view (associated with the naturalistic fallacy argument) according to which goodness is not identical with any natural property. Veatch subjects these doctrines to close scrutiny, arguing that neither is tenable and that, accordingly, we have no reason for rejecting a philosophical examination of normative ethical questions.

Dewey Hoitenga, Jr., in "Motives and Obligations," considers the opposition, in contemporary moral philosophy, between those who believe that someone is under moral obligation to perform a given action only if he has a motive for performing it and those who deny that motivation is a necessary condition of obligation. He then shows that this opposition appears in theological writings on Christian Ethics and suggests a way of resolving it.

"A Restricted Motive Theory of Ethics," by Fred Brouwer, is a development of a motive theory of ethics. Professor Brouwer develops the theory by comparing and contrasting it with Utilitarianism and Deontologism in their various forms and by availing himself of a distinction similar to that between traditional Utilitarianism and Rule Utilitarianism. He then defends the theory against various objections and asks how one is to choose between it and its rivals.

In "Love and Principle in Christian Ethics," Professor William Frankena points out certain illuminating parallels between issues arising in Christian ethical theory and issues which are under intensive discussion by contemporary philosophers. Arguing that Christian theologians could profit from the work of these philosophers, Frankena carefully and thoroughly outlines a variety of possible positions in Christian ethics and discusses the question how a Christian can decide which of these positions he ought to accept.

—ALVIN PLANTINGA

Contents

1

Faith and Philosophy

NICHOLAS P. WOLTERSTORFF, Associate Professor of Philosophy, Calvin College. A.B., Calvin College; A.M., Ph.D., Harvard University. Articles in *Philosophical Review, Philosophical Quarterly, Journal of Philosophy, Philosophical Studies*.

Faith and Philosophy

BY NICHOLAS P. WOLTERSTORFF

SOCRATES ASKS CEPHALUS, "WHAT IS JUSTICE?"

Cephalus replies, "Telling the truth and keeping your promises."

"But that does not seem right," says Socrates. "Suppose you have borrowed a weapon and promised to return it at a certain time, but in the meanwhile the lender goes mad. Would giving back the weapon be the just thing to do?"

"No, I suppose it would not," says Cephalus.

"Well, it seems to me," says Polemarchus, "that justice is helping your friends and harming your enemies."

"Fine," says Socrates; "but what do you mean, 'friend'? Suppose a man seems to be concerned over your welfare but really is not. Is he a friend?"

"No, I think I would say that he is not," says Polemarchus.

I

On the face of it, philosophy is a hodge-podge, a *Gemisch* of the most diverse utterances. No philosopher is willing, however, to conclude that this is what it really is. We all try to spy some order, some pattern, beneath its surface disarray. We look for a model, clearly structured, of such a sort that we can say: Philosophy is *really*, though perhaps not apparently, like this model. Is not the discussion above as good a model as any? Can we not see in this microcosm the macrocosm of philosophy? All the essential features seem to be present: A problem is posed; an answer to the problem is offered;

3

when necessary the answer is clarified so that we know exactly what is being said; then the answer is held up to the facts[1] to see whether or not it is correct. A question asked; a thesis proposed; the meaning clarified; and then confirmed or disconfirmed. Our goal in philosophy is truth: We are to accept what a philosopher has said on the basis of whether he has spoken truthfully or not. To speak truthfully is to report the facts correctly.

Have any, or very many, philosophers really seen this sort of pattern in philosophy?

Dominant in the consciousness of every philosopher since the Middle Ages is the fact that philosophers have made no progress in reaching agreement. Bacon says, "Observe also, that if [philosophy and the intellectual sciences] had any life in them, that could never have come to pass which has been the case now for many ages — that they stand almost at a stay, without receiving any augmentations worthy of the human race; insomuch that many times not only what was asserted once is asserted still, but what was a question once is a question still, and instead of being resolved by discussion is only fixed and fed. . . ."[2] Descartes says, "I shall not say anything about Philosophy but that . . . it has been cultivated for many centuries by the best minds that have ever lived, and that nevertheless no single thing is to be found in it that is not subject of dispute, and consequently dubious. . . ."[3] Kant says, "Whether then we demonstrate our knowledge or our ignorance [in metaphysics], we must come once for all to a definite conclusion respecting the nature of this so-called science, which cannot possibly remain on its present footing. It seems almost ridiculous, while every other science is continually advancing, that in this, which pretends to be wisdom incarnate, for whose oracle everyone inquires, we should constantly move round the same spot, without gaining a single step."[4] And G. E. Moore says, "It appears to me that in Ethics, as in all other philosophical studies, the difficulties and disagreements, of which its history is full, are mainly due to a very simple cause: namely to the attempt to answer questions, without first discovering precisely *what* question it is which you desire to answer."[5]

---

[1] In what follows, I shall use "fact" in a sense which allows us to say that it is a fact that p entails q, when (it is true that) p entails q.

[2] *The Great Instauration*, Preface.

[3] *Discourse on Method*, translated by E. S. Haldane and G. R. T. Ross in *The Philosophical Works of Descartes* (Cambridge, 1911), Part I.

[4] *Prolegomena to Any Future Metaphysics*, translated by L. W. Beck (New York, 1950), Introduction.

[5] *Principia Ethica* (Cambridge, 1903), Introduction.

Philosophy is ill, these men are saying. Generation after generation the same old questions are raised, but none of them are ever answered. Round and round go philosophers in the same old tracks and never do they get anywhere.

What must we conclude from this? Why is it that in philosophy "things stand almost at a stay"? Why is philosophy not cumulative? Why can one philosopher not pick up where another has left off? Is it perhaps that this is the fate of mortals — doomed always to search and never to find? Or is it perhaps that our minds are feeble, or clouded, or that Reality is too much for us?

Certainly none of the modern philosophers ever thought so. Since the rise of our modern era we have seen ever more vividly that in mathematics and natural science disputes *are* settled and progress *is* achieved. Why then should we despair? In science and mathematics we have a glimpse of the promised land, perhaps even a guide to it. Bacon continues by saying, "In the mechanical arts we do not find it so: they, on the contrary, as having in them some breath of life, are continually growing and becoming more perfect. . . ." And Descartes prefaced the remarks quoted above by saying, "Most of all was I delighted with Mathematics because of the certainty of its demonstrations and the evidence of its reasoning; but I did not yet understand its true use. . . ."

What *then* is the source of those fundamental disputes of which philosophy is so full? The source, say the modern philosophers, is a mistaken method, or some crucial mistaken assumption. Science and mathematics have found their correct method, philosophy has not. Method for what? For seeing the facts aright, for getting at the truth. Men purge their lives of disagreements in many ways: by threats, by persuasion, by appeal to authority. But the great modern philosophers are all apostles and ministers of reason, so these techniques are not available to them. It is their conviction that philosophical disputes can be settled by a calm objective appeal to the facts. Our difficulties arise from not approaching the facts aright, from somewhere making crucial and mistaken assumptions and thereby coloring the whole landscape. What is necessary, then, is not a more industrious attack along the same lines as heretofore, but the removal of the faulty spectacles. What is needed is a new approach for philosophy, and once this new approach is found and adopted, philosophical disputes will be settled in the same way scientific disputes are settled — by objective appeals to the facts. Philosophers have spun theories and invented hypotheses; but in doing so they have been beating air. For there have been no agreed criteria for accepting or rejecting what a philosopher says. The right approach will finally enable the philosopher, like the scientist and the mathematician, to get at the facts. Philosophy needs a Newton.

From our own historical standpoint the irony of this persistent belief is that each of the great modern philosophers thought that the correct philosophical approach had already been discovered — by himself. Moritz Schlick might well have been speaking for all of them rather than for himself alone when he says, "I refer to this anarchy of philosophical opinions which has so often been described, in order to leave no doubt that I am fully conscious of the scope and weighty significance of the conviction that I should now like to express. For I am convinced that we now find ourselves at an altogether decisive turning point in philosophy, that we are objectively justified in considering that an end has come to the fruitless conflict of systems. We are already at the present time, in my opinion, in possession of methods which make every such conflict in principle unnecessary. What is now required is their resolute application."[6] Schlick's logical positivism is already not the last so-called "revolution" in philosophy.

Why, though, should philosophers have supposed that the discovery of a new approach would *settle* disputes? Why not rather suppose that it would give new opportunities for disagreement, as in fact it has always done? Granted that a philosophical approach is, in part at least, a method for reaching agreement. Why should other philosophers accept the approach?

To raise this question is to see what *must* be its answer: Behind the confidence of modern philosophers lies the assumption that the acceptance of the new approach is itself to be secured simply by a confrontation with the facts. Fundamental to the positivist conception of philosophy, for example, are certain views concerning knowledge and meaning. These views lead to the result that, according to the positivist, a genuine philosophical question — that is, a question which is at once meaningful and truly philosophical — must be answered by investigating the logical structure of the language of science. Once a person accepts this whole approach, then he has indeed a definite method for settling philosophical disputes. The fact that it may be difficult to decide whether a certain proposition does or does not entail a certain other proposition is nothing against the method; disputes on such matters are no longer *fundamental* dis-

---

[6] "The Turning Point in Philosophy," in *Logical Positivism*, edited by A. J. Ayer, (Glencoe, Illinois, 1959).

putes. Schlick's confidence that this approach is in principle capable of settling all philosophical disputes surely rests, then, on his belief that any man of reason will acknowledge that this is the correct approach. The basic conviction of the modern philosopher is that previous methods and assumptions can be shown to be unacceptable by the clinching counter-example and the inescapable distinction.

We might have reached this same conclusion by showing that the modern philosophers have all wanted to make philosophy scientific, and then discussing their conception of science.

Thus the model of philosophy which lies behind most of modern philosophy is this: The philosopher is confronted with certain problems. In answering the problems he makes certain claims concerning the facts, and perhaps cites what he regards as evidence or proof for his claims. But almost invariably fundamental mistakes are made in his formulation. And we can show to any man willing to use his unbiased reason that mistakes have been made, by citing counter-examples which cannot reasonably be denied and by making distinctions and clarifications which cannot reasonably be avoided.

Suppose now that this view of the philosopher as a man who makes and tries to establish claims concerning certain facts, or certain sorts of claims concerning all the facts, is accepted. What then could faith have to do with philosophy, and what could philosophy have to do with faith?

What we might expect is that philosophy and faith would now and then conflict. But surely in all such cases faith must be the loser! The philosopher is the avenging angel of the land of Truth, Reason, Objectivity, Fact. What mortal, if he could, would dare strike swords with him? Only a madman, out of his mind — an Irrationalist: Tertullian, Kierkegaard. Or Abraham, who, about to kill childless Isaac, believed that Isaac would be the father of a star-like host. But could there be an Abraham?

The philosopher had better take steps then to see that no irrational bias influence his work. He had better see to it that, if he has faith at all, it be the faith of a rational man. "Whatever God hath revealed is certainly true; no doubt can be made of it. This is the proper object of faith: but whether it be a divine revelation or not, reason must judge; which can never permit the mind to reject a greater evidence to embrace what is less evident, nor allow it to entertain probability in opposition to knowledge and certainty. . . . And therefore *nothing that is contrary to, and inconsistent with, the clear and self-evident dictates of reason, has a right to be urged or assented to, as a matter of faith, wherein reason hath nothing to do.*"[7]

The man of faith, for his part, had better see to it that faith nowhere tries competing with philosophy.

Perhaps philosophy and faith are related like the stories of a house, philosophy on the ground floor and faith on the top. Philosophy deals, in principle, with all the propositions available to "natural man," propositions whose truth or falsity can be ascertained by the careful and unflagging exercise of "unaided human reason." Faith deals with those propositions whose truth or falsity cannot be ascertained by reason but must be accepted on trust, propositions for which neither demonstrative nor probable reasons can be given. On this view, philosophy and faith both make claims concerning facts, but different sorts of facts.

Or perhaps philosophy along with the sciences is capable of dealing with all the facts. Faith must then comprise some non-cognitive segment of man's life. On one version, a man's faith is his ultimate concern, or the whole pattern of his values and concerns — what he thinks worth striving, fighting, and dying for, what he admires and emulates, what he despises, what he chooses to do and think and feel. On another version, a man's faith is his outlook on life as a whole, the whole armor of attitudes and emotions with which he surrounds himself, his fears, his hopes and aspirations, his stance towards death, towards suffering and war, his feelings of guilt and awe and mystery.

It needs no saying that all these possibilities and others besides have already been canvassed in the long history of philosophy; there is no point in elaborating them here beyond the mere hints I have given. What may be noted, however, is that they all have this important feature in common: in one way or another they claim that there is or ought to be a barrier between the realm of philosophy and the realm of faith which prevents any crossing, and especially prevents a man's faith from interfering with his pursuit of philosophy and with his attempt to solve the philosophical problems. Objectivity is assured for philosophy and face is saved for faith by allowing no interaction.

In what follows I want to discuss some aspects of the relation between faith and philosophy. And especially I want to discuss this view that philosophy makes objective appeals to the facts; and that whatever else faith does, it cannot hope to compete with philosophy, at the cost of irrationality. I shall take note first of certain

[7] John Locke, *An Essay Concerning Human Understanding*, IV, xviii, 10.

relevant features of philosophy, and then of certain relevant features of faith.

II

Philosophers spend a great deal of time composing, reformulating, and criticizing arguments. True, arguments do not always enjoy and have not always enjoyed the same status among philosophers. Sometimes philosophers come close to identifying philosophy with philosophical arguments, whereas at other times the role of arguments in philosophy is very much subordinate to that of insight, vision, scope, etc. But philosophy is never wholly devoid of arguments; it is never merely an outpouring of "this I believe" utterances. An insight into the working of philosophical arguments is thus an insight into the nature of a large component of philosophy. But we have a right to expect more than this from a study of philosophical arguments. Often when we are puzzled to know what sort of claim a man is making, it helps to know the arguments and reasons, if any, that he would give for making the claim. There is every reason to suppose that the same is true for philosophy, and that an insight into philosophical arguments will hence serve in large measure to illuminate the rest of philosophy.

We may begin by asking why it is that, in spite of all their arguments, philosophers disagree. The obvious answer is that so few, if any, philosophical arguments are proofs — strict, rigorous, deductive proofs; or even inductive proofs. Of course, many philosophers have *claimed* to give strict proofs, but that is another matter; for a philosophical argument which is absolutely conclusive in one man's eyes often has no force whatsoever in another's. But to say that philosophical arguments are not conclusive is not to say much. *Why* are they not conclusive?

Philosophical arguments come in too many different sorts to make it worthwhile trying to say something informative about all of them at once. What I shall do instead, then, is consider only one sort of argument; namely, the counter-example argument. I choose this partly because it is a very common sort of argument in philosophy but also because it seems especially relevant to the view of philosophy outlined above. The prevalence of counter-example arguments in philosophy seems in large measure responsible for the view that the philosopher is a man who makes very special sorts of claims concerning the facts, or claims concerning very special sorts of facts.

When do philosophers cite counter-examples? One circumstance in which they do so, it seems obvious, is when someone has made a generalization to the effect that all x's are P, and someone else finds or thinks he finds an x which is not P. Some philosophers have indicated that they believe this sort of argument to constitute a large part of philosophy. They have spoken of appealing to the evidence, of finding the evidence decisive or indecisive for or against a certain view; and they have accused other philosophers of overlooking and ignoring certain facts: Whitehead held that Hume overlooked the "connectedness" of our experience, phenomenologists typically accuse analytic philosophers of overlooking the richness and variety and complexity of human experience, and Hume claimed that prior philosophers had overlooked the fact that the negation of a causal proposition is never self-contradictory. Now if this sort of argument did indeed play a significant role in philosophy, one would certainly be justified in emphasizing the alliance of philosophy to science. I think it is very difficult, however, to find any examples which are clearly and unambiguously of this sort.

As promising an example as any perhaps is Hume's claim that we cannot imagine a certain shade of color unless first we have seen the color, and his own counter-claim that we probably could imagine a certain shade of blue without ever having seen it, if all the blues but this were arrayed in front of us. Now it should be noted at once that if this is a generalization at all, it is so in a very special sense. Hume is not claiming that we never *do* imagine without first seeing, but that we *cannot* imagine without first seeing. He is not presenting a hypothesis concerning how things are, but rather a claim concerning how things can and cannot be. I think that the vast majority of philosophical "generalizations" turn out similarly on close scrutiny to be claims concerning what can and cannot be. That this raises difficulties in the way of accepting the view of philosophy suggested above will be argued later.

It should be admitted at once, though, that from the fact that a man makes a claim concerning what can and cannot be, it does not follow that there is no objective way of determining whether his claim is correct or not. For such claims, too, we sometimes have agreed criteria for determining whether they are true or false. And does not Hume show that this one is false by citing his counter-example? The claim that there *are* no black swans, and the claim that there *cannot be* any black swans, may both be refuted by pointing to a black swan. And is not this latter analogous to what Hume is doing? We are still in the land of Fact.

Instead of investigating this view directly, let us consider another example, namely, the frequent claim of philosophers that no one can know whether anything "outside" himself exists. It would seem that there are a great many obvious counter-examples to this claim; for instance, don't I know that I have hands, legs, a head, etc., all of them things "outside" myself? Indeed, an important element in the common sense views of all normal human beings is that we know that we have hands, legs, a head, etc.; and a philosopher who claims that none of us knows any of these things is making a simple though at the same time rather incredible mistake.

But the sceptic might refuse to admit that any real counter-examples to his claim have been cited. On what grounds might he refuse to do so? For one thing, he might dispute the truth of the premise. He might claim that the ordinary man does not really hold that he knows that he has hands, legs, a head, etc. He might claim, with some plausibility, that once we make clear to the ordinary man what is at stake, by asking him whether it has never happened that he thought some physical thing existed when later it became clear that it did not, the ordinary man might no longer be so willing, or even be at all willing, to hold that we *know* we have hands. Instead he might agree that to speak thus is to speak loosely, and that at most what we do is *believe* that we have hands, legs, a head, etc. *Does* the ordinary man hold that he knows that he has hands? How do we tell?

On the other hand, instead of disputing the premise the philosopher might rather question the connection between the premise and the conclusion by saying that he does not see that the views of the ordinary man have anything to do with the matter. Then the argument will have taken a wholly new turn. What was at first a simple question concerning the truth of someone's defense of the claim to have found a counter-example has turned into a question concerning the *relevance* of that defense. Our philosopher does not see why he has to, or should, accept the conclusion once he has accepted the premise. How can we show him that he should, or must? How can we show him that this argument based on an appeal to common sense is relevant to the philosophical issue at stake?[8] Since the diffi-

---

8 "It is indeed a great gift of God to possess right or (as they now call it) plain common sense. But this common sense must be shown in action by well-considered and reasonable thoughts and words, not by appealing to it as an oracle when no rational justification for one's position can be advanced. To appeal to common sense when insight and science fail, and no sooner — this is one of the subtle discoveries of modern times, by means of which the most superficial ranter can safely enter the lists with the most thorough thinker and hold his own. But as long as a particle of insight remains, no one would think of having recourse

culty is not that our philosopher fails to see the validity of a formally valid argument, it seems that what we must do is find some additional premise, such that he would be willing (forced) to accept it, and such that if he accepted both premises he would (would have to) accept the conclusion. I wish to postpone for a while the question of whether such additional premises are available in philosophy. But whether they are or are not, there have certainly been many philosophers who regarded arguments based on an appeal to common sense as relevant to (at least some) philosophical disputes; and for some such philosophers the counter-example argument suggested has been regarded as decisive.

We can now look back and ask why the counter-example in the Hume case looked so uncomplicated. I think the answer is that if we *do* regard it as uncomplicated, we are in effect regarding it as a scientific matter, to be settled by an empirical psychological investigation. But is it clear that this is what it really is? And if it really is this, does it strictly belong to philosophy?

Another circumstance in which a philosopher may offer a counter-example is in answer to a proposed definition. Consider, for instance, the selection from the *Republic* which is paraphrased at the beginning of this paper. Cephalus is not offering a generalization or hypothesis concerning just actions, but rather a *definition* of "justice." And defining is very different from generalizing. For one thing, in defining we do not simply say how things are, but rather, in a special sense, how they can and cannot be. Now this might be admitted; and again it might be claimed that there are nevertheless objective standards for the correctness or incorrectness of definitions, and hence that there are decisive or at least reasonably convincing counter-examples which can in principle be brought against any mistaken definition. To this extent philosophy can here, too, touch the bedrock of facts.

The fact that Socrates' counter-example works, as it does, depends on the willingness of Cephalus to regard the case Socrates imagines as not a case of justice. It seems quite possible, however, for someone to refuse to grant this and to insist that it is never right to break promises. What might be said then is that this sort of response would introduce a new factor into the discussion; it would change it, in effect, from a philosophical into a moral discussion; it

---

to this subterfuge. Seen clearly, it is but an appeal to the opinion of the multitude, of whose applause the philosopher is ashamed, while the popular charlatan glories and boasts in it." Kant, *op. cit.,* Introduction.

would be a counter-example to a proposed moral law and not to a proposed definition.

How can this be shown? How can it be shown that when one man says it is always wrong to break one's promises, and another that sometimes it is not, that then they are disagreeing on the acceptibility of a certain moral law and not on the meaning of the word "wrong"? How does one show when a definition is at stake in a certain disagreement and when something else?

Instead of elaborating these difficulties let us evade them by taking a different sort of definition. Consider Plato's definition of "art" as *representation of physical reality*. Suppose that I present Plato with a late non-representational work of Mondrian, and claim that Plato's definition is mistaken, since this is a work of art. What now could Plato say? One thing he could say is that this work too really does represent something physical — lines, colors, planes, etc. Another thing he could do is insist that this is not a work of art. Suppose he does the latter. What then could I say in response? What I might say, in defense of my claim that this *is* a work of art, is that as the English language is now used it is quite proper to call Mondrian's paintings "art"; if Plato then wishes to say it is not a work of art, he must be using the word "art" in an unusual sense. Plato then could either dispute my claim that it is proper to call such a painting a "work of art," or he could say that the ordinary use of words has nothing to do with the philosophical issue at stake. And if he held the latter, then again we would have a case in which a philosopher admits the truth of the premise in a philosophical argument and questions its relevance to the conclusion.[9] The premise made an appeal to the ordinary use of language, and the conclusion drawn was that a certain definition was mistaken. But to make the

---

[9] "What, then, is good? How is good to be defined? Now, it may be thought that this is a verbal question. A definition does indeed often mean the expressing of one word's meaning in other words. But this is not the sort of definition I am asking for. Such a definition can never be of ultimate importance in any study except lexicography. If I wanted that kind of definition I should have to consider in the first place how people generally used the word 'good'; but my business is not with its proper usage, as established by custom. I should, indeed, be foolish, if I tried to use it for something which it did not usually denote: if, for instance, I were to announce that, whenever I used the word 'good,' I must be understood to be thinking of that object which is usually denoted by the word 'table.' I shall, therefore, use the word in the sense in which I think it is ordinarily used; but at the same time I am not anxious to discuss whether I am right in thinking that it is so used. My business is solely with that object or idea, which I hold, rightly or wrongly, that the word is generally used to stand for." G. E. Moore, *op. cit.*, Section 8.

argument sound and convincing it seems that we shall have to sup-
plement the premise offered with certain propositions concerning
meaning, definitions, concepts, etc.

A third situation in which a philosopher may offer a counter-
example is in answer to a claimed implication. To claim that p entails q is to claim that if p, then necessarily also q; or, in other words,
that if p is true it cannot also happen that q is false. It is clear at a
glance that this, too, is not a hypothesis concerning what is the case,
but rather a claim concerning what, in a certain sense, can and cannot be. Again, though, this is not to impugn the "objectivity" of
the claim; so let us consider the structure of the counter-example.
The claim can be refuted by finding a case in which p is true and q
false. And is this not a simple direct matter? Not at all. Can one
have a toothache and not know it? Can a man know how to tell
one cat from two cats and not know what the number one is? Could
it be that God does not exist? Can a man err knowingly? Where
are the premises which will lead to agreement on these issues? Suppose we ask whether it can *clearly and distinctly* be conceived that
God does not exist. Then obviously we can have disagreement on
whether it can or cannot be distinctly conceived; and we can also
have disagreement on the relevance of such considerations to the
issue.

We have considered three typical cases in which philosophers
offer counter-examples. What is the upshot of our discussion? For
one thing, we found that in most cases the claim against which the
counter-example is offered is not a claim concerning what is or
is not the case, but is rather a claim concerning what can or cannot
be the case. Furthermore, we found that the arguments were indecisive for two reasons. In the first place, we found that the truth
of the premises could frequently if not always be brought into question. And secondly, we found that even if the philosopher accepted
the premise offered, he could still question the relevance of the premise to the conclusion and insist that he did not see why, if he accepted
the premise, he should or must also accept the conclusion. Thus the
question arose of whether, in principle at least, such arguments could
be completed by adding premises, premises of a very general sort,
concerning definitions, the relevance of common sense beliefs to
philosophical arguments, etc.

Considerations concerning what can and cannot be the case turn
out to be crucial in philosophy — a point first made in detail by Kant.
We have seen why it is that arguments against such claims are often
indecisive; let us now see why it is that arguments *for* such claims are

equally indecisive. Where is solid ground? Can it be said that philosophers make objective appeals to the facts, when they agree neither on which facts support their claims nor on which refute them?

Near the beginning of *The Blue Book*, Wittgenstein says, "The difference between the grammars of 'reason' and 'cause' is quite similar to that between the grammars of 'motive' and 'cause.' Of the cause one can say that one can't *know* it but can only *conjecture* it. On the other hand one often says: 'Surely *I* must know why I did it,' talking of the *motive*. When I say: 'We can only *conjecture* the cause but we *know* the motive,' this statement will be seen later on to be a grammatical one. The 'can' refers to a *logical* possibility."[10]

Here we have a claim concerning what can and cannot be: We cannot know the cause of an action but can only conjecture it. Wittgenstein hints that his ground for saying this has something to do with grammar and logic. It has nothing to do, let us say, with certain observations he has made concerning human frailty. The question we want answered can now be anticipated: Supposing that Wittgenstein's grammatical observations are correct, how will he show the relevance of these grammatical observations to his conclusion concerning what can and cannot be done? How will he show us that the word "can" here bears a logical or grammatical, and not a physical, sense?

Wittgenstein says that later we will *see* his point to have been correct. He does not specifically say what later passage he has in mind, but probably it is this:

> What we did in these discussions was what we always do when we meet the word "can" in a metaphysical proposition. We show that this proposition hides a grammatical rule. That is to say, we destroy the outward similarity between a metaphysical proposition and an experiential one, and we try to find the form of expression which fulfils a certain craving of the metaphysician which our ordinary language does not fulfil and which, as long as it isn't fulfilled, produces the metaphysical puzzlement. . . . When we say "I can't feel his pain," the idea of an insurmountable barrier suggests itself to us. Let us think straight away of a similar case: "The colours green and blue can't be in the same place simultaneously." Here the picture of physical impossibility which suggests itself is, perhaps, not that of a barrier; rather we feel that the two colours are in each other's way. What is the origin of this idea? — We say three people can't sit side by side on this bench; they have no room. Now the case of the colours is not analogous to this; but it is somewhat analogous to saying: "3 x 18 inches won't go into 3 feet." This is a grammatical rule and

---

10 *The Blue and the Brown Books*, (Oxford, 1958), p. 15.

states a logical impossibility. The proposition "three men can't sit side by side on a bench a yard long" states a physical impossibility; and this example shows clearly why the two impossibilities are confused.[11]

We want to know why the colors green and blue *cannot* be in the same place simultaneously. What sort of a claim is being made when someone says this? Wittgenstein holds that it is the logical grammar of our words which makes the claim true. To get us to accept this view he mentions two other propositions, "3 x 18 inches won't go into three feet" and "three men can't sit side by side on a bench a yard long"; and then he says: Now don't you *see* that the business about colors is like the former case and not like the latter? and don't you see that the former "is a grammatical rule and states a logical impossibility"? *No premises!*

Philosophers do not agree on how a philosophical proposition concerning what can and cannot be is to be supported. They do not agree on the *sense* of these words. Where must we look, then, for an objective appeal?

Wittgenstein's procedure in general corresponds to the pattern above. In another place he says, "If we scrutinize the usages which we make of such words as 'thinking,' 'meaning,' 'wishing,' etc., going through this process rids us of the temptation to look for a peculiar act of thinking, independent of the act of expressing our thought, and stowed away in some peculiar medium."[12] Wittgenstein indicates here that he is opposed to certain views of thinking, meaning, wishing, etc. The way that we can see they are mistaken, he says, is not by introspecting more carefully than we have ever done before, and not by attaching electrodes to the brain or to the muscles, but by scrutinizing the usages we make of words. But he nowhere tries to persuade us that this is the correct technique by giving us premises which are probably or self-evidently true. He just tries to get us to *see* it.

What is true in Wittgenstein's case is true in others as well. If we look to Moore for solid and complete arguments in favor of his view that common sense beliefs are often a relevant appeal in philosophy, we find nothing. If we look to Descartes for solid and convincing arguments in favor of his view that the relative clarity and distinctness of an idea is often or always a relevant appeal in philosophy, we find nothing. And so also for Hume, Kant, Schlick, *et al.*

---

11 *Op. cit.,* pp. 55-56.
12 *Op. cit.,* p. 43.

Why is this? Why this gap between the premises philosophers offer and the conclusions they draw?

One possibility is this: Philosophers are grossly negligent, careless, and incompetent. No doubt they are. But always? This is incredible.

A more attractice possibility is that philosophers fail to state clearly and exactly what it is that they are claiming. Wittgenstein holds that we cannot know the cause of our actions. His reason for saying this is that if someone did speak of knowing the cause of his actions, he would be misusing the word "cause" or "know." Now someone might hold that our feeling that there is a gap here between the premise offered and the conclusion drawn is wholly due to the vagueness of the original claim: "We cannot know the cause of our actions." Suppose instead we said, from the beginning: "To speak of knowing the cause of one's actions is to use the word 'know' (or, 'cause') incorrectly." Then our feeling that there was a gap, is seen to be illusory; for we have an objective claim, to be verified or falsified by looking to see how in fact the language *is* properly used.

I think this view, attractive as it has proved, is unsatisfactory on two counts. In the first place, I think philosophers would in general refuse to make this sort of translation. Wittgenstein *wants* the conclusion from his grammatical survey to be that we cannot know the cause of our actions. And Moore *wants* the conclusion from his survey of common sense beliefs to be, not that ordinary men believe, or say, they know that they have hands, but that they *know* they have hands. The nominalist who tries to translate statements about universals into statements about particulars, holds that in answering the question, "Can statements about universals be translated into statements about particulars," he is answering the question (or a question close to the question), "Are there universals?" This is how this question *really must be answered*, he wants to say. Philosophical problems are expressions of unease. The philosopher tries to soothe that unease, not ignore it.

Also, what is clarity? Surely it is more than a stylistic matter. But the history of analytic philosophy is the history of the building and wrecking of various formulations of philosophical clarity. Why can philosophers not agree on what constitutes clarity? It is obvious that to pursue the answer to this question would be to retrace steps we have already taken. What is the meaning of a word?

So why the gap between premise offered and conclusion drawn?

Does heat ever cause water to boil? Most of us would hold that it does. We have often put kettles with water on fires, and, after waiting a bit, have seen the water begin to boil. What better evidence could one want? George Berkeley denied, however, that heat is ever the cause of water boiling. Did he discover, or think he had discovered, some subtle new factor, closely associated with heat, which is the real cause of liquids boiling? Not at all. Berkeley held that no matter how much evidence we might gather concerning regular sequences of heat applied and water boiling, this would make it neither certain nor probable that heat causes water to boil. It would have nothing to do with the issue. For Berkeley holds that it is incoherent to suppose that an impersonal thing like heat could cause water to boil. What Berkeley is doing then is dismissing our ordinary ways of finding out the answer to the question "What makes water boil?" and insisting that by following such procedures we will never find the answer. This is quite a different thing from accepting the ordinary procedure, and denying that the evidence is sufficient to justify the usual conclusion.

Many similar disputes can be found in the history of thought. Ernst Mach, for example, denied that there were atoms. And his ground for doing so was not that he thought the evidence still insufficient, nor that he had some shreds of counter-evidence and wished for the time being to suspend his belief, but rather that he thought no evidence of the sort that scientists customarily assemble in favor of the conclusion that there are atoms, had anything to do with the issue. Again, many philosophers and psychologists have disputed Freud's conclusion that there is a human subconscious, not on the ground that Freud's evidence was insufficient to warrant so radical a conclusion, nor that there was a certain amount of counter-evidence of which Freud took insufficient notice, but rather on the ground that no evidence of the sort Freud assembled either entailed or made likely the conclusion that there is a human subconscious. Or again, if a neurologist contended that thought was such and such a brain wave, one might disagree either on the ground that really it was a different sort of brain wave, or on the ground that propositions concerning brain waves have nothing to do with propositions concerning the nature of thought. And the same, *mutatis mutandis*, for the denial of the existence of external objects, or of other minds.

I suggest that many basic philosophical disagreements, perhaps most, should be interpreted in the light of these examples.

Sometimes a philosopher takes a question for which there is a widely accepted procedure or method for determining the answer, and disputes the acceptability of that procedure or method. This is what Berkeley did for all questions concerning the cause of physical events, what Mach did for all questions concerning microscopic particles, what Wittgenstein did for all questions concerning mental processes. The philosopher tries to show us a chasm where previously we saw nothing but solid ground. Sometimes, on the other hand, a philosopher discovers or comes across a question for which there is no agreed procedure or method for determining the answer. Examples of such are Augustine's question, "How can time be measured?" Kant's question, "How is pure geometry possible?" and the question of every man, "Why is there anything at all?" Such questions are peculiarly philosophic questions. For them, the philosopher tries to get us to accept a certain procedure or method for answering the question; only when that has been done can there be any thought of deciding what *is* the answer. In this case he tries to show us solid ground where previously we saw only empty space.

Of course, philosophers do not typically try to persuade us, by any non-violent means whatsoever, to accept a certain procedure. Rather, they try to get us to "see" that a certain procedure is the *correct* one and that a certain other procedure is *incorrect;* and consequently that there is a definitely correct answer to the question. But enough has been said to make us wary here. If we ask the philosopher why a certain procedure is the correct procedure, and why a certain answer is the correct answer, all the same questions can be asked about his response to us: Why must we accept his premise? And why, if we accept his premise, must we also accept his conclusion? If there are no conclusive arguments in philosophy, there are none here either. "Seeing" that a certain method is the correct one is more like being converted than like following a proof.

And now it is time to say something about those premises — not the premises we have been looking for, but the ones we had or thought we had all along. If it cannot be *shown* that Berkeley is wrong, then is it a *fact* that heat causes water to boil? And if a philosopher should sometime use "Heat causes water to boil" as a premise in an argument, is he then reporting a *fact?* And is it a *fact* that we cannot properly speak of knowing the causes of our actions? Whatever our procedure for determining the proper use of a word, cannot someone question the acceptability of that procedure? And then what has happened to the fact? A method is a method for determining the facts, for deciding whether an utterance is true or false. But if we cannot prove the correctness of the method, will the method lead us to the facts? Will *every* method lead us to the facts if we but follow it? Where *are* the facts? The ground opens before and beneath us. How can there be bias in philosophy when there is no objectivity?

Is there then no truth in philosophy? Suppose that in a certain puzzle I see a duck and a rabbit, whereas my friend sees only the rabbit. I then trace the outline of the duck, to get him to see it. But now it develops that where I see lines he sees only dots, etc. That is philosophy. Did I then not see the duck? Was there no duck to be seen? And what if I see only the duck and he sees only the rabbit? *That* is even more like philosophy.

If we stopped our discussion here we would leave the impression that philosophy is piecemeal, and philosophy is not at all piecemeal.

The philosopher, in "seeing" how to go about answering one question, typically feels that a great light has been shed on *all* the philosophical questions. He feels that he has gained an insight into the manner in which all, or a great many, of the philosophical questions must be answered, and an insight into the source of all, or a great many, of the prior confusions and mistakes. He feels that scales have fallen from his eyes. Descartes' initial excitement over the discovery of his new method can still be discerned in the *Discourse on Method;* and what gave rise to this excitement was not his conviction that he had discovered the method for solving one particular philosophical problem, but that he had discovered the method for solving all philosophical problems. In the hands of a great philosopher an insight into one philosophical problem is an insight into all.

Thus a philosophical perspective is born. Philosophy is always or almost always synoptic. This is not, as some have suggested, because philosophers have felt it their duty to talk about everything. Too obviously many have not. Philosophy is not a super-science. Rather, philosophy is synoptic because the growth of a philosophical perspective cannot be stopped. A philosophical perspective is inherently expansive, dynamic, proliferative: the procedure, the method, the court of appeal, the authority which the philosopher regards as competent to solve one philosophical problem he also regards as competent to solve a great many more, and perhaps *all*, philosophical problems. Descartes and all the rationalists abhorred Imagination; the sole ground for acceptance of any claim at all ought to be Reason — clear and distinct ideas. This is what gives unity and dynamic to the Cartesian philosophy. For Hume, the court of appeal is always whether we do or do not have certain mental images; for the positivist, the court of appeal is science and logic; for Moore, common sense and logic; for the later Wittgenstein, logical grammar.

What is important in a man's philosophy is not his detailed opinions on a number of topics, not his skill as a technician, but rather his fundamental method and appeal.

It would be drastically misleading, however, to separate the method of a philosopher from the results of that method in his hands; to separate the appeal of a philosopher from the answers which he thinks that appeal gives. To understand what the appeal to clarity and distinctness amounts to for Descartes we must investigate Descartes' use of this appeal. Similarly, one cannot separate Wittgenstein's appeal to logical grammar from the consequences of this appeal in his hands, namely, a deep-going conventionalism; and one cannot separate Hume's appeal to the presence or absence of mental images from what he regarded as the chief result of that appeal, namely, that "custom is the great guide of human life."

A sharp distinction between method and results might be satisfactory if the structure of a philosophical perspective were like that of a mathematical proof — axioms, rules of inference, and theorems. But its structure is more like that of a sonata movement. The musician starts with a theme and then develops it — plays it backwards, upside down, backwards and upside down both, faster, slower, broken up. Still, it is always the same theme; and in each new development we see a new facet of the old theme. We see more "in it" than we saw previously. Someone else might have taken the same theme and written a very different movement. But on the other hand, an unfinished sonata movement can be completed by someone else. A composer's style is not something separable from his works; yet it is something more than his works. One can accept a philosopher's method and disagree with some of his results; yet a philosopher's method is seen in his results.

Philosophy today is no different in fundamentals from what it has always been. It is indeed less "systematic" and "speculative"; but it is no less synoptic. The notion that philosophers today are mere technicians solving problems, that all they do is describe and prove, is a delusion. Philosophy is today, as always, the elaboration and defense of a *Weltanschauung;* an interpretation of our human condition. The philosopher is after the meaning and "hang" of things; today as always he has a vision of the whole structure of men's thoughts. The rise of analytic philosophy, like the rise of any other philosophy, has caused a change in the whole intellectual scene. The fact that there are today a great many things about which the philosopher does not wish to talk, topics which he regards as outside his field of competence, is part of his conception of how things hang together. To see nothing but technical "objective" discussions in present-day philosophy is to come in at the middle of the development section and insist that there is no theme, only notes. In Schoenberg too there are themes; only, it takes some listening.

III

What is faith?

I do not propose to answer this question.

If by the question is meant, "What are the necessary and sufficient conditions for calling something 'faith'?" then I do not know the answer. If the question is understood in a looser sense, as meaning "How is the word 'faith' normally used by English-speaking people?" then I also do not know the answer. In short, I do not know how to *define* "faith."

Let us instead begin this way: Let us consider a case of conversion, a case of change of faith; and let us ask, "What changed?" St. Paul is perhaps as good an example as any. What changed when St. Paul was converted from Judaism to Christianity?

"A man's faith consists of his religious beliefs."

Were any of Paul's beliefs changed? All or most of his life Paul had had religious beliefs. Being a Jew, he had believed that there was a supernatural and eternal person called "God," that everything in our world depended on Him for its existence, that He guided the destinies of all things but in some very special way had now for many centuries guided the historical destiny of the Jewish people, and that to the Jews He had promised one day to send His Messiah. All these beliefs, and more, Paul had held. In his conversion these beliefs were radically reorganized: some were dropped, others were added, and in general the whole structure was seen in a different light. The crux of this re-organization was that now Paul believed that in the risen person of Jesus Christ God had revealed Himself and the way of salvation for men, and that the message of this Jesus was the message of God.

I shall not here consider the much worried question of the logical status of such beliefs: Are they propositions? or expressions of attitude? or expressions of worship? or what? I shall simply call them religious beliefs and let it go at that. But let us notice that in his conversion some of Paul's beliefs about ordinary straightforward empirical facts were also changed. Now he believed, in a literal sense, that Jesus Christ, after being dead for three days, arose from the dead; whereas previously he had regarded this as a despicable lie propagated by the Christians.

"A man's faith is his ultimate concern"; or, "A man's faith is the whole structure of his values and concerns."

Were St. Paul's concerns and values changed? Prior to his conversion, Paul had devoted his life to the cause of the Jews — to the preservation of their nation and the defense and propagation of their religious practices and rituals. For he held that the righteousness to be found in the strict observance of the Jewish law was the only thing which, without fail, gave point and meaning to human life. Now all this was changed. He no longer cared about the Jewish nation; his message was to all peoples. He no longer cared about the Jewish ritual practices; though he still followed them by and large, he did so as a concession and not as something essential. For though he still saw in righteousness the point and meaning of human life, he no longer believed that this righteousness could be achieved by man's strict observance of the Law, but only by following "the Way" of Jesus Christ and being accepted by God. This now was the cause which he held and espoused. He says, "I am not ashamed of the Gospel. I see it as the very power of God working for the salvation of everyone who believes it, both Jew and Greek. I see in it God's plan for imparting righteousness to men, a process begun and continued by their faith."[13]

If St. Paul's ultimate concern changed, so also did his moral outlook as a whole. A man's moral outlook is manifested in his actions and decisions, and Paul's actions were radically changed. Where once he had persecuted Christians, he now tried with even greater zeal to persuade men to become Christians. It is true, of course, that a change in a man's activities is not a decisive criterion for a change in his moral principles. A man's moral principles may remain the same and yet his actions may change — if, for instance, he changes his mind concerning the facts. But it is perfectly clear, from the letters which later he wrote, that this was not St. Paul's case. His moral principles were changed: "If I speak with the eloquence of men and of angels, but have no love, I become no more than blaring brass or crashing cymbal. If I have the gift of foretelling the future and hold in my mind not only all human knowledge but the very secrets of God, and if I also have that absolute faith which can move mountains, but have no love, I amount to nothing at all. If I dispose of all that I possess, yes, even if I give my own body to be burned, but have no love, I achieve precisely nothing."[14]

---

13 Romans 1 (Phillips).
14 I Corinthians 13.

"A man's faith consists of his attitudes toward the fundamental features of human life."

Were St. Paul's attitudes changed in his conversion? Beyond a doubt. Love and hate, pain and grief, death and birth — toward all of them Paul's stance was changed.

"A man's faith consists of what he worships, and the rituals he follows in his worship."

Did St. Paul worship differently? Certainly he did.

And let us not forget the role of "religious experience" in Paul's conversion. Did he have a sense of *mysterium tremendum*, of the numinous? Perhaps so; he never really says. Did he have a sense of the awe and mystery and deep-down freshness of things; was he filled with wonder when he looked at the stars; did he have a "sense sublime" of "a motion and a spirit, that impels/ All thinking things, all objects of all thought,/ And rolls through all things. . ."? Perhaps so. The only thing we know for sure is that once he had a vision, a vision which led to his conversion, a vision so overwhelming that, coupled with the tremendous emotional upheaval which it produced, made him unable to see for several days afterwards. Paul himself seems hesitant to speak about the matter; all he tells us is that it was a vision of Christ. But here is how Luke relates it:

> But on his journey, as he neared Damascus, a light from Heaven suddenly blazed around him, and he fell to the ground. Then he heard a voice speaking to him,
> "Saul, Saul, why are you persecuting me?"
> "Who are you, Lord?" he asked.
> "I am Jesus whom you are persecuting," was the reply. "But now stand up and go into the city and there you will be told what you must do."
> His companions on the journey stood there speechless, for they had heard the voice but could see no one. Saul got up from the ground, but when he opened his eyes he could see nothing.[15]

Enough has been said to make it clear what a tremendously comprehensive thing happened when St. Paul was converted. Whether one wants to say that all these changes were actually components in or aspects of his change of faith, or rather wants to say that some of them were grounds for and others consequences of his change of faith, makes no difference here. We are not trying to define "faith." The point is simply that, as the New Testament puts it, Paul became "a new being."

Is it fair to take Paul as an example? Is it not the case that sometimes a religious conversion is a very localized change in a per-

---

15 The Acts of the Apostles, 9 (Phillips).

son's life, and not at all so comprehensive and pervasive as it was in Paul's? Yes, indeed it is. But it is also the case that in some conversions the changes are even more pervasive; this would be the case if, let us say, a Buddhist or a Logical Positivist became a Christian. The point I wish to make is not that a change in faith is always thus pervasive, but rather that it *may* be. And more strongly, that there is apparently no facet whatsoever of a person's existence, provided it lies in some way within his control, which might not be changed in some conversion or other. In this sense, no part of human life is immune to faith.

To say this, though, is not to say that a given man's faith pervades or may pervade every aspect of his life. A certain feature of a man's life may change when he changes his faith, even though that feature has nothing to do with his new faith — if, for instance, that feature was an important element in his old faith, or if it had nothing to do with either his old or his new faith and its change was a mere coincidence. Conversely, however, a certain feature of a man's life might *not* change when he changes his faith, even though it is an important feature in his new faith — if, for instance, it was also an important feature in his old faith. Thus to show the pervasiveness of the change which took place in Paul's life is not to show the pervasiveness of his new faith. I think, however, that it is clear from our discussion and citations that the pervasiveness of the changes which took place in Paul's life was due to the pervasiveness of his Christian faith.

Another important feature of the changes which took place in Paul's life is their unity. The various changes did not take place independently; what is more, it seems that features of Paul's life which at first he regarded as having no particular relevance to his new faith he later regarded as having such relevance. Paul's faith was dynamic and expansive.

In the first place, what led to most of the other changes in Paul's life were his special experiences on that Damascus road. Paul might of course have come to Christianity in some other way — most people do; and in general, Paul seems very suspicious of any claim on the part of others to special experiences. Furthermore, it is obvious that the experiences neither entail nor lend probability to the "truth" of Christianity; they are not relevant to the existence of God and the divinity of Christ in the way in which a person's claim that he seems to be seeing something is relevant to the claim that a physical object exists. So far as the character of the experience is concerned, Paul, instead of saying "Who are you, Lord?"

might instead have said, "Good heavens, the heat and the exhaustion are making my mind reel." Yet, when all these points are made, it is still the case that Paul's experiences led to his conversion. What is the force of "led to" here? Is it causal? I do not know.

What seems to play a far more crucial role in Paul's own faith, and what certainly plays a more crucial role in his presentation of the claims of Christ to others, is his belief that Christ arose from the dead. From his writings it seems that Paul held this belief to be so crucial that if he had, for whatever reasons, given it up, he would have given up his Christian faith as a whole. He *need* not have done so, however; there are plenty of men who agree with Paul on most other matters and still hold that Christ did not in a literal sense arise. And, conversely, the resurrection is neither a demonstrative nor a probable reason for the truth of Christianity. But this is what Paul says: "If Christ was not raised then neither our preaching nor your faith has any meaning at all . . . if Christ did not rise your faith is futile and your sins have never been forgiven. . . . But the glorious fact is that Christ *did* rise from the dead. . . ."[16]

Just as, in somewhat different ways, Paul's religious experiences and his belief in Christ's resurrection function as "grounds" for his faith in Christ, so also Paul's faith in Christ functions as the ground for his moral beliefs. Paul cites his confidence that salvation is to be found through faith in Christ as the basis for the moral injunctions which he gives to his readers: "With eyes wide open to the mercies of God, I beg you, my brothers, as an act of intelligent worship, to give him your bodies, as a living sacrifice, consecrated to him and acceptable by him."[17] "Avoid sexual looseness like the plague! Every other sin that a man commits is done outside his own body, but this is an offense against his own body."[18] Again, however, Paul's faith in Christ is not the ground for his moral principles in the sense that it constitutes a sufficient or forceful condition for them; it does not seem that a man would be irrational, in any specifiable sense, if he agreed with Paul on all other matters but disagreed with some of his moral convictions. Still, "by their works ye shall know them."

Finally, Paul even argues that given his basic faith, certain feelings and attitudes become appropriate and others inappropriate. "Let us not allow slackness to spoil our work and let us keep the fires of the spirit burning, as we do our work for God. Base your happiness

16 I Corinthians 15 (Phillips).
17 Romans 12 (Phillips).
18 I Corinthians 6 (Phillips).

on your hope in Christ. When trials come endure them patiently...."[19]

The various changes which took place in Paul's life, then, are unified in the sense that one facet is treated by Paul as ground for some other. What sort of ground, we have of course not even pretended to say; all we have said is that, in most cases at least, they are not grounds in the sense of premises in either inductive or deductive arguments. Indeed, in most cases here the notion of an inductive or deductive argument seems irrelevant, since in most cases it is not a belief which is at stake but rather some attitude or feeling or action. Paul is more concerned to give grounds for deciding than grounds for believing. For a full understanding of the unity of Paul's faith we should require then an understanding of the nature of grounds for doing, and trusting, and feeling, as well as of all the various grounds for believing. I am incapable of fulfilling this requirement. All I wish to do at present is *point* to the unity, not *explicate* it.

Paul's faith is perhaps more unified than we have even yet indicated. We have said that his belief in the resurrection serves as a ground for his faith in Christ. But perhaps it is the other way round as well. Paul seems to have come to believe in the resurrection *at the same time* that he came to have faith in Jesus; he did not go out first to conduct elaborate historical investigations. One gets the impression that Paul would have believed in the resurrection even if all the historical evidence were against it. And, indeed, what kind of historical research would lead Christians in general to abandon their faith? Suppose some historian would claim, on good grounds, that the New Testament was a sixth-century forgery. No doubt many Christians, if they believed this, would give up their faith. But would they believe it? For that matter, how long must capitalism survive to persuade the Communist that Marxism is a tissue of errors? And how often must science disappoint us to persuade the Positivist that his hopes are misplaced? Has it not done so often enough already?

Someone might protest against our discussion thus far that we have missed the essential thing in faith. We have talked about the changes which took place in Paul's life and emphasized their pervasiveness and unity; but we have said nothing about the *focus* of all these changes. What was the *essential* thing which changed in Paul's life? What is faith for? What does it do for men? What role does it play in human life? Why is it around? What do men expect of it? What do they ask of it? And what do they get from it?

[19] Romans 12 (Phillips).

There is no one answer to these questions. Faith is different things to different people. There is no one role which it plays in human life. For some, it is the resolution of a sense of guilt so deep and pervasive that nothing in the world will free them. For some, it is a way of calming fears and anxieties and finding the peace that passes understanding. For some, it provides inspiration and drive where otherwise they would flag in performing the tasks and duties of life. For some, it is a response to feelings of absolute dependence or ultimate security or awe and mystery. For some, it "explains" things — explains strange experiences they have, explains striking and miraculous happenings, explains the design and order of things, explains why there is anything at all. For some, it is an alternative and preferable way of organizing their beliefs about the universe to that which can be found in natural science. For some, it answers the riddle of human existence and reveals the meaning of human life. The character of a man's faith depends on which of these needs he feels; its focus depends on which of these needs he feels most deeply.

Which sort of faith shall we select for our purposes? Or all of them?

Luther somewhere says, "What does it mean to have a god, or what is God?" "Trust and faith of the heart alone make both God and idol. . . . For the two, faith and God, hold close together. Whatever then thy heart clings to . . . and relies upon, that is properly thy God." Luther is here stressing the centrality of trust ("relies upon") and loyalty ("clings to") in religious faith. Indeed, he seems to *equate* this with faith. But quite obviously he cannot be speaking of *every* sort of trust and loyalty. What sort then? Some sort of *ultimate* trust and loyalty apparently. What sort would that be? A trust in something and a loyalty to something as giving meaning to our lives as a whole — something whose removal would open before us the abyss of meaninglessness and absurdity, destroy the point of everything we were doing, and deprive our lives of significance. A man's faith is his way of life as determined by what he thinks worth his ultimate trust and loyalty.

I propose to follow Luther's guidance here and take ultimate trust and loyalty as the core of faith. I do so not because I think this constitutes the definition of "faith," nor because I think it is the dominant feature in every man's religious faith, but only because I think a faith with this as its dominant or one of its dominant features bears the most significant relations to philosophy. Furthermore, it was the dominant feature of Paul's faith: witness his repeated use of the concept *"faith in."* It was Paul's faith in God as revealed in Christ which constituted the essence of his faith.

If we do take as our standard case a religious faith in which *faith in* constitutes the dominant and organizing feature, then we can understand something else which Luther hints at, and which a good many religious people claim — namely, that the opposite to a particular faith is not an absence of faith, but rather a different faith. If we understood this as the claim that everyone has religious beliefs, or that everyone has some faint glimmering of religious feelings, or that everyone has a pervasive sense of guilt and some way of assuaging that sense, or that everyone follows some ritual and accepts some "myth," then the claim seems in all likelihood false. But if we understand it as the claim that every man or almost every man trusts and serves something as giving meaning and value to his life, then it seems to me that the claim is correct. It seems most unlikely that some men have no ultimate faith in anything at all — though "ultimate" has to be understood here in the somewhat odd sense of allowing several competing faiths to be equally ultimate. Whether we put our trust in science, or reason, or humanity, or the nation, or the Party, still it is trust. It is not, then, that some men have a way of life determined by a trust and loyalty, and that others do not; but rather that their ways of life are different, determined by different trusts and loyalties. I think it should be admitted, however, that a man could in this sense have faith without in the usual sense having a "religious" faith. He may in fact be irreligious. Or his *faith in* may be relatively independent of his religion.

Let us from now on, then, take as our standard case this Pauline, "Lutheran" sort of faith, recognizing that if we took a faith with a different sort of focus as our standard case, our results might be quite different.

IV

Enough has been said to show that there is every likelihood of conflict between one man's philosophy and some other man's faith, and between one man's faith and some other man's philosophy. Indeed, this is a well-known and very obvious truth; since the pre-Socratics there have been conflicts between faith and philosophy. What we have gained, however, is some understanding of why this is, and of why it will in all likelihood continue.

We have seen that in the background of a philosophical claim there is often a philosophical perspective, which in turn is based on a philosophical method or appeal which is expansive in the sense that it leads the philosopher to take a position on a great many philosophic issues, thus to function in organizing all or a large segment of his beliefs.   Even though Kant or Descartes or Hume did not discuss a certain issue, we can still often answer the question of what a Cartesian or Kantian or Humean treatment of that issue would be; and it also often happens that a philosopher, in order to disagree with a philosophical claim, finds himself forced to disagree with an entire philosophical method and perspective.

Similarly, we have argued that a man's ultimate trust and loyalty can and often does serve as an organizing principle for his entire way of life; we saw, in fact, that there seems to be no feature of man's life which cannot, in principle at least, be linked to some man's faith.   Paul's faith was unusually comprehensive in just this way: he held beliefs on the happening of certain very remarkable natural events, on the existence and nature of supernatural beings, on the origin of things, on the destiny of man, on the nature of man, on what men ought to do and why, and on what the consequences of their not doing so would be; and his views on these matters were all linked, in one way or another, to his faith in God as revealed in Jesus and His message.   Paul's faith is intimately bound up with the rudiments of an anthropology, a cosmology, an ethics, etc.

As a result of the expansiveness of a philosophical appeal and the pervasiveness of faith, there are a number of issues which are typically raised both when men are discussing philosophy and when they are discussing ways of life, among them being these: the origin of all things, the nature of man, the foundation of moral principles, the existence of supernatural beings, etc.   One man's view of the world and some other man's (or his own) way of life thus tend to intersect.   In any such case of intersection, however, what is crucial is not the *particular* issues involved, but rather the basic appeal of the philosopher and the basic trust and loyalty of the man of faith.   This is so because even though the specific views of a philosopher and the specific views of a man of faith nowhere conflict, it may still be that if we pressed the "implications" of the philosopher's appeal and of the man of faith's trust, we would find conflicts.   It is also so because a given conflict may be superficial; the relation between a philosopher's basic method, and his views on various specific issues, is not so tight but that sometimes at least he may surrender these views without surrendering his method; and the same, *mutatis mutandis*, for faith.

In some cases, however, the possibility of conflict between one man's philosophy and some other man's (or his own) faith is even stronger; for it sometimes happens that those features of the universe to which the philosopher appeals in justifying his philosophical views are also quite clearly those in which he places his faith. Descartes, for instance, announces that he wishes to accept nothing unless it be so clear and distinct that it cannot be doubted. Imagination was to be wholly cast out, and Reason alone followed. Now of course Descartes did believe in God; but he did so on the basis of an argument which, to his mind, fitted his rational standards. And if we are to believe him, if he had found it impossible to form such an argument, or if he had found it impossible to form a clear and distinct conception of the Christian God, he would have given up his belief. This in fact is the consequence which Spinoza drew. Thus not only did Descartes think that the appeal to clear and distinct ideas would settle theoretical disputes, but he also held that this was the proper appeal in the sphere of religion and morals. It seems clear then that Descartes' ultimate trust and loyalty was to Reason, rather than to God. Similar things must be said for all the great rationalists, including Locke and Kant. And though perhaps the case is somewhat less clear, I think a similar point can be made for some of the positivists and some of the pragmatists. In them we see a fundamental trust in natural science, as we now know it, as capable of solving man's deepest difficulties and serving as a guide to a better life. In place of the right reason of the eighteenth century we have the scientific attitude of the twentieth. In all these cases, and more, philosophy becomes a secular theology — the elaboration and defense of a man's faith.

What I wish to conclude from our discussion thus far is that a philosophical appeal is typically not neutral with respect to faith — meaning that, given any philosophical appeal, there are usually certain trusts and loyalties which conflict in one of the ways indicated with that appeal. And conversely, an ultimate trust and loyalty is typically not neutral with respect to a philosophical appeal — meaning by this, that given any trust and loyalty, there are usually certain philosophical appeals which conflict in the ways indicated with that way of life. I doubt, however, that for the words "typically not" in these formulations we can substitute "never"; and for "usually," "always." Some faiths are not very pervasive, and some philosophical methods are not very expansive; and there seems no reason to suppose that a philosophical appeal *must* also function as an object of trust and loyalty for someone's way of life.

The matter may be considered from a different direction. Suppose we take a case in which we are clearly dealing with a philo-

sophical perspective. Is it possible, in every such case, to infer what
must be the philosopher's faith and his way of life? And suppose
we take a case in which we are clearly dealing with a faith. Is it
possible, in every such case, to infer what *must be* such a person's
philosophical perspective, if he but bothered to elaborate it? In some
cases we can make such inferences. Can we always? Well, what is
the force of "must be" in these questions? Must be, *if what?* Apparently, if he is to be consistent. But what can "consistency" mean
here? If we answer "Yes" to these questions, I think we are again
tacitly construing both faith and philosophy on the model of a
mathematical system in which we can accuse men of straightforward
inconsistencies. But if we have seen anything, we have seen that
the connections between the various elements of a man's philosophical
perspective, and between the various features of his way of life, are
rarely deductive connections. In principle at least it seems possible
for a man's philosophical perspective and his way of life to be independent — for his philosophical appeal to be independent of his ultimate trust. Philosophical problems arise in all sorts of contexts; it
is not the case that the dominant *philosophical* interest of every man
lies in the problems posed by his own particular faith. Especially,
then, if the focus of a philosopher's attention is not on his own faith,
it seems possible that his philosophical appeal will have no positive
and direct relation to his ultimate trust. Is G. E. Moore an example?
Can one infer, from Moore's appeal to Common Sense and logic, anything positive about his way of life?

     What is left to consider is whether in cases of conflict between
philosophy and faith, or in cases where a man's faith exercises a
formative influence on his philosophy, or vice versa, we have a contrast between reason on one side and faith on the other. Can these
be viewed as cases of rational objectivity versus bias? It is clear by
now that they cannot. It may indeed be the case that Reason, interpreted let us say as "clear and distinct ideas," can serve as a man's
ultimate appeal in philosophy, and even as his ultimate trust; but in
such cases, too, we have a conflict between two trusts, or a conflict
between an ultimate appeal and an ultimate trust, and not a conflict
between bias and objectivity. For we have seen that no conclusive
"rational" defense can be given for a man's ultimate philosophical
appeal. In cases of conflict between philosophy and faith a man
will have to choose; but this choice, in the last resort, cannot be represented as a choice between rationality and irrationality, or rationality and non-rationality.

     I wish, in closing, to consider one objection to our thesis. St.

Paul, for the most part, presented his beliefs in what has variously been called a mythical or symbolic language. This is very different from the language which is customarily used by philosophers. And it is sometimes claimed, on the ground that these *are* two different languages, that anybody who tries to draw connections here fails to understand that these *really are* two different languages. Now I think that the attempt to translate the symbolic statements of religion into the language of philosophers is indeed fraught with difficulties. Is Aquinas in his first cause argument trying to prove what the Scriptures claim when they say that God created the heavens and the earth? Is the heart of which the Scriptures speak the same as the transcendental ego of the philosophers? Can Romans 7 be used in defense of the dictum that no man errs knowingly? Is the teleological argument only restating what the Psalmist says when he utters, "The heavens declare the glory of God, and the firmament showeth his handiwork"? Does the doctrine of predestination conflict with the theory of indeterminacy? In particular, how are we to tell in a given case whether two utterances really are in conflict, or whether one of them just means something different from what we may think on first glance? Is it a mistake to speak of the sun rising? Or is it merely a quixotic way of uttering a truth?

In spite of all these difficulties, however, I see no reason to suppose that we never can answer any such questions. A similar situation arises in poetry. Though a paraphrase of a poem is not to be identified with the poem, and though the paraphrase plays a different function from that of the poem, it does not follow from this that paraphrases are impossible. Or the situation is similar to that of a boy who loves a girl and a psychologist who studies the girl. The description the boy gives of the girl will be very different from the one the psychologist gives of the girl, and the two descriptions no doubt have different functions; yet it is not impossible that the one may claim that the other has made mistakes. The situation is not, I think, very much like the relation between a carpenter's description of a painting and a critic's description of the same painting. The depth of the painting, in the critic's sense, has nothing at all to do with the carpenter's claim that the painting will require a deep crate.

2

Traditional Reason and Modern Reason

Francis H. Parker, Professor of Philosophy, Haverford College. A.B., Evansville College; A.M., Indiana University; Ph.D., Harvard University. Author of (with Henry Veatch) *Logic as a Human Instrument;* essays in *The Return to Reason* (ed. John Wild), *The Philosophy of Knowledge* (ed. R. Houde and J. Mullally), *Twentieth Century Encyclopedia of Religious Knowledge* (ed. L. Loetscher) , *Collier's Encyclopedia;* articles in *Review of Metaphysics, International Philosophical Quarterly.*

Traditional Reason and Modern Reason

BY FRANCIS H. PARKER

IN MUCH OF CONTEMPORARY PHILOSOPHY THERE IS A BELIEF, AMOUNTING almost to a dogma, that no proposition can be both necessarily true and also about real existence. I want to try to defeat this belief by arguing the four following points: (1) The belief that no proposition can be both necessary and also existential or factual is necessarily connected with a peculiarly modern conception of reason (and, correlatively, a peculiarly modern conception of experience). (2) Fundamentally opposed to this is a conception of reason (and correspondingly of experience) which is central to the tradition of classical and medieval philosophy and which implies that there *can* be propositions which are both necessary and existential, both necessarily and factually true. (3) While the issue between these two conceptions of reason is so basic that neither can be strictly, logically demonstrated, it can be demonstrated that *belief* in or *assertion* of the traditional conception of reason is inescapable, even for the modern philosopher. Consequently, (4), there is compelling reason to believe that there can be, and actually are, propositions which are both necessarily and existentially true.[1]

A proposition can be necessarily true only if its terms signify

---

[1] An appreciation of the nature and importance of the traditional conception of reason is chief among my many philosophical debts to Professor William Harry Jellema — my teacher, friend, and one-time colleague — whom we strive to honor with this volume.

repeatable, complex structures — forms, universals, sets, or the like.[2] And a necessary proposition can be factual or existential only if these universals or complex formal structures are primary data of awareness, immediate intuitions. If, on the contrary, experience includes only particulars, then the universals requisite for necessary propositions, and consequently the necessary propositions involving these universals, must be *a priori*, uninformative, vacuous, non-factual, or non-existential. Thus any philosophy which excludes universals, forms, or essences — intelligible structures — from what it finds given in experience, must also exclude the possibility of propositions being both necessarily and factually true.

The most obvious and most influential historical examples of this double exclusion are Hume and Kant. Of these two Kant seems especially interesting and instructive in view of the ironical fate of his own contention that there are propositions about facts which are necessarily true. When his followers remembered the dictum of Leibniz and Hume that only "analytic" propositions, only "truths of reason" or "relations of ideas," can be necessarily true, Kant's view that all necessary factual truths are "synthetic," that "analytic" propositions are always *a priori*, led to the conclusion that there are no necessary truths of fact at all, that necessary propositions are always *a priori* and without experiential reference. But why should Kant

2 This is certainly true of so-called analytic propositions, since there can be no analysis of simple terms. While bare tautologies of the form "A is A" *need* not have terms which signify complex structures (e.g., "That's that"), they *may* have (e.g., "A rose is a rose"); and, moreover, many philosophers would hesitate to denominate such unanalyzable tautologies *propositions*. I myself am in the habit of following the predominant current custom of regarding the class of necessary propositions as co-extensive with the class of analytic propositions (while believing, as this essay indicates, and contrary to the predominant current attitude, that some analytic propositions are existential or factual). Professor Henry Veatch has advised me to rid myself of this habit, however, both on the ground that "analytic" now *means* "non-factual" or "uninformative" and also on the ground that the analytic-synthetic distinction is philosophically untenable, or at least badly misplaced. Concerning the first of these two points, I myself would hope that the notion of "analytic" could be divorced from the notion of "non-factual," since I believe that these two notions are quite independent of each other. Concerning the second point, I have not yet straightened out in my own mind the philosophical problems involved in the analytic-synthetic distinction, although I have been greatly helped in this regard by personal correspondence with Professor Veatch and by his excellent unpublished essay entitled "On Trying to Say and to Know What's What." Because of these considerations I have decided to avoid describing necessary propositions as analytic in this essay while hopefully awaiting later clarity concerning the appropriateness or inappropriateness of the term "analytic." This decision does not, I believe, affect the argument of this essay, since necessary propositions are currently held to be non-factual or uninformative whether or not they are said to be analytic.

say that no necessary truth is *a posteriori,* derivable from experience
and possessing experiential, existential reference? Because, he tells
us, "necessity . . . cannot be obtained from experience."[3] But why
should Kant say that necessity cannot be obtained from experience?
Because he equates experience with *sense* experience, and Kant rightly
sees that sensed items are, as sensed, always particular and contingent.
"The sum of the matter is this," the Prussian Hume pronounces,[4]
"All our intuition takes place by means of the senses only; the understanding intuits nothing but only reflects." Given a stock of intuited
sensory particulars as materials, the understanding can set about its
proper business of constructing orderly phenomenal objects according to its purely *a priori* blueprints. But the understanding has no
peculiar intuitions, no proper objects of its own; universals, the proper
concern of the understanding, are *a priori,* non-empirical. Since all
empirical data or intuitions are sensory and therefore particular and
contingent, and since necessary propositions essentially involve universals, no necessary proposition can be empirical, *a posteriori,* or
factual. The conception of understanding, intelligence, or reason
underlying this belief, the conception of reason as non-intuitive and
purely reflective, I shall call "constructive reason."

The alternative conception of reason which I want to consider
is essentially foreign to modern thought. It is peculiarly classical
and medieval, and it originates most clearly in Aristotle. So fundamental to his thought as to be both ubiquitous in his philosophy and
yet rarely self-consciously expressed is the conception of reason as an
intuitive agency, a mode of cognition distinct both from sensation
on the one hand and from reflective, discursive reason on the other.
"The thinking part of the soul must . . . be capable of receiving the
form of an object," the philosopher tells us;[5] and this "thinking part
of the soul" whose apprehension of the forms of things gives rise to
"universal and necessary judgments" and "the first principles of scientific knowledge" he calls "intuitive reason" (*voûs*).[6] Intuitive reason has peculiar data of its own, its own proper objects; and these
proper objects of intuitive reason are forms, essences, characteristics,
or universals rather than particulars. Thus their apprehension and
formulation can give rise to essential or necessary propositions.
Furthermore, these forms intuited by reason are given empirically,
embedded in the particular, contingent data of sensation. "The ob-

---

3 *Prolegomena to Any Future Metaphysic,* Section 2, c, 2.
4 *Ibid.,* Sections 22 & 13, Remark II.
5 *De Anima,* 429a, 14-16.
6 *Nicomachean Ethics,* 1139b, 31-1140a, 8.

jects of thought are in the sensible forms," Aristotle says,[7] "viz., both the abstract objects and the states and affections of sensible things." Thus propositions definitive of these forms are also *a posteriori*, factual, or existential. Consequently the assumption of rational intuition of formal structures coeval with and immersed in sensory data implies the possibility of propositions which are both essential and *a posteriori*, both necessarily and factually true.

Such necessary, existential propositions are, to be sure, completely certified prior to all *subsequent* experience; since they are true by virtue of their meanings alone, no *further* experience is required. But these meanings by virtue of which alone they are completely certified are still themselves factually real since they are, as the proper objects of intuitive reason, embedded in empirical reality. One may of course object, as Kant does, that "all analytic judgments are *a priori* even when the concepts are empirical," on the ground that *qua* "analytic" they "depend wholly on the law of contradiction,"[8] which cannot itself, Kant believes, be derived from experience. But such an objection only begs the question, for it is possible, assuming intuitive reason, for the law of non-contradiction itself to be factual or existential as well as necessary. All that is required for the actualization of this possibility is that the universals which are the proper objects of intuitive reason include among them at least one that is completely universal, such as *being* or *thing*. We shall return to this point later.

Thus constructive reason is revelatory only of our attitudes toward things, while intuitive reason is revelatory of factual reality. At this point an analogy may possibly be helpful in clarifying these contrasting conceptions of reason. Let us imagine that in the midst of a raging battle each contending army sends a messenger back to its own headquarters. Each message has been codified, and each code has been withheld from the messenger lest he be captured and reveal it under torture. But one of the messages has been garbled by a snafu coder. Thus while neither messenger can read the inscription that he carries, only one of the inscriptions contains any message to be read. When the two messengers arrive at their respective headquarters, the inscriptions they delivered are run through decoders. In the case of the message-bearing inscription the intelligence officer reads the original message, thus discovering the true facts of the matter at the front. The other intelligence officer, however, finds only gibberish. But gibberish cannot determine strategy, so the inscription

[7] *De Anima,* 432a, 4-6.
[8] *Op. cit.,* Section 2, b.

must be made to make sense. And so it is; the intelligence officer constructs meaning where he cannot find it.

The inscription, in this analogy, stands in both cases for the data of sensation. The first intelligence officer is intuitive reason, and the message he discovers in the inscription is the statements of the formal structure embodied in the data of sensation but given only to intuitive reason. The second intelligence officer is constructive reason, and the meaning he constructs is an *a priori* statement, a truth of reason, a relation of ideas, imposed upon the data of sensation.

Thus we have two alternative conceptions of reason: the conception of reason as intuitive, and the conception of reason as constructive.[9] The replacement of intuitive reason by constructive reason might well be regarded as a fundamental theme of the rise and development of modern philosophy. If medieval man is created lower than the angels but higher than the brutes, his definitive in-betweenness lies most of all in his possession of intuitive reason. The angelic factor above medieval man is divine revelation, a participation in God's vision rather than in man's own peculiarly human vision. The brute factor below medieval man is sense experience, that power of observing particulars and storing those observations which man shares in common with the brute animals. And man's in-betweenness, that which differentiates him from the angels above and the brutes below, that in him which is peculiarly human, is his reason: man's natural faculty of discerning universals in and through particular sense experiences. The brutes discern universals not at all, and the angels discern them without abstracting them from sensation. As a result man possesses the power of acquiring a specifically human wisdom, a knowledge and appreciation of universal, abiding truths gained in and through common sense experience.

The classical and medieval tradition in philosophy is, I believe, most basically characterizable by its recognition of this essential in-betweenness of man, by the presence of reason defined as the power of discerning universals in sensations. In ancient philosophy the struggle was primarily for the distinctness of reason from sensation, for the distinctness of the specifically human from the brute; and in the great ancient philosophers, especially Plato and Aristotle, this struggle was successful. In medieval philosophy the struggle was primarily for the distinctness of reason from revelation, for the distinctness of the specifically human from the angelic and divine; and, once more, this struggle was successful in the great medieval philoso-

9 The first is central to what Professor Jellema calls the tradition, and the second is central to what he refers to as modernity.

phers, especially Augustine and Thomas. From this point of view the basic character of the late medieval and early modern period was a revolt against reason as it had been conceived in the tradition, a revolt against man's essential in-betweenness. Such a revolt could take only two different forms: a reduction of reason to sensation and a reduction of reason to revelation. The reduction of reason to sensation meant the substitution of empirical science for rational philosophy, the confusion of philosophy with science. The reduction of reason to revelation meant the substitution of religious faith for rational philosophy, the confusion of philosophy with religion. These two forms of the revolt against traditional reason developed concurrently, and, indeed, were often combined in the same persons: science and religion without philosophy as a distinct discipline, sensation and revelation without reason as a distinct faculty. This double-phased revolt continued down into and through modern times, and it led to the development of the conception of reason as constructive.

The early stages of the reduction of reason to sensation are found most notably in William of Ockham and Nicholas of Autrecourt, and the early stages of the correlative reduction of reason to revelation are to be found especially in Meister Eckhart and Nicholas of Cusa. What is not sensorily observable is a matter of faith, so all things formerly grasped by reason and formulated in rational philosophy — e.g., the existence and nature of God, the soul, and moral principles — become the concern solely of revelation. Thus is the world partitioned into science and religion, sensation and revelation. From this point of view the Renaissance may be regarded as the social manifestation of the reduction of reason to sensation, of the merging of man with the brute animal; and the Protestant Reformation may be regarded as the social manifestation of the reduction of reason to revelation, of the merging of man — in so far as he is more than a brute — with the angelic and divine. Just as no institution shall stand between the individual man and his God, so shall no rational system — the core of institutions — intervene between the individual human and God. The next stage in this story of the loss of traditional reason and the development of constructive reason is the rise of a new, intermediate conception of reason in Descartes and his followers, the continental "rationalists," the conception of reason as a faculty of deducing universal truths *a priori* from innate ideas which are wholly independent of sense experience. When this conception of reason was discarded by the British "empiricists," it required the revolution of Kant to develop the conception of reason as constructive, modernity's fully developed conception of reason which we are here contrasting with the tradition's conception of reason as intuitive. For the tradition the intelligence officer — in our previous analogy — finds meaning in experience; for continental "rationalism" meaning is deduced from innate ideas independently of experience; for British "empiricism" meaning is imparted only by the subrational faculties of passion and habit; and for Kant and his voluntarist and pragmatist followers, utilizing the conception of reason as constructive, meaning is created out of the mind itself.

Here, in summary form, are what I believe to be the two major competing conceptions of reason: the conception of Aristotle and the tradition of reason as intuitive, which conception makes possible truths which are both factual and necessary, and the conception of Kant and modernity of reason as constructive, which conception excludes the possibility of such existential yet necessary truths. How now are we to decide between these two conceptions of reason — or can we decide between them at all? Well, why did Kant make the choice he made? Because he identified experience with sense experience. But why did he do this? Because it was the modern thing to do? Because it was done both by the characters inhabiting his dogmatic slumber and also by the rude fellow who awoke him? Distinctively rational factors were innate for the "rationalists" and psychological (if present at all) for the "empiricists." Neither school found them in experience. So Kant didn't find them there either, and given this fact it took the genius of Kant to connect them plausibly with experience. But these *causes* of Kant's acceptance of the conception of constructive reason cannot be regarded as *reasons*.

Why, then, did Aristotle accept the conception of intuitive reason? Because it seemed obvious to him, because he thought he saw a non-sensuous type of intuition. But why did he think this? Because he studied twenty years with Plato? Again we may have historical causes, but no reasons. Indeed, the issue is so basic as to raise serious question whether any reason could be given for either position. If we examine what is involved in each of these conceptions, however, we may yet find grounds for accepting one or the other of them. We have already seen that one consequence of the conception of intuitive reason is the possibility of necessary factual truths, and that this is precluded by the conception of constructive reason. Put more strictly, the possibility of necessary factual propositions and the conception of intuitive reason would seem to be mutually implicative. But is there anything else of consequence involved in, even though not a co-implicant of, the conception of intuitive reason which would therefore be a ground for accepting or rejecting that conception?

One important, already adumbrated, factor involved in the conception of intuitive reason is the possibility of an empirical ontology. Put more strictly, intuitive reason is a necessary condition of an empirical ontology. As already mentioned, if among the structured forms given to rational intuition there are any which are completely universal, as wide as being itself, then the propositions formulating these structures will be, on the one hand, ontological and, on the other hand, both necessarily and factually or existentially true. This possibility is excluded by the conception of reason as constructive. The "very concept" of "metaphysical knowledge," Kant tells us,[10] "implies that they [its sources] cannot be empirical. Its principles (including not only its maxims but its basic notions) must never be derived from experience. It must not be physical but metaphysical knowledge, namely, knowledge lying beyond experience. It can therefore have for its basis neither external experience, which is the source of physics proper, nor internal, which is the source of empirical psychology." One is tempted to say that Kant is here punning on the word "metaphysics," but in any event his statement is doubtless true of *meta-physics* thus conceived. But it is not true of an empirical, existential ontology. Whether we do in fact possess this other condition necessary for an empirical, existential ontology, whether, that is, there are in fact given to intuitive reason data which are completely universal, is another question, which I now leave open. Likewise, the exact statements constituting any such empirical ontology is quite another matter. That the conception of reason as intuitive is a necessary condition of an empirical ontology, and that the conception of reason as purely constructive excludes the possibility of an empirical ontology, would seem, however, to be sufficiently clear. But does this mean that the conception of reason as intuitive is therefore the correct one, that we ought to accept it? Not necessarily, of course. It means only that *if* an empirical ontology is possible, or *if* we believe, or want to believe, that it is possible, then we must accept the conception of intuitive reason — that if we reject this conception we reject all possibility of an empirical ontology. Seeing this connection may persuade some to accept one conception of reason, but it will probably also persuade just as many to accept the other. In any event, therefore, the argument is inconclusive.

[10] *Op. cit.,* Section I.

Perhaps a connection between the conception of intuitive reason and the possibility of empirically necessary axiological truths may be persuasive, however. It seems clear that a conception of reason as intuitive is also a necessary condition of necessary, existential truths about values. If there are among the proper objects of intuitive reason value structures not completely reducible to facts, then the propositions definitive of these structures will be, on the one hand, axiological and, on the other hand, both necessarily and existentially true. This possibility is excluded by the conception of reason as constructive. On the basis of that conception value truths are either *a priori*, as with Kant, or contingent, as with Moore, or non-existent, as with the non-cognitivists. Whether we do in fact possess this other condition requisite for existentially necessary axiological propositions, the condition, that is, that intuitive reason find among its data non-reducible value structures, it is not my purpose to discuss. Likewise whether any such value data would include distinctively moral, or aesthetic, or religious ones is another matter. That the conception of reason as intuitive is a necessary condition for any existential yet necessarily true value propositions, and that a conception of reason as entirely constructive precludes the possibility of any such propositions, would seem, however, to be sufficiently clear. Now is *this* connection a compelling reason for the acceptance of one or the other of these alternative conceptions of reason? Again, not necessarily. We can only say — but we can say this — that *if* necessary *a posteriori* truths of value are possible, or believed or hoped to be possible, the conception of intuitive reason must be accepted.

A third consideration is the connection between intuitive reason and natural or rational theology. In so far as there are or may be necessarily true propositions about God as a real existent, the conception of intuitive reason is presupposed as a necessary condition. If there are among the peculiar objects of intuitive reason either aspects of God Himself or situations entailing aspects of God, then the propositions definitive of these aspects will be necessarily true (as definitive) and existential (as concerning a real being) as well as theological. Such propositions are impossible on the basis of the constructivist conception of reason. On the basis of that conception propositions of natural theology are either *a priori and* non-existential, as with Kant, or merely probable, as with Mill and James, or entirely non-existent, as with the positivists. Whether or not we do in fact possess this other condition requisite for necessary existential theological propositions, the condition, that is, that intuitive reason find among its data aspects of God as a real being or situations entailing aspects of God, it is not my purpose here to discuss. That the conception of reason as intuitive is a necessary condition of any existential yet necessarily true theological propositions, and that the conception of reason as entirely constructive precludes the possibility of any such propositions, would seem, however, to be sufficiently evident. But is this connection any more of a compelling reason for the acceptance of one or the other of these conceptions of reason than were the other two connections? Once more, not necessarily. We can only say — but we must say this — that *if* necessary existential theological propositions are possible, or believed or hoped to be possible, the intuitivist conception of reason must be accepted.

It is also appropriate at this point to note that there is good reason to believe that the conception of intuitive reason receives support, if not its origin, from a belief in God as the source of the possibility of intelligible traffic between man and nature. The conception of intuitive reason involves the idea of a bond of intelligibility between the mind of man and the structure of nature, a rational pattern in which both nature and the human mind participate. If intelligible forms come into being in and pass away from nature or the human mind or both, then they are independent of and prior to both nature and the human mind. If we attend to this transcendent priority and independence rather than to the immanence of those forms in nature and mind, then we have the Forms of Plato; and if we attend to the unity of these forms as intelligible rather than to their multiplicity, then we have — to cite only a few examples — the Good or the One of Plato, the Pure Actuality of Aristotle, the λογος of the Stoics and of the fourth Gospel. the voῦs and the One of Plotinus, or the Divine exemplars of Augustine and Thomas. The late medieval and early modern loss of intuitive reason as man's definitive in-betweenness also meant, I believe, the loss of God as rational mediator between man and nature — though not necessarily the loss of God as completely transcendent and rationally unknowable. Without a source and home for those intelligible forms which mediated between the mind of man and the structure of nature, man's bond with nature was broken. Thus arose the subjectivism, *a priorism*, and constructivism definitive of modernity — though whether the loss of God as λογος caused the loss of reason as intuitive, or vice versa, I do not know.

Our results so far are disappointingly inconclusive, however. Can we not find a strictly compelling reason for a selection from these two alternative conceptions of reason? Well, what would be a strictly compelling reason? Why, a logical one, of course. And, indeed, it does seem possible to produce a logical reason for a selection, for careful analysis seems to indicate that the conception of reason as purely constructive involves a contradiction.[11]

According to the purely constructivist conception of reason, reason constructs its objects out of certain materials; it makes phenomena out of the "manifold of intuition" or constructs out of sense data. Now this means that rationally to know anything is to transform it into something else, to construct some other thing out of it. But this is to assert that the rational knowing of a thing is *not* a rational knowing of *that* thing *itself* at all, but rather of something *new* and *different*. And this position is, I believe, self-contradictory. At this point, however, the advocate of constructive reason will object that the antecedent thing is not an object of reason at all before its transformation, that it is only the material for such an object. It is rather the transformed thing, the construct, the phenomenon, which is the object of rational knowing; and as soon as we see this, we see that there is no contradiction at all. Be it so. But exactly how, then, is the construct, the phenomenon, rationally known on the basis of a purely constructivist conception of reason? Since the phenomenon or construct is by hypothesis an object of rational knowledge, and since rational knowledge is regarded as a purely constructive activity, then we must say of the construct that it too is transformed or constructed, or better, *re*-constructed, by the act of rationally knowing it, into a still different something. But then once more, to know something is not to know that something, but rather something else — and so on. In each case there is a contradiction, and the contradiction is continued in an infinite regress.

At this point, however, the advocate of constructive reason may again object that for any given object the constructing process occurs only once, and that after it has occurred so as to produce an object, phenomenon, or construct, then that constructed object is just simply known. By saying this we stop the regress and avoid the contradiction. This is, indeed, just what Kant seems to say. But the point to be noted is that to say this is to invoke the conception of intuitive reason; to say that the rational construction is followed by a rational intuition of the construct is to abandon the conception of reason as purely constructive. This does avoid the contradiction,

11 The two following paragraphs are an abbreviated form of an argument I have used elsewhere for a different, though related, purpose — most recently in "A Demonstration of Epistemological Realism," *International Philosophical Quarterly*, II, 3 (Sept. 1962), 382-384.

but only at the cost of conceding the point. Indeed, Kant's theory is plausible only because it tacitly assumes that phenomena, once constructed, are simply intuited exactly as they are.

Thus it would seem that we have finally arrived at a compelling reason for accepting the conception of intuitive reason and rejecting the conception of reason as purely constructive — namely, that the latter either involves a contradiction or else abandons its position. And of course any conception which is self-contradictory is thereby false.

Or is it? Can we really be sure that any conception which involves a contradiction is thereby false? To say that a claim made upon reality is false *because* it involves a contradiction is to assume that the law of non-contradiction is true of *reality*, of *fact*. But this is to assume that at least one necessarily true proposition is also existentially or factually true, and this in turn entails the conception of intuitive reason which we are trying to establish. So the argument that the conception of constructive reason is false because it involves a contradiction is itself based upon the assumption of intuitive reason, and specifically upon the assumption that the law of non-contradiction is necessarily true of real, factual existence. But of course this is just what the advocate of constructive reason does not admit. No necessary propositions "provide any information about matters of fact," Ayer reminds us.[12] "Analytic propositions are necessary and certain" because "they simply record our determination to use words in a certain fashion. . . . As Wittgenstein puts it, our justification for holding that the world could not conceivably disobey the laws of logic is simply that we could not say of an unlogical world how it would look."[13] Since the necessity of even the laws of logic is contingent upon our linguistic or conceptual conventions, even the law of non-contradiction could be abandoned. True enough, as C. I. Lewis points out, "The higher up a concept stands in our pyramid, the more reluctant we are to disturb it. . . . The decision that there are no such creatures as have been defined as 'swans,' would be unimportant. The conclusion that there are no such things as Euclidean triangles, would be immensely disturbing. And if we should be forced to realize that nothing in our experience possesses any stability — that our principle, 'Nothing can both be and not be,' was merely a verbalism, applying to nothing more than momentarily — that denouement would rock our world to its foundations."[14] And

---

12 *Language, Truth, and Logic* (London, 1946), p. 79.
13 *Ibid.*, p. 84.
14 *Mind and the World Order*, p. 306.

yet such a world-shaking event is still quite possible — in some ineffable use of the word "possible" — simply because, on this view, not even the law of non-contradiction is necessarily true of the real world.

And so our final effort seems also to have failed, simply because it begs the question. The conception of intuitive reason cannot be demonstrated to be factually, existentially true even by showing that its denial involves a contradiction, because to say that contradictoriness implies falsity concerning the real, factual world is to assume at least one necessarily true existential proposition and hence also the conception of intuitive reason.

Yet perhaps we should not give up quite so easily. While it does seem that the issue between these two conceptions of reason is too basic to be resolved by logical demonstration, may there not be some other way of justifying one conception over the other? Here one is reminded of Aristotle's argument that the skeptic refutes himself by reducing himself to the vegetative state. Is it possible for us as humans, as thinking beings, to avoid believing that the law of non-contradiction is necessarily true of the real world? To say that "the law of non-contradiction does not hold true of objective reality" is to allow that the contradictory of this very proposition itself may also be true, that it may also be true that the law of non-contradiction *does* hold true of objective reality. As we have seen, however, this latter proposition is precisely the fundamental position of the advocate of the conception of reason as intuitive. Hence the advocate of the conception of reason as constructive is, at bottom, in the self-defeating position of denying his thesis in the same breath with which he affirms it, of granting the conception of reason as intuitive at the same time that he denies it. And this is exactly not to maintain any position at all. This being the case, the intuitivist need pay no more attention to the constructivist than Aristotle did to his vegetable. Thus while the conception of reason as intuitive might possibly *be* false, by some unspeakable use of the word "might," it cannot be *asserted* or *believed* to be false. Put differently, while the *proposition* that reason is intuitive can only be rationally intuited and cannot be rationally demonstrated to be true, the *assertion* of or *belief* in that proposition can be demonstrated to be inescapable by any being who makes any assertion or holds any belief at all.

Contemporary philosophers are therefore obliged to admit that at least one proposition, the law of non-contradiction, is both necessarily true and also true of real, factual existence just in order to maintain their position — or any position at all. And they must therefore also accept the conception of reason as intuitive, at least in addition to if not in place of the conception of reason as constructive. Here the reason of modernity must, just in order to assert itself, become the reason of the tradition.

3

First Steps in Mysticism

JESSE DE BOER, Professor of Philosophy, University of Kentucky. A.B., Calvin College; A.M., University of Illinois; Ph.D., Harvard University. Contributor to *The Return to Reason* (ed. John Wild).

First Steps in Mysticism

BY JESSE DE BOER

INTRODUCTION

A PASSAGE IN THE *Upanishads* OPENS WITH THE REMARK THAT THIS world is "woven" on water, the world of water on wind, that on the sun, . . . the moon, . . . stars, they on gods, they on Indra, Indra on Prajapati, and Prajapati on Brahman.

> "On what then, pray, are the worlds of *Brahman* woven, warp and woof?"
>
> Yajnavalkya said: "Gārgi, do not question too much, lest your head fall off. In truth, you are questioning too much about a divinity about which further questions cannot be asked. Gārgi, do not over-question." *Brhadaranyaka Upanishad* III.vi. RM 84[1]

This passage exhibits a familiar first step in religious thought. I shall not now argue with people who forbid taking it. Instead, I wish to understand what sort of movement this is and at least some of the various modes in which it may be made.

This step consists in saying that something is dependent on something independent. It presents a contrast between what we may call the finite and what we may call the infinite. Passages like the one above point out that the man who asks for the cause or explanation of what is infinite has not understood the sense of saying that

---

[1] The symbol *RM 84* is a page reference to *A Source Book in Indian Philosophy*, edited by Sarvepalli Radhakrishnan and Charles A. Moore (Princeton, 1957). I shall use like symbols throughout.

it is infinite. It is senseless to ask about the infinite the very question which, when it is asked about the finite, has led to the conception of the infinite, viz., what is its cause or ground? Augustine made this point when he said that it is absurd to ask what God was doing a week before He created the world or why He did not create it earlier than He did.[2]

Involved in taking this step is the act of giving sense to the expression "this world." This world is somehow distinguished from something else, viz., God or the infinite. It is spoken of as finite or dependent. I wish to stress that it is important to clear up if possible the respect in which, or the feature(s) in virtue of which, a given thing or type or collection of things is said to be finite. Why do speakers in the *Upanishads* attribute finitude to this or that and to this world? What makes something finite? Is it because a cow is not a windmill that each is finite? Is a wagon finite because there are many wagons? Or perhaps because wagons are made in the wagon shop, or because they wear out and end up in the wagon graveyard? Or is a dog finite because it often gets hungry and needs a beef bone and dog biscuits?

According as the respect varies in which things are said to be finite, so will vary the conception of the infinite. This, I would say, is to be expected. I at least do expect it. There is no reason, is there, despite the efforts of such writers as Professor W. T. Stace to persuade us that religion always teaches the same thing,[3] to suppose that men agree on these matters. Certainly the spokesmen of various religions do not sound like an orchestra performing the same piece.

Let us see. It will be useful to call attention to a few passages in Plato. I start with him because he is uncommonly clear on the topic before us, and because it is fairly safe to suppose that Western students of philosophy and religious thought are more familiar with his work than with that of any other equally important writer. The passages I shall refer to show Plato making a distinction between the

2 I am paraphrasing a few lines from *The City of God* XI. 5, 6.

3 See his *Time and Eternity,* e.g. (Princeton, 1952). On p. 22 he writes: "But religion . . . is the same for all men." And he means mysticism: "The mystic — and we must remember that this means every one of us — . . . " (p. 125). See also pp. 15, 17, 18, 144. Professor Stace gives the impression of being uneasy until he can assure himself that all men are ready to say what he wants to say. Apparently his chance to be correct varies in proportion to the decrease of dissent. What he identifies as essential to religion turns out to be mysticism not Platonism or Theism. So his confidence in the consensus is bought at the price of interpreting several writers as "really" saying what they did not at all intend to say.

finite and the infinite, and what is more, doing so in a special way, a way that is not at all the same as another we might think of.

Begin with a few lines from the *Phaedrus*, where Plato, in an address attributed to Socrates, offers an explanation of motion through soul as self-moving. At present I am interested, not in his concept of soul but in his movement from something taken to be dependent to something taken to be self explanatory, i.e., final and ultimate. In this passage Socrates offers us "the truth about the soul divine and human. . . ."

> Every soul is immortal. For that which is ever moving is immortal; but that which moves something else or is moved by something else, when it ceases to move, ceases to live. Only that which moves itself, since it does not leave itself, never ceases to move, and this is also the source and beginning of motion for all other things which have motion. But the beginning is ungenerated (*archē de agenēton*). For everything that is generated must be generated from a beginning, but the beginning is not generated from anything; for if the beginning were generated from anything, it would not be generated from a beginning. *Phaedrus* 245 c-d. (I am using the translations of Plato found in the Loeb Library series.)

The key sentence is "But the beginning is ungenerated." Whatever is moved by something can be understood only by reference to something which, since it moves itself, and thus can move whatever does not move itself, does not refer to something further as cause of its motion. The explanation for secondary motion is primary motion, i.e., a self-mover as the first cause of all motion. (See also *Laws* X 894b-d.) So far as Plato here moves toward something self-explanatory, and clearly understands what this entails, his discussion is like Yajnavalkya's saying, "Gārgi, do not over-question." Furthermore, Plato here calls on soul for explanation of what is dependent; the self-explanatory or infinite is soul, which is self-moving and so the cause of secondary motion. His thought here virtually compares this world to an animal, whose motions are explained by saying that it is alive, not dead. Certain passages in the *Timaeus* (e.g., 36d ff.) are similar: here Plato speaks of a world-soul bearing the relation to the cosmos that life has to a living organism.

There is, however, in the *Timaeus* another conception based on an especially important analogy. In order to introduce this notion I wish to present a brief tract occurring early in the *Philebus*. Socrates is proposing that four great Kinds (*eidē*, *genē*) or ultimate factors be distinguished; his opening suggestion is that all things now existing be divided into a number of types or classes. These he calls the infinite (*apeiron*), the limit or finite (*peras*), the combination or mixture of the first two (*mixis* or *mikton*), and last the cause (*aitia*) of the mixture. (One of these, the third, is not an ultimate principle: it is what when analyzed leads Plato to propound his *three* ultimate factors. At this point, however, he lists it along with the explanatory principles and so makes a total of four.) Now, I am interested in the analogy used by Plato to clarify the role of these factors, and in particular the words he employs for "cause" which exhibit the character of his analogy. The passage begins where Socrates sets out to present the fourth factor, viz., cause.

> Soc. But we said there was, in addition to three classes, a fourth to be investigated. Let us do that together. See whether you think that everything which comes into being must necessarily come into being through a cause.
>
> Pro. Yes, I do; for how could it come into being apart from a cause?
>
> Soc. Does not the nature of that which makes or creates (*poiountos*) differ only in name from the cause (*aitias*), and may not the creative agent (*poioun*) and the cause (*aition*) be properly considered one?
>
> Pro. Yes.
>
> Soc. And again, we shall find that, on the same principle, that which is made or created (*poioumenon*) differs in name only from that which comes into being (*gignomenon*), shall we not?
>
> Pro. We shall.   *Philebus* 26e-27a

A bit later we come upon a few further statements in which Plato explains the aim he has been pursuing in making the distinction between the four principles. I call special attention to his word "*dēmiourgos*" as the name of the fourth factor, cause.

> Soc. Did not the things which come into being and the things out of which they come into being furnish us all the three classes?
>
> Pro. Certainly.
>
> Soc. And that which produces (*dēmiourgoun*) all these, the cause (*aitian*), we call the fourth, as it has been satisfactorily shown to be distinct from the others?
>
> Pro. Yes, it is distinct.
>
> Soc. It is, then, proper, now that we have distinguished the four, to make sure that we remember them separately by enumerating them in order.
>
> Pro. Yes, certainly.
>
> Soc. The first, then, I call infinite (*apeiron*), the second limit or finite (*peras*), and the third something generated by a mixture of these two (*miktēn kai gegenēmenēn ousian*). And should I be making any mistake if I called the cause of this mixture and creation the fourth (*tēs mixeōs aitian kai geneseōs*)?
>
> Pro. Certainly not.   *Philebus* 27a-c

Plato's descriptive title "Mixture" is intended to cover every sensible object, i.e., the whole of this world of "nature," "all the choir of heaven and furniture of the earth, in a word all those bodies which compose the mighty frame of the world." This is the finite order, dependent on something else. It is defined by the feature of coming to be. The word "nature" itself derives from a stem that signifies being born (*nascor, natus*). Why is something finite? Because it comes to be. The cosmos comes to be, and is explained by what it comes to be out of. It is plain to Plato that what comes to be cannot originate itself; hence there must be a cause. And it is equally plain to him that a cause is a maker; and a maker is a craftsman, an artificer. The translator obscures the thought by using two words, "makes" and "creates," for Plato's single word *poioun*. Creating is not making, as *ex nihilo* is not *ex materia*. Plato says explicitly that the concept of making is the same as that of cause, so that for him everything that comes to be is a thing made: something contrived or constructed. He proceeds at once to identify the concepts "made" and "having come into being." This comment is justified by his introducing (27b) the word *dēmiourgos* as equivalent to *aitia*. What has to be explained is whatever comes into being. This is a mixture of *apeiron* and *peras*, a composite of two factors. A cause is required to do the mixing, and this cause is a *poioun* or *dēmiourgos*. This world, then, is a product of craftsmanship; the model in Plato's thought is the craftsman introducing form into material.

I turn now to a longer and more detailed account, occurring early in the *Timaeus*.

> Tim. Nay, as to that, Socrates, all men who possess even a small share of good sense call upon God always at the outset of every undertaking, be it small or great; we therefore who are purposing to deliver a discourse concerning the Universe, how it was created (*gegonen* — has come to be) or haply is uncreate (*agenes* — has not come to be), must needs invoke Gods and Goddesses. . . .
>
> Now first of all we must, in my judgement, make the following distinction. What is that which is Existent always and has no Becoming? And what is that which is Becoming always and never is Existent? Now the one of these is apprehensible by thought with the aid of reasoning, since it is ever uniformly existent; whereas the other is an object of opinion with the aid of unreasoning sensation, since it becomes and perishes and is never really existent. Again, everything which becomes must of necessity become owing to some Cause; for without a cause it is impossible for anything to attain becoming. But when the artificer of any object, in forming its shape and quality, keeps his gaze fixed on that which is uniform, using a model of this kind, that object, executed in this way, must of necessity be beautiful;

but whenever he gazes at that which has come into existence and uses a created model, the object thus executed is not beautiful. Now the whole Heaven, or Cosmos, or if there is any other name which it specially prefers, by that let us call it, — so, be its name what it may, we must first investigate concerning it that primary question which has to be investigated at the outset in every case, — namely, whether it has existed always, having no beginning of generation, or whether it has come into existence, having begun from some beginning. It has come into existence; for it is visible and tangible and possessed of a body; and all such things are sensible, and things sensible, being apprehensible by opinion with the aid of sensation, come into existence, as we saw, and are generated. And that which has come into existence must necessarily, as we say, have come into existence by reason of some Cause. Now to discover the Maker (*poiētēn*) and Father (*patera*) of this Universe were a task indeed; and having discovered Him, to declare Him unto all men were a thing impossible.

Timaeus 27c-28c

At this point Plato has Timaeus support the view that the model followed by the Demiurge was eternal, not one that came to be, for the Cosmos is beautiful and the Demiurge is "the best of all the Causes" (29a). To proceed:

TIM. Let us now state the Cause wherefore He that constructed (*ho zunistas*) it constructed Becoming and the All. He was good, and in him that is good no envy ariseth ever concerning anything; and being devoid of envy He desired that all should be, so far as possible, like unto Himself. This principle, then, we shall be wholly right in accepting from men of wisdom as being above all the supreme originating principle of Becoming and the Cosmos. For God desired that, so far as possible, all things should be good and nothing evil; wherefore, when He took over all that was visible, seeing that it was not in a state of rest but in a state of discordant and disorderly motion, He brought it into order out of disorder, deeming that the former state is in all ways better than the latter. For Him who is most good it neither was nor is permissible to perform any action save what is most fair.   *Timaeus* 29d-30a

I digress a moment to call attention to one of the more interesting features of this passage. It may not be very prominent, but I think it has some importance for the student of philosophy. The opening lines (at 27c) express Plato's genuine piety. He suits his language, or adjusts his diction, to the sublimity of his topic; and he acknowledges the propriety of prayer at the outset of such a vast undertaking. And at 29e he states that the principle of the generosity of God (is this not another signal expression of piety?) comes to him from "men of wisdom." I take it that he has in mind religious teachers, not men engaged in the professional work of the philosopher. Similar passages are easy to find: e.g., *Gorgias* 523ff., *Phaedo* 61d ff.

and 107d ff. In all of these Plato listens with respect to the teachings of religious spokesmen; his procedure is tantamount to disclaiming originality in point of the teaching itself. It is careless to suppose that since Plato wrote the *Timaeus* this dialogue is chiefly a philosophical work. The theme is of interest to the religious man; it is a treatise on the relation of this world to the eternal principle or principles. Besides, it is a piece of religious writing: it both expresses and evokes the proper personal or existential posture. The philosophy in it, I judge, is confined to the exercises in elucidation of thought.

To return from the digression. The particular form of the finite-infinite distinction in Plato's mind is that between what comes to be and that which is. What comes to be is what needs explanation. To see what he means we may observe that he proposes to discuss the Universe or Whole (*to pan*), the whole Heaven or Cosmos (*ho pas ouranos hē kosmos*). This I have spoken of as nature or the entire mass of sensible items, distributed in time and space.

Being, says Plato, is existent always, i.e., eternal; thus it contrasts with Becoming. The first is object of reason, the second of sense and opinion. Under Being he includes the Forms. Their eternity, I would say, consists merely in the impropriety of applying temporal predicates to the supposed entities named by general words. How old is triangularity or duality? Later passages in the *Timaeus* present the Receptacle as a further eternal principle. (It is called *hypodochē* at 49b and 51a, *chōra* at 52b.) Its eternity consists, I surmise, in duration lacking a foothold for dates and numeration. For Time, which comes into being with the Cosmos, imitates eternity ("moving image of eternity") by making possible the business of the calendar. (See 37d-e.) One may be excused for feeling that Plato is a bit obscure; be that as it may, what he calls Becoming is exemplified by any sensible object we care to indicate: this table, that tree. Each of these is mortal: it begins and ends. Not being eternal, either as the Forms are eternal or as the Receptacle is eternal, it does not exist. (A grammatical comment?)

And as not existing but coming to be, it requires a cause. Nothing can come into being apart from a cause. Do tables make themselves? And what produces a thing like a table is a craftsman. The whole cosmos is like a table. Has it existed always? Of course not: it is visible, object of sense and opinion, corporeal; and every such thing has come into being and been generated. And the cause is a craftsman. Plato speaks of the world-craftsman as Maker (*poiētēs*) and Father (*patēr*); the slide in these metaphors feels smooth, though the

two notions are in conflict. Overlooking this difficulty, it is plain
that the dominant analogy is that of the craftsman: God is to the
world as the furniture maker is to the table.

This is underscored by the concluding portion of the passage
quoted. God is devoid of envy, He is a flawless craftsman — neither
technically incompetent nor morally corrupt; so He tried to make
the cosmos as good and beautiful as possible. He used as model an
eternal pattern, not a picture made from a visible, changing object.
When He set to work He found the material on which He was to
work in disorderly motion. Thus the furniture maker begins with
pieces of wood which, relative to the table, are ill-shaped: matter
for construction through in-formation. By introducing pattern into
the visible chaos He made the cosmos, thus bringing order out of
disorder. What I call the visible chaos is Plato's first mention, though
not by name, of the principle which later he will call the Receptacle,
an eternal factor which, besides the Forms, will have to be included
under the head of the always existent. It too is ultimate inasmuch as
it does not come to be. God finds it, He takes it over, and out of it
and something else He makes (constructs, contrives) the cosmos, the
total sensible world.

In sum, Plato thinks of the finite world as a product of craftsmanship. There is an eternal pattern on which God looks as He
shapes and in-forms the eternal Receptacle, combining the two as He
constructs the sensible world. If I am permitted to use terms of
Aristotle's which developed from those of Plato, the world is a composite of two eternal factors, Form and Matter. Just as a table is a
composite of pattern and materials, so with the world. And as a table
is made by a furniture maker, the world is made by a divine craftsman. Thus God is the efficient cause of the cosmos; and His generosity, in the shape of His desire to make the world as good as
possible, as like to Himself as possible, is its final cause. The dominant model in Plato's religious cosmology is that of the craftsman;
the same can be said of Aristotle's treatment of the four causes of
change in *Physics* II.

So much for Plato's religious thought. I have presented this
slight sketch in order to exhibit Plato as making the initial step of
identifying something as finite and of relating it to something infinite,
and as being the exponent of one, and not the only possible, view
of precisely what makes a thing finite and what its relation is to the
infinite. His view, surely, is radically unlike that which finds its
base in the Bible. I take it to be obvious that the Scriptures say some-

thing about God and His relation to the world that is utterly different from what Plato says. Biblical teaching contrasts God and creature; and there is no eternal factor in the creature. The created world is not dependent on God for the in-forming of material by the agency of a craftsman, but for its entire being. And there is no analogy drawn between a familiar process in the world, such as furniture making, and the creative act. "To whom then will ye liken me. . .? saith the Holy One" (Isaiah 40:25). God's holiness signifies His separateness or transcendence, His distance from everything creaturely.[4]

There is no difficulty, I believe, in seeing that the notions of creation and construction are sharply different. This difference is overlooked by Professor Stace when he says that all religion is the same. Platonism and Theism are not the same. What he mistakenly takes to be the teaching of religion is a third type of religious thought. His studies in religious thought present, I think, a handy summary and interpretation (though not a clear one in every part) of a third type of religious thought, viz., that of mysticism or mystical monism. They certainly do not explain the thinking of Plato and the Gnostics, or that of Augustine and Thomas Aquinas and John Calvin.

I submit that there are at least three major types of religious thought, each of which has its own distinctive way of diagramming the character and the interrelation of the finite and the infinite. I shall now, in concluding this introductory section, present certain passages from the *Upanishads* in order to illustrate my third type, viz., mysticism.

4 "And what is this? I asked the earth; and it answered, 'I am not He'; and whatsoever are therein made the same confession. I asked the sea and the deeps, and the creeping things that lived, and they replied, 'We are not thy God, seek higher than we.' I asked the breezy air, and the universal air with its inhabitants answered, 'Anaximenes was deceived, I am not God.' I asked the heavens, the sun, moon, and stars. 'Neither,' say they, 'are we the God whom thou seekest.' And I answered unto all these things which stand about the door of my flesh, 'Ye have told me concerning my God, that ye are not He; tell me something about Him.' And with a loud voice they exclaimed, 'He made us.'
"All these things praise Thee, the Creator of all. But how dost Thou make them? How, O God, didst Thou make heaven and earth? Truly, neither in the heaven nor in the earth didst Thou make heaven and earth; nor in the air, nor in the waters, since these also belong to the heaven and the earth; nor in the whole world didst Thou make the whole world; because there was no place wherein it could be made before it was made, that it might be; nor didst Thou hold anything in Thy hand wherewith to make heaven and earth. For whence couldest Thou have what Thou hadst not made, whereof to make anything? For what is, save because Thou art? Therefore Thou didst speak and they were made, and in Thy Word Thou madest these things." Augustine, *Confessions*, X. vi, and XI. v.

As a spider emits and draws in [its thread],
As herbs arise on the earth,
As the hairs of the head and body from a living person,
So from the Imperishable arises everything here.
Mundaka Upanishad i. 7. RM 51

This says, very simply, that the finite world, composed of many things, diverse and changing, is made out of the ultimate, is the same in substance with it. This is said again as follows:

He knew: "I, indeed, am this creation, for I have emitted it all from myself." Thence arose creation. . . .
Brhadaranyaka Upanishad I.iv.5. RM 78

. . . Having performed austerity he created this whole world, whatever there is here. Having created it, into it, indeed, he entered. Having entered it, he became both the actual [here] and the yon, both the defined and the undefined, both the based and the nonbased, both the conscious and the unconscious, both the real and the false. As the real, he became whatever there is here. That is what they call the real. . . .   <i>Taittiriya Upanishad</i> II.6. RM 60

These lines say that this world, the finite order, is composed of this and that, of what is thus and not-thus — of whatever is other than any given thing. The finite is the definite, whatever is unlike any other specified thing. And the infinite becomes the finite.

Verily, at that time the world was undifferentiated. It became differentiated just by name and form, as the saying is: "He has such a name, such a form. . . ."
He entered in here, even to the fingernail tips, as a razor would be hidden in a razor-case, or fire in a fire-holder. Him they see not, for [as seen] he is incomplete. When breathing, he becomes breath by name; when speaking, voice; when seeing, the eye; when hearing, the ear; when thinking, the mind. These are merely the names of his acts. . . .   <i>Brhadaranyaka Upanishad</i> I.iv.7. RM 78

The expression "at that time" has the same force as "in the beginning"; i.e., the talk is about the infinite considered in itself. The Bible says: "In the beginning God. . . ." Here, however, the infinite becomes the finite; this world is the infinite, when the infinite has differentiated, divided itself. The <i>Brhadaranyaka Upanishad</i> says (at I.iv.1, 3) that in the beginning the world was Self alone; then this Self caused itself to divide into parts. Why did this happen? On this crucial question, let me present a few passages.

The Lord of Creation (<i>Prajapati</i>), verily, was desirous of creatures (offspring, <i>praja</i>). . . .   <i>Prasna Upanishad</i> I.4. RM 50

This is not very clear. Why does the Lord have a desire? And what will be the relation of the "offspring" to Him? This lack of clarity or definition is found in two more passages.

... He desired: "Would that I were many! Let me procreate myself!"   *Taittiriya Upanishad* II.6. RM 60

"It bethought itself: 'Would that I were many! Let me procreate
myself.'"   *Chandogya Upanishad* VI.ii.3. RM 68

The fullest and clearest passage, with which I close, is the following.

1.   In the beginning this world was Self (*Atman*) alone in the form
of a Person. Looking around, he saw nothing else than himself.
He said first: "I am ...."

2.   He was afraid. Therefore one who is alone is afraid. .... ((But
the fear left him for, being alone, he had nothing to fear.))

3.   Verily he had no delight. Therefore one alone has no delight.
He desired a second. He was, indeed, as large as a woman and a
man closely embraced. He caused that self to fall into two pieces.
((So, as man and woman, arising by division of the original self,
they changed into the forms of animals, and men came to be.))

5.   He knew: "I, indeed, am this creation, for I have emitted it all
from myself." Thence arose creation. ...

11.   Verily, in the beginning this world was *Brahman,* one only.
Being one, he was not developed. ... ((He produced the ruling
gods, and other gods, and the *sudra* caste, and *Dharma,* which is
Law.))

17.   In the beginning this world was just the Self, one only. He
wished: "Would that I had a wife; then I would procreate. Would
that I had wealth; then I would sacrifice." So far as he does not
obtain any one of these, he thinks that he is, assuredly, incomplete.
Now his completeness is as follows: his mind truly is his self
(*atman*); his voice is his wife; ... his body (*atman*), indeed, is
his work, for with his body he performs work. ...

Brhadaranyaka Upanishad I.iv. RM 77-79

I. The Whole

Religious thought commonly distinguishes something as finite
or dependent from something else taken to be infinite, the ground or
explanation of the finite. So far diverse religious traditions are alike.
But they differ in point of the manner in which the two poles of
contrast are conceived, in point of the conception of what makes
an item finite and of what its relation is to the infinite. Certainly
Platonism and Theism differ sharply. A third thought pattern has
been illustrated by passages from the *Upanishads;* these give expression to the conception of an identity of substance between finite
things and their cause or principle. This world, composed of a mass
of differentiated items, individual, diverse and changing, each of them
a "this," is the eternal Brahman. The eternal Being "at that time"
gave rise to this world by emission from itself, pictured in some

passages as a process of God dividing Himself into His bodily members. I call this third way mysticism or mystical monism.

In what follows I shall be busy studying certain central doctrines of mysticism as they occur in a classical collection of writings, the *Upanishads*. These writings are not systematic in form; I run the risk of distorting them and weakening their effect by pursuing the aim of arranging and clarifying the pattern of doctrine. I accept the risk, because there is in the *Upanishads* a pattern of doctrine, and after one has looked squarely at the separate elements he can return to the total picture, perhaps with improved vision. Moreover, I shall on occasion look at the same passage several times over, in order to note diverse aspects of such a passage as they bear on stages in my program of analysis.

My first objective is to examine and clarify the way in which, in the *Upanishads*, the pattern of the finite-infinite relation is drawn. Can we map the basic maneuver whereby the infinite Being is defined and its relation to the ordinary and familiar contents of this world is specified?

The basic move is to contrast whatever is a "this," each item in the entire welter of differential items met with in experience and characterized in descriptions and definitions, with a something that includes, embraces, contains or envelops them all. The infinite is the Totality, the Whole within which finite items are contained; finite things are parts in a whole.

> By the Lord (*Isa*) enveloped must this all be —
> Whatever moving thing there is in the moving world. . . .
>
> *Isa Upanishad* 1. RM 39

> Manifest, [yet] hidden; called "Moving-in-secret";
> The great abode! Therein is placed that
> Which moves and breathes and winks.
>
> *Mundaka Upanishad* II.ii.1. RM 53

Here the image is that of vessel, storehouse or reservoir. The *Mundaka Upanishad* speaks (at III.ii.5) of those wise men who, when reaching the divine, "into the All itself do enter." In this All the finite items are unified. Three sections later there occurs the familiar passage likening the infinite to an ocean wherein rivers disappear, losing their individuality.

> As the flowing rivers in the ocean
> Disappear, quitting name and form,
> So the knower, being liberated from name and form,
> Goes unto the Heavenly Person, higher than the high.
>
> *Mundaka Upanishad* III.ii.8. RM 55

This spatial metaphor corresponds to the image of the unity of all times and events.

> *Om!* — This syllable is this whole world.
> Its further explanation is:—
> The past, the present, the future — everything is just the word *Om*.
> And whatever else that transcends threefold time — that, too, is just the word *Om*.
> For truly, everything here is *Brahman;* this self is *Brahman.* . . .
> *Mandukya Upanishad* 1, 2. RM 55

Another text presents the figure of container or receptacle as follows:

> 1.   Verily, this whole world is *Brahman*. Tranquil, let one worship It as that from which he came forth, as that into which he will be dissolved, as that in which he breathes.
> 2.   He who consists of mind, whose body is life *(prana)*, whose form is light, whose conception is truth, whose self is space, containing all works, containing all desires, containing all odors, containing all tastes, encompassing this whole world, the unspeaking, the unconcerned — . . .
> 4.   Containing all works, containing all desires, containing all odors, containing all tastes, encompassing this whole world, the unspeaking, the unconcerned — this is the Self of mine within the heart, this is *Brahman.* . . .   *Chandogya Upanishad* III.xiv. RM 65

The final lines above identify Brahman, the great Self, with the small self within me ("smaller than a grain of rice, . . . or a mustard seed"). This move I shall take up later. I proceed to a few more texts that exhibit the container theme, one of them working with the figure of rivers and the ocean.

> 1.   "These rivers, my dear, flow, the eastern toward the east, the western toward the west. They go just from the ocean to the ocean. They become that ocean itself. As there they know not 'I am this one', 'I am that one' —
> 2.   even so indeed, my dear, all creatures here, though they have come forth from Being, know not We have come forth from Being. . . ."
> *Chandogya Upanishad* VI.x. RM 69

> Higher than this is *Brahman*. The Supreme, the Great,
> Hidden in all things, body by body,
> The One embracer of the universe —
> *Svetasvatara Upanishad* III.7. RM 90.

> This whole world is pervaded
> With beings that are parts of Him.
> *Ibid.* IV.10. RM 91

> The Creator of all, of manifold form,
> The One embracer of the universe —
> *Ibid.* V.13. RM 92

As finite items are present in the infinite as in a receptacle, so the infinite is present in each finite item. It is present as salt is present in every portion of salt water: the salt dissolves, cannot be found apart; the water is salty in every part. So Being is in all things, though it cannot be perceived apart by itself.

> "It is — as a lump of salt cast in water would dissolve right into the water; there would not be [any] of it to seize forth, as it were (iva), but wherever one may take, it is salty indeed — so, lo, verily, this great Being (bhuta), infinite, limitless, is just a mass of knowledge (vijnana-ghana). . . ." Thus spake Yajnavalkya.
>
> Brhadaranyaka Upanishad II.iv.12. RM 82;
> cf. Chandogya Upanishad VI.xiii.1-2. RM 69-70

Certain passages combine statements of Brahman's presence in with statements of Brahman's transcendence to every limited object.

> 5. It moves. It moves not.
> It is far, and it is near.
> It is within all this,
> And it is outside of all this.
> 6. Now, he who on all beings
> Look as just in the Self (Atman),
> And on the Self as in all beings —
> He does not shrink away from Him.
>
> Isa Upanishad. RM 40

> [Yajnavalkya said:] "He who, dwelling in all things, yet is other than all things, whom all things do not know, whose body all things are, who controls all things from within — He is your Self, the Inner Controller, the Immortal. . . ."
>
> Brhadaranyaka Upanishad III.vii.15. RM 84

The infinite Being is unlike every limited object in not being differentiated from anything: its unlikeness to every finite item consists in the impropriety of predicating of it anything unlike what can be predicated of any different thing. A thing is finite when it is limited, i.e., if it has properties the presence of which forbids or prevents the compresence of others. A windmill is finite because, being so, it is not a locomotive or an apple. Wherever there is difference (i.e., negation), multiplicity, or change, there is finitude. Reality is without these: it is eternal, one, and undifferentiated. It is the limitless. Thus it is *outside* "all this," other than everything that is other than any given thing. And it contains, envelops every "this," it is the abode, the ocean, the reservoir. At the same time it is *within* "all this," the universally present medium pervading every item in the welter of finite things.

These two assertions occur in two texts occurring near each other in the same *Upanishad*. Gārgi asks Yajnavalkya what it is on which are based the parts of time and the whole of space. The answer is as follows:

> He said: "That, O Gārgi, *Brahmins* call the Imperishable. It is not coarse, not fine, not short, not long, not glowing [like fire], not adhesive [like water], without shadow and without darkness, without air and without space, without stickiness (intangible), odorless, tasteless, without eye, without ear, without voice, without wind, without energy, without breath, without mouth, (without personal or family name, unaging, undying, without fear, immortal, stainless, not uncovered, not covered), without measure, without inside, without outside. . . ."
>
> *Brhadaranyaka Upanishad* III.viii.8. RM 85

> Verily, this self is *Brahman,* made of knowledge, of mind, of breath, of seeing, of hearing, of earth, of water, of wind, of space, of energy and of non-energy, of desire and of non-desire, of anger and of non-anger, of virtuousness and of non-virtuousness. It is made of everything. This is what is meant by the saying "made of this, made of that."
>
> *Ibid.* IV.iv.5. RM 87

Let me try to go through the movements again. I wish to get clear the respect in which a given thing is said to be finite and thus contrasted with what is infinite. A finite thing is a "this" or a "that." This means, I take it, that wherever something can be distinguished from anything else, we have a finite thing. A book is not a cow, a cow is not a juniper bush. Each is a "this" and is finite. Why? Because it is differentiated. It has properties or functions unlike those of other things. Anything other than anything else is finite. It is limited because it is *not* the same as something else. As *not being* something else it is unreal: it has negation, it is Non-Being. Spinoza said: *Omnis determinatio est negatio.* The infinite, now, is the non-finite, i.e., it is what is *not* differentiated from anything else. It is not-not a cow or a tree. There is in it no feature whereby it excludes any predicate: it includes all differences, all opposites. It is unlike a particular "this" only in the sense that, while it contains the properties of the particular, it also contains all the properties not possessed by that particular. The infinite is Being insofar as it is not differential: there is no predicate to be denied of it. It is the whole or totality of all predicates and of all finite items possessing such predicates differentially. This fits the Hegelian slogan: The Truth is the Whole. Suppose one takes the Real to be the infinite Being so characterized, he can go on to say that finite things are unreal or non-existent. "Lead me from the unreal to the real!"

One question remains to be asked. How or why does the infinite give rise to finite things? In the introduction to this study I presented texts in which the Eternal is likened to a person who feels lonely and for the sake of company divides himself into limbs and members. Is this a way of asserting the incompleteness of the Eternal? Hegel talks of Being as in itself abstract and vacuous; thus it is identical with Non-Being, its antithesis; and the synthesis is Becoming, in which Being actualizes itself. (I shall not remark here on his failure to understand that the concept of Being is not a sort-concept.) Schiller has the lines:

> *Freundlos war der grosse Weltenmeister*
> *Fuehlte Mangel —.*   J. C. Friedrich Schiller, *Die Freundschaft*

Let us see how the *Upanishad* talks about this point.

> He knew: "I, indeed, am this creation, for I emitted it all from myself." Thence arose creation. . . .
> *Brhadaranyaka Upanishad* I.iv.5. RM 78

> The One Who, himself without color, by the manifold application of his power
> Distributes many colors in his hidden purpose,
> And into whom, its end and its beginning, the whole world
>   dissolves — He is God (*deva*)!
> *Svetasvatara Upanishad* IV.1. RM 91

> 9. As the one fire has entered the world
>   And become corresponding in form to every form,
>   So the one Inner Self (*antaratman*) of all things
>   Is corresponding in form to every form, and yet is outside.
> 12. The Inner Self of all things, the One Controller,
>   Who makes his one form manifold —.
> *Katha Upanishad* IV. RM 48

These texts speak of self-division, a distribution of unity into difference. They speak in a bit more sophisticated way of the same picture as was presented in the introduction, of God emitting all things out of Himself, producing the finite world by dividing into His own parts and members.

And why is this thesis offered? There is no answer; there is nothing back of it. It is simply offered. As the *Brhadaranyaka Upanishad* says (at I.iv.7), the world in the beginning was undifferentiated; then it became differentiated by name and form. The expression "name and form," I take to signify the differential aspect of the finite. As this passage says, Brahman became voice by name when speaking. To worship Brahman under such a limited aspect is to be misled. "Whoever worships one or another of these — he knows not; for he is incomplete with one or another of these" (RM 78). The worshiper is incomplete when so approaching the Eternal; likewise the Eternal would be incomplete if it were voice or light, or any other finite thing. There is no reason to be sought why the

Eternal is defined as it is, and why it differentiates itself. The passages here adduced present the teaching of the *Upanishads* as the last word. They state how these teachers see everything, and to ask why they see it so is to ask why thy do what they do. "Do not over-question, Gārgi."

The infinite is the non-finite, limitless, different from nothing and so unlike whatever does differ from anything. It is one and Real: all else is unreal. The world is illusion.

> 9. The past, the future, and what the Vedas declare —
> This whole world the illusion maker (*mayin*) projects out
> of this [*Brahman*].
> And in it by illusion (*maya*) the other is confined.
> 10. Now, one should know that Nature (*Prakriti*) is illusion (*maya*),
> And that the Mighty Lord (*Mahesvara*) is the illusion-maker
> (*mayin*).
> This whole world is pervaded
> With beings that are parts of Him.
>
> *Svetasvatara Upanishad* IV. RM 91

To exist is to be the infinite, the totality of all attributes, all opposites, all differential items. They, not being infinite, do not exist; they are unreal, an illusion.

II. Predication Is Illicit

The doctrine outlined in the preceding section is, I judge, the heart of mysticism. Two of its corollaries form the subject of this section. (1) It is improper to apply predicates to the infinite; and consequently (2) there is no discursive knowledge of the infinite — the best speech about Brahman is silence. When the mystic does go on to speak of "knowing" the Eternal, he will insist that it lacks the shape of rational discourse; he will compare it, perhaps, to contact or to the melting of one thing into another, or perhaps to the experience of lovers in sexual embrace.[5]

I shall now exhibit the presence in the *Upanishads* of the two views just mentioned. As for (1) the denial of the propriety of ap-

---

5 Some people talk of this experience as directed upon the dissolution of the two into one. I question whether such talk is accurate description of the event, or is rather an account drawing on a general theory which rises from a longing to remove finite individuality. Perhaps Tristan and Isolde feel as they do because of their allegiance to Gnostic beliefs; they seem to depreciate their personal separateness and to long for escape from it. Mr. W. H. Auden says: "Tristan and Isolde are tormented because they are compelled to count up to two when they long to be able only to count up to one; . . ." *The Portable Greek Reader*, edited, and with an introduction, by W. H. Auden (New York, 1948), p. 28.

plying predicates to the infinite, this is conspicuous and emphatic.
Speaking of Brahman, one text says:

> Wherefrom words turn back,
> Together with the mind, not having attained —.
>
> *Taittiriya Upanishad* II.4. RM 60

Another makes the same point, rejecting a list of possible predicates;
and it adds that he who fails to see the true doctrine is fated to remain fast to the wheel of repetitive birth and death.

> What is soundless, touchless, formless, imperishable,
> Likewise tasteless, constant, odorless,
> Without beginning, without end, higher than the great, stable —
> By discerning That, one is liberated from the mouth of death.
>
> *Katha Upanishad* III.15. RM 47

In the foregoing section I quoted two passages from the *Brhadaranyaka Upanishad* (viz., III.viii.8. RM 85; and IV.iv.5. RM 87)
which supply the reason why Brahman has no attributes. In the
former of these Yajnavalkya says that Brahman is without this or
that attribute, organ, or function. All are denied because the infinite
Being contains all differences, all opposites. It is not more short than
it is long; it is both and therefore neither. The second says that
Brahman is "made of this, made of that," i.e., all differences and opposites are present in the one totality; hence none can describe it.
The ordinary use of predicates is for the purpose of characterizing
a given thing. Predication consists in noting and marking what a
given thing is or does, or what a group or class of things is or does.
To predicate is to differentiate. "That's a cow." "The whale is a
mammal." In mystical monism the infinite Being is made of all
definite items in sum. Their mode of being is that of being determinate; thus predication fits them. But "determination is negation";
whatever is determinate is short of reality; the infinite is plainly in-
determinable and hence indescribable.

> 19. By the mind alone is It [the ancient, primeval *Brahman*] to be
>   perceived.
>   There is on earth no diversity.
>   He gets death after death,
>   Who perceives here seeming diversity.
> 20. As a unity only is It to be looked upon —
>   This indemonstrable, enduring Being,
>   Spotless, beyond space,
>   The unborn Self, great, enduring.
>
> *Brhadaranyaka Upanishad* IV.iv. RM 88

> Manifest, [yet] hidden; called "Moving-in-secret";
> The great abode! Therein is placed that
> Which moves and breathes and winks.

What that is, know as Being and Non-Being,
As the object of desire. . . . *Mundaka Upanishad* II.ii.1. RM 53

4. . . . Then they said to him:
5. "*Brahman* is life (*prana*). *Brahman* is joy. *Brahman* is the void." Then he said: "I understand that *Brahman* is life. But joy and void I do not understand." They said: "Joy (*ka*) — verily, that is the same as the void (*kha*). The Void — verily, that is the same as Joy. . . ." *Chandogya Upanishad* IV.x. RM 66

That which is beyond this world
Is without form and without ill.
                          Svetasvatara Upanishad III.10. RM 91

19. Not above, not across,
    Nor in the middle has one grasped Him.
    There is no likeness of Him
    Whose name is Great Glory.
20. His form is not to be beheld.
    No one soever sees Him with the eye. . . .
                                    Ibid. IV. RM 91

These passages have the same thrust. Diversity belongs to finitude: a finite item can be characterized. But it is unreal. The infinite is "indemonstrable," i.e., beyond the reach of predication; there is as good reason to apply one opposite predicate to it as another. And something composed of opposite attributes, Being and Non-Being, is void: devoid of character, empty, inconceivable, ineffable.

Verily, this Self (*Atman*) — poets declare — wanders here on earth from body to body, unovercome, as it seems, by the bright or dark fruits of action. He who on account of his unmanifestness, subtility, imperceptibility, incomprehensibility, and selflessness is [apparently] unabiding and a doer in the world — he, truly, is not a doer, and he is abiding. Verily, he is pure, steadfast and unswerving, stainless, unagitated, desireless, fixed like a spectator, and self-abiding. As an enjoyer of righteousness, he covers himself with a veil made of qualities; [but] he remains fixed — yea, he remains fixed!
                                    Maitri Upanishad II.7. RM 94

This is a comment on the hidden, ineffable Self withdrawn from the finite self; but the comment applies equally to Brahman. The two are the same, as we shall see later. The qualities that distinguish things one from another are only a veil; action is unreal and is performed in the unreal, for it too involves differentiation. Brahman is void.

(2) Therefore it cannot be reached by discourse. I am sure that the thought here is clear and simple, but I do wish to exhibit a number of characteristic texts.

4. Unmoving, the One is swifter than the mind.
   The sense-powers reached not It, speeding on before.

10. Other, indeed, they say, than knowledge!
Other, they say, than non-knowledge.
11. Knowledge and non-knowledge —
He who this pair conjointly knows,
With non-knowledge passing over death,
With knowledge wins the immortal.

Isa Upanishad. RM 40-41

There the eye goes not;
Speech goes not, nor the mind.
We know not, we understand not
How one would teach it.
Other, indeed, is It than the known,
And moreover above the unknown.

Kena Upanishad I.3. RM 42

It is conceived by him by whom It is not conceived of.
He by whom It is conceived of, knows it not.
It is not understood by those who [say they] understand It.
It is understood by those who [say they] understand It not.

Ibid. II.3. RM 42

This Self is not to be obtained by instruction,
Nor by intellect, nor by much learning.

Katha Upanishad II.23. RM 46

An intelligent man should suppress his speech and his mind.
The latter he should suppress in the Understanding Self (*jnana atman*).
The understanding he should suppress in the Great Self.
That he should suppress in the Tranquil Self. . . .

Ibid. III.13. RM 47

The opposites, knowledge and non-knowledge, are unified, their difference cancelled, in the effort to say what knowing Brahman is like. This is because of what Brahman is. Because Brahman is without properties, discourse cannot make an approach.

6. The separate nature of the senses,
And that their arising and setting
Is of things that come into being apart [from itself],
The wise man recognizes, and sorrows not.
10. When cease the five
[Sense-] knowledges, together with the mind,
And the intellect [*buddhi*] stirs not —
This, they say, is the highest course.
11. This they consider as *yoga* —
The firm holding back of the senses.
Then one becomes undistracted.
Yoga, truly, is the origin and the end.
12. Not by speech, not by mind,
Not by sight can He be apprehended.

How can He be comprehended
Otherwise than by one's saying "He is"? . . .

13. He can indeed be comprehended by the thought "He is"
And by [admitting] the real nature of both [his comprehensibility
and his incomprehensibility].
When he has been comprehended by the thought "He is"
His real nature manifests itself.

Katha Upanishad VI. RM 49-50

Not by sight is It grasped, not even by speech,
Not by any other sense-organs, austerity, or work.
By the peace of knowledge, one's nature purified —
In that way, however, by meditating, one does behold Him who is
without parts. *Mundaka Upanishad* III.i.8. RM 54

The approach to the infinite is "the peace of knowledge," i.e., withdrawal from whatever can be said to be "this" or "that." This peace is silence, inaction. A final passage is as follows:

By knowing Him only, a wise
brahmin should get for himself intelligence;
He should not meditate upon many words,
For that is a weariness of speech.

Brhadarunyaka Upanishad IV.iv.21. RM 88

III. BRAHMAN IS ATMAN

The crowning mystical thesis of the identity of the self (Atman) with God (Brahman) has already appeared. I propose now to examine how the *Upanishads* present it. I shall try to do so in four stages: (1) a direct statement of the thesis; (2) a partial survey of the attribution of the same predicates (or lack of them) to the self and to Brahman; (3) the particular reason offered for asserting the thesis; (4) and finally, the great doctrines of the self after its identity with Brahman is seen. The third stage is the most difficult.

There is no room for doubt about the importance attached by the *Upanishads* to the identity of Atman and Brahman. He who does not realize it wanders in ignorance.

"In this which vitalizes all things, which appears in all things,
the Great —
In this Brahmā-wheel the self flutters about,
Thinking that itself and the Actuator are different."

Svetasvatara Upanishad I.6. RM 89

The self is helpless as a moth, lost in the whirling wheel of finitude, as long as it takes itself to be distinct. To attain the opposite position to this delusion is salvation.

—(1)—

One of the *Upanishads* contains two simple assertions of the identity of Brahman and Atman.

> When a seer sees the brilliant
> Maker, Lord, Person, the *Brahman*-source,
> Then, being a knower, shaking off good and evil,
> Stainless, he attains supreme identity with Him.
>
> *Mundaka Upanishad* III.i.3. RM 54

> He, verily, who knows that supreme *Brahman,* becomes very *Brahman.* . . .   *Ibid.* III.ii.9. RM 55

These are simple statements because the finite person is characterized no further than by describing him as a seer or knower. Nothing is said so far about the need to work out a distinction between the self as an ordinary empirical person (that man saying his prayers, who took a bath before breakfast), and the self as a hidden something which is not noticed until after one has learned what Brahman is and how (in mystery) the self is united with it. I am here trading on Kant's distinction between the empirical ego and the transcendental ego. Only a hint is given, in the phrase "being a knower," as to how there may be developed a definite conception of the respect in which, and the reason why, the self is one with Brahman.

Now for a very interesting couplet.

> The Self-existent pierced the openings [of the senses] outward;
> Therefore one looks outward, not within himself.
>
> *Katha Upanishad* IV.1. RM 47

My looking outward through my sense organs, as though looking through windows, is the act of Brahman.[6] Brahman is myself engaging in sense experience. Brahman is the knowing self.

> Then Usasta Cakrayam questioned him. "Yajnavalkya," said he, "explain to me who is the *Brahman* present and not beyond our ken, him who is the Self in all things. . . ."
> "He is your self (*atman*), which is in all things. . . ."
>
> *Brhadaranyaka Upanishad* III.iv.1. RM 83

> "Verily, he is the great, unborn Self, who is this [person] consisting of knowledge among the senses. In the space within the heart lies the ruler of all, the lord of all, the king of all."
>
> *Ibid.* IV.iv.22. RM 88

---

6 St. Augustine: "God hath given thee eyes in the body, reason in the heart, wake up the interior inhabitant of thine interior eyes, let it take to its windows, examine the creature of God." From Sermon CXXVI.

The questioner here seems to fear that he cannot grasp the eternal Brahman; his fear is allayed by the tidings that his own self is Brahman. The concepts of the two are the same.

For final notice I call attention to the formula "That art thou" (*Tat tvam asi*) occurring several times in the *Chandogya Upanishad*. One text begins with an allusion to the way in which the essences of various trees are lost in the unity of honey.

> "That which is the finest essence — this whole world has that as its self. That is Reality. That is *Atman*. That art thou [*Tat tvam asi*], Svetaketu. . . ."
>
> *Chandogya Upanishad* VI:ix.4. RM 69

A few lines farther on there occurs the simile of rivers losing their identity in the unity of the ocean. Then the familiar formula is repeated. Twice more it recurs after presentation of two more similes. (*Ibid.* VI.x.3; xii.3; xiii.3.)

−(2)−

We are now prepared for many passages in which Brahman and the self are similarly described. They join the two notions and apply to them the same attributes. In a number of cases the identification is so thorough that one has difficulty making out whether the title "Self" is being used to refer to Brahman or to the personal self.

I begin with a passage in which only the expression, "the Self of the discerner," ties the remarks on to the personal self; otherwise one might read the passage as straightforward description of the eternal Being. Then I add a similar text.

> 8. Now, he who on all beings
> Looks as just in the Self (*Atman*),
> And on the Self as in all beings —
> He does not shrink away from Him.
> 7. In whom all beings
> Have become just the Self of the discerner —
> Then what delusion, what sorrow is there,
> Of him who perceives the unity!
>
> *Isa Upanishad.* RM 40

> 18. The wise one [i.e., the *Atman*, the Self] is not born, nor dies.
> This one does not come from anywhere, has not become any one.
> Unborn, constant, eternal, primeval, this one
> Is not slain when the body is slain.
> 19. If the slayer thinks to slay,
> If the slain thinks himself slain,
> Both these understand not.
> This one slays not, nor is slain.

20. More minute than the minute, greater than the great,
Is the Self that is set in the heart of a creature here.
One who is without the active will beholds Him, and becomes
freed from sorrow —

Katha Upanishad II. RM 45-46

The 19th stanza just quoted has particular interest. In the *Bhagavad-Gita* Krishna encourages Arjuna to join in the impending battle by reciting words almost identical with these. Taking a man's life is not taking life; for a man's self is one with Brahman, and the eternal does not admit of birth and death. Accordingly, the same description (i.e., the rejection of differential predicates) applies to both.

2. For truly, everything here is *Brahman;* this self is Brahman. This same self has four fourths. ((These four, presented earlier, are waking, sleep with dreams, deep sleep free from dreams, and "*turiya,*" i.e., the state of salvation. This last is spoken of as follows.))

6. This is the lord of all. This is the all-knowing. This is the inner controller. This is the source of all, for this is the origin and the end of all beings.

7. Not inwardly cognitive, not outwardly cognitive, not both-wise cognitive, not a cognition mass, not cognitive, not non-cognitive, unseen, with which there can be no dealing, ungraspable, having no distinctive mark, non-thinkable, that cannot be designated, the essence of the assurance of which is the state of being one with the Self, the cessation of development, tranquil, benign, without a second (*a-dvaita*) — [such] they think is the fourth. He is the Self. He should be discerned.

12. The fourth is without an element, with which there can be no dealing, the cessation of development, benign, without a second.
Thus *Om* is the Self (*Atman*) indeed.
He who knows this, with his self enters the Self — yea, he who knows this.

Mandukya Upanishad. RM 55-56

Insofar as my self is the pure subject, the pure possibility of experience, undetermined as to how or what I observe or say, I am Brahman. As such I have no differential attributes. Hence there is no second item, nothing is distinct from me. This self of mine is the Self: the word first applied to me is applied to Brahman. One of the *Upanishads* makes the point several times over that I am Brahman in my capacity to know anything anywhere and anywhen.

1. Verily, this whole world is *Brahman.* Tranquil, let one worship It as that from which he came forth, as that into which he will be dissolved, as that in which he breathes. . . .

2. He who consists of mind, whose body is life (*prana*), whose form is light, whose conception is truth, whose self is space, containing

all works, containing all desires, containing all odors, containing all tastes, encompassing this whole world, the unspeaking, the unconcerned — this Self of mine within the heart is smaller than a grain of rice, or a barley-corn, or a mustard-seed, or a grain of millet, or the kernel of a grain of millet; this Self of mine within the heart is greater than the earth, greater than the atmosphere, greater than the sky, greater than these worlds.

4.   Containing all works, containing all desires, containing all odors, containing all tastes, encompassing this whole world, the unspeaking, the unconcerned — this is the Self of mine within the heart, this is *Brahman*. Into him I shall enter on departing hence. . . .
Chandogya Upanishad III.xiv. RM 65

Where one sees nothing else, hears nothing else, understands nothing else — that is a plenum. But where one sees something else — that is the small. Verily, the plenum is the same as the immortal; but the small is the same as the mortal.   *Ibid.* VII.xxiv.1. RM 72

1.   That [plenum], indeed, is below. It is above. It is to the west. It is to the east. It is to the south. It is to the north. It, indeed, is this whole world.
"I [the ego], indeed, am below. I am above. I am to the west. I am to the east. I am to the south. I am to the north. I, indeed, am this whole world.

2.   ". . . The Self (*Atman*), indeed, is below. The Self is above. The Self is to the west, . . . east . . . south . . . north. The Self, indeed, is this whole world. . . ."   *Ibid.* VII.xxv. RM 72

One final passage.

"Verily, this self is *Brahman*, made of knowledge, of mind, of breath, of seeing, of hearing, of earth, of water, of wind, of space, of energy and of non-energy, of desire and of non-desire, of anger and of non-anger, of virtuousness and of non-virtuousness. It is made of everything. This is what is meant by the saying 'made of this, made of that.' . . ."   *Brhadaranyaka Upanishad* IV.iv.5. RM 87

Brahman is all, made of everything — this being surveyed by a list of differential predicates, including opposites. In itself Brahman is undifferentiated; it became differentiated "by name and form." The self too is everything. In itself it is pure possibility, neither inward nor outward, neither this nor that; as knower of everything knowable, it contains all; every item that can be known is a differentiation of the initial undifferentiated. Thus to understand the self is the same act as to understand Brahman, though in either case the understanding is non-understanding. Being what it is, Brahman is indescribable, unthinkable: it is the whole. So too the self is unthinkable, and for the same reason: it is the receptacle for all acts, notions, opinions, strivings, predications. There is no second thing (*a-dvaita*).

—(3)—

Now let us see if we can pick out the reason or argument for
affirming the identity of self and Brahman. Or, if the course of reflection is less formal than an argument, is there a pivotal maneuver
about a key analogy which can be isolated and inspected?

I pause a moment to notice a couple of barriers to this project.
First is the point that search for the argument is unnecessary. Statements of the identity of self with Brahman are numerous. Thus the
central doctrine is before us; what more is needed? This is a fact, of
course; but there remains a question as to how the mystic arrives
at his thesis. I wish to trace if possible the essential movement.

The second point is more serious. Perhaps the mode of self-
expression or self-consciousness offered in the *Upanishads* is too un-
sophisticated, too close to the initial leap of conviction, for the teacher
to have asked himself, and told his listener, precisely what he has been
doing. A man can become skillful in performing a complicated intellectual move without acquiring *pari passu* the complementary skill
of explaining that move. He can master a given know-how without
mastering the further know-how of telling about the first know-how.
There may be an extended lag between learning the first and learning the second skill. This lag is what Hegel alludes to, I think, in
his famous remark about the owl of Minerva not taking flight until
nightfall. It may be a fact of cultural history that a people acquire
their most important convictions before they are conscious of precisely what these are or of how they compare with equally possible
though alternative fundamental ideas. (One of the main services of
philosophy is to bring such fundamental beliefs into the purview
of reflection and to compare them with other fundamental beliefs.)
A man's most basic beliefs are like his spectacles: he sees all that he
sees through them, and they affect how he sees whatever he sees;
yet only rarely does he look at them or take occasion to inspect
them. A special occasion and a special pressure may be indispensable
to a man's engaging in the derivative exercise of intellectual self-
analysis and explication which is part of that examined life of which
Socrates spoke. This derivative exercise is not more intelligent than
the initial act of taking a stand, of acquiring one's spectacles; it is
simply a further skill, and one which it has been the business of the
philosopher to develop.

What this second point poses is a difficulty, not an objection to
my project. I think that it will be difficult to tease out of the
Upanishads a theoretical diagram of the crowning mystical thesis.

I am not sure that I have found anything like a satisfactory account of the mystic's move. I shall offer only a suggestion as to what that movement is. In order to do so I shall single out certain texts in the *Upanishads* which at least hint at the form of reasoning one might offer as a ground for saying that Brahman and Atman are the same. And I shall have to return to passages that have been noticed before.

The self is identified with Brahman in its capacity as a knower. In this capacity it contains all things and is therefore ungraspable, beyond all predication or description. How does one come to see the propriety of this insight? Attention to the following text may show us the clue we want.

> The Self-existent pierced the openings [of the senses] outward;
> Therefore one looks outward, not within himself.
> A certain wise man, while seeking immortality,
> Introspectively beheld the Self face to face.
>
> *Katha Upanishad* IV.1. RM 47

It is Brahman that looks outward through my eyes and hears through my ears. My senses are directed outward in the normal course of things (the soul looks out through the windows); and my experience of the environment is here characterized, with the help of the mystical thesis, as in fact Brahman's experience carried on "through the openings" of my senses outward. None of this is unexpected. But then there is an unexpected development. A wise man (he is Brahman looking out through the windows of his soul) turns around and looks the other way. He looks back, or reflects. This, I think, is signified by "introspectively beheld the Self face to face"; the normal outward gaze is reversed. The man had been looking at things, at the items surrounding him. Now he looks at himself: at what sees, hears, imagines, supposes, etc. He has been saying, "That is a tree," "That is a cow." Now he says, "I see a tree," "I hear a cow," "I taste . . .," "I touch . . .," "I'm scared," etc. Attention is turned backward on myself seeing, fearing, thinking, dreaming, sleeping (?). What is this like? What does one see when he sees himself?

The very last answer to this question is, of course, the eternal Brahman: which the ego is. But what does one go through before reaching that reply? The self has turned back to see itself. It notices that it is the speaker, the asserter of all that is asserted. This is my suggestion as to what sets the dance in motion. The self can prefix every assertion with "I say." Every expression it offers can be *owned*. "I suppose . . .," "I fear . . .," "I know. . . ." Every conceivable item of thought or expression (and this means everything contained in Brahman) can be regarded as included in the self. This is said, I suggest, in the following lines:

> That [plenum], indeed, is below. It is above. It is to the west . . . east . . . south . . . north. It, indeed, is this whole world.
> "I [the ego], indeed, am below. I am above. I am to the west . . . east . . . south . . . north. The Self, indeed, is this whole world."
>
> *Chandogya Upanishad* VIII.xxv.1. RM 72

I am above, below, to the east, the west, etc., in the sense that I know, surmise, am aware of every item that can be mentioned: or rather, I am able to know . . . I am able to say everything that is said or can be said. As saying or apprehending whatever is apprehended, I am not to be identified with any particular item or any differential operation, performance, or action, whether "subjective" or "objective." The self is the pure potentiality of apprehending anything, withdrawn from any specific determination. Consider the following:

> 7. Gone are the fifteen parts according to their station,
>   Even all the sense-organs in their corresponding divinities!
>   One's deeds and the self that consists of understanding —
>   All become unified in the supreme Imperishable.
> 8. As the flowing rivers in the ocean
>   Disappear, quitting name and form,
>   So the knower, being liberated from name and form,
>   Goes unto the Heavenly Person, higher than the high.
>
> *Mundaka Upanishad* III.ii. RM 55

> One should worship with the thought that he is just one's self, for therein all these [breathing, speaking, thinking — names of his acts] become one. That same thing, namely, this self, is the trace of this All, for by it one knows this All. . . .
>
> *Brhadaranyaka Upanishad* I.iv.7. RM 78

This last text is crucial; especially the line, "That same thing, namely, this self, is the trace of this All, for by it one knows this All. . . ." The self is the trace or image of Brahman because it is the unity of all one's acts. Who or what is the "I" which serves as the subject of all possible sentences of the form "I see . . .," "I hear . . .," "I imagine . . .," etc., etc.? It is the unity of all acts whose assertion can be prefixed to every possible sentence. And no matter whose acts! The "I" is not Socrates, Molly Bloom, or Yajnavalkya. It is the "transcendental ego" of German idealism. This ego is not seeing or hearing to the exclusion of any other conscious function; these are parts composing it. It is their totality, undifferentiated in itself but capable of differentiation, receptive to specification "by name and form."

It is the pure potentiality of awareness and response. It can be differentiated so as to become any conscious act, and the totality of conscious acts embraces as content all possible objects of reference, every item mentionable in the totality of possible assertions. To know this unity, this self, is to know this All, i.e., Brahman.

> . . . being a knower, shaking off good and evil,
> Stainless, he attains supreme identity with Him.
> *Mundaka Upanishad* III.i.3. RM 54

—(4)—

I have tried to show how mysticism arrives at the thesis, "I, indeed, am this whole world." The *Upanishads* go on to say that the self is, first, the creator of all things, and that, second, it is a void, wholly lacking attributes.

7. "Which is the self?" . . .

"The person here who among the senses is made of knowledge, who is the light in the heart. He, remaining the same, goes along both worlds, appearing to think, appearing to move about, for upon becoming asleep he transcends this world and the forms of death.

8. "Verily, this person, by being born and obtaining a body, is joined with evils. When he departs, on dying, he leaves evils behind.

9. "Verily, there are just two conditions of this person: the condition of being in this world and the condition of being in the other world. There is an intermediate third condition, namely, that of being in sleep. By standing in this intermediate condition one sees both these conditions, namely, being in this world and being in the other world. Now, whatever the approach is to the condition of being in the other world, by making that approach one sees the evils [of this world] and the joys [of yonder world].

"When one goes to sleep, he takes along the material of this all-containing world, himself tears it apart, himself builds it up, and dreams by his own brightness, by his own light. Then this person becomes self-illuminated.

10. "There are no chariots there, no spans, no roads. But he projects from himself chariots, spans, roads. There are no blisses there, no pleasures, no delights. But he projects from himself blisses, pleasures, delights. There are no tanks there, no lotus-pools, no streams. But he projects from himself tanks, lotus-pools, streams. For he is a creator." *Brhadaranyaka Upanishad* IV.iii. RM 86

13. He who has found and has awakened to the Self
That has entered this conglomerate abode —
He is the maker of everything, for he is the creator of all;
The world is his; indeed, he is the world itself.

22. Verily, he is the great, unborn Self, who is this [person] consist-

ing of knowledge among the senses. In the space within the heart
lies the ruler of all, the lord of all, the king of all. . . .

Ibid. IV.iv. RM 88

Thus the self and Brahman are one in containing all items; the
self projects all things from itself. The world is the dream of the
self. As Brahman is the sole ultimate Being, so with the self. There
is no second thing. The self is a plenum; and a plenum exists "Where
one sees nothing else, hears nothing else, understands nothing else. . ."
(*Chandogya Upanishad* VII.xxiv.1. RM 72).

> "For where there is a duality (*dvaita*), as it were (*iva*), there one
> sees another; there one smells . . . hears . . . speaks to . . . thinks of
> . . . understands another. Where, verily, everything has become just
> one's own self, then whereby and whom would one smell . . . see . . .
> hear . . . understand? Whereby would one understand him by whom
> one understands this All? Lo, whereby would one understand the
> understander?"   *Brhadaranyaka Upanishad* II.iv.14. RM 82

> 30.   "Verily, while he does not there know, he is verily knowing,
> though he does not know (what is [usually] to be known); for
> there is no cessation of the knowing of a knower, because of his
> imperishability [as a knower]. It is not, however, a second thing,
> other than himself and separate, which he may know.
> 31.   "Verily, where there seems to be another, there the one might
> see . . . smell . . . taste . . . speak to . . . hear . . . think of . . .
> touch . . . know the other.
> 32.   "An ocean, a seer alone without duality, becomes he whose world
> is *Brahman*, O King!" — thus Yajnavalkya instructed him. . . .

Ibid. IV.iii. RM 86-87

How can one be said to know when what he knows is himself
and there is no second thing? What one knows is not a "something"
about which something is said. To use the favorite idealist formula,
subject and object coalesce. And the self is Brahman, the all-encom-
passing, the undifferentiated totality embracing all differences. So
its nature is best pictured by the state of dreamless sleep. The self
is without predicates; it is not an agent, it does not suffer. It is the
knower considered in itself, apart from every act and every content.

> He who consists of mind . . . containing all desires . . . encompass-
> ing this whole world, the unspeaking, the unconcerned —.

Chandogya Upanishad III.xiv.2. RM 65

The self has four parts: waking, sleep with dreams, deep dreamless
sleep (where one is a "cognition-mass," i.e., potential knowing), and
last, the state of *turiya*, bliss. The last, while praised as "the lord of
all . . . the all-knowing" (*Mandukya Upanishad* 6. RM 55), is em-
phatically deprived of properties.

7. Not inwardly cognitive, not outwardly cognitive, not both-wise cognitive, not a cognition-mass, not cognitive, not non-cognitive, unseen, with which there can be no dealing, having no distinctive mark, non-thinkable, that cannot be designated, the essence of the assurance of which is the state of being one with the Self, the cessation of development, tranquil, benign, without a second (*a-dvaita*) — [such] they think is the fourth. He is the Self. He should be discerned.

12. The fourth is without an element, with which there can be no dealing, the cessation of development, benign, without a second.
Thus *Om* is the self (*Atman*) indeed.
He who knows this, with his self enters the Self —
yea, he who knows this.

Mandukya Upanishad. RM 56

"Now, when one is sound asleep, composed, serene, and knows no dreams — that is the Self (*Atman*)," said he. "That is the immortal, the fearless. That is *Brahman*. . . ."

Chandogya Upanishad VIII.xi.1. RM 68

IV. REBIRTH AND DETACHMENT

The culminating doctrine of mysticism which I have sought to sketch is not offered out of theoretical interest only; it is offered "unto salvation." A man is not attracted to it as he might be to a piece of information the sole use of which is to allay curiosity, or as he might be to a discussion of which species of nonsense is exemplified by "Saturday is in bed." On several occasions Aristotle describes the philosopher's interest in the highest science as interest in knowledge for its own sake; yet at the end of his *Nicomachean Ethics* he argues for preferring intellectual activity to practical activity on the ground (not the only one, but the chief one) that its exercise enables a man more nearly to imitate the divine life. Here he exhorts the reader; his discussion takes on the cast of religious persuasion. Plato also urges his reader to strive to imitate the gods, and as a means thereto he recommends attention to the majestic circular movements of the heavenly bodies: such attention can train the rational soul to move on the same course, over and over, about the same point, and thus to come as close as may be to fixity. For Plato and Aristotle no argument is needed to show that not to move is better than to move, that change is a blot on existence.

The *Upanishads* state many times over that the key to salvation is grasp of the truth that Brahman and Atman are identical. He who can realize this and hold to it firmly, conforming his practice and his attitudes to this doctrine, is free, liberated from sorrow, delusion, and every form of ill; he has peace, tranquillity. I wish to present this view of salvation, aiming to sharpen its outline by attention to what this salvation saves us from and to the type of practice or personality-set which is recommended as both required for and constituting the saved life. I shall not offer extensive comment on the relevant texts, nor shall I take occasion to express my own attitude toward the doctrine.

> 6. Now, he who on all beings
> Looks as just in the Self (*Atman*),
> And on the Self as in all beings —
> He does not shrink away from Him.
> 7. In whom all beings
> Have become just the Self of the discerner —
> Then what delusion, what sorrow is there,
> Of him who perceives the unity!
>
> *Isa Upanishad.* RM 40

I am the Whole. If I see my unity with all, I have no sorrow. What is better than to be Brahman? Than to be divine? Who needs to argue for the glory of this?

> When a seer sees the brilliant
> Maker, Lord, Person, the *Brahman*-source,
> Then, being a knower, shaking off good and evil,
> Stainless, he attains supreme identity [with Him].
>
> *Mundaka Upanishad* III.i.3. RM 54

Seeing the identity is to enter Brahman, it is to attain *turiya*, the fourth or blessed state. There is sorrow for him who does not realize the unity.

> More minute than the minute, greater than the great,
> Is the Self that is set in the heart of a creature here.
> One who is without the active will beholds Him, and
> becomes freed from sorrow —.
>
> *Katha Upanishad* II.20. RM 45-46

A close connection is claimed to hold between attaining unity with Brahman and what is signified by the beautiful words "freedom" and "tranquillity." The anxiety of passion, the complexity of finite striving and performance, the diversity of faculties, vanish in the exaltation of the unification.

> 5. Attaining Him, the seers who are satisfied with knowledge,
> Who are perfected selves, from passion free, tranquil —
> Attaining Him who is the universally omnipresent, those wise,
> Devout selves into the All itself do enter.
> 7. Gone are the fifteen parts according to their station,
> Even all the sense-organs in their corresponding divinities!
> One's deeds and the self that consists of understanding —
> All become unified in the supreme Imperishable.

8. As the flowing rivers in the ocean
Disappear, quitting name and form,
So the knower, being liberated from name and form,
Goes unto the Heavenly Person, higher than the high.
9. He, verily, who knows that supreme *Brahman*, becomes very *Brahman*. . . . *Mundaka Upanishad* III.ii. RM 55

Brahman is the All; it is unlimited, free from subjection to influence; it is undetermined. So I , too, can be undetermined, unaffected by anything outside myself. This is perfect autonomy.

Containing all works . . . desires . . . odors . . . tastes, encompassing this whole world, the unspeaking, the unconcerned — this is the Self of mine within the heart, this is *Brahman*. Into him I shall enter on departing hence. . . . *Chandogya Upanishad* III.xiv.4. RM 65

". . . The Self, indeed, is this whole world.
"Verily, he who sees this, who thinks this, who understands this, who has pleasure in the Self, who has delight in the Self, who has intercourse with the Self, who has bliss in the Self — he is autonomous; he has unlimited freedom in all worlds. But they who know otherwise than this are heteronomous; they have perishable worlds; in all worlds they have no freedom." *Ibid.* VII.xxv.2. RM 72

I take it that the teaching in such texts is clear enough. Brahman, by being All, is unlike any finite item in not having anything to affect it; it is related to nothing and so cannot undergo passion. Thus it is free. A finite item is finite because it is unlike others; so it is limited, determined. The form this situation takes, when there is capacity to feel it, is the experience of need or striving: passion, aspiration, action and suffering. So far as I am a living body I need nourishment: if I am deprived I suffer; if privation is prolonged I perish. My wants are legion; not a moment passes in which I am not seeking something, concerned about something: the mark on my existence is dread, the possibility of anxiety. But I am, as a knower, one with Brahman; so I can, by intention or taking into account, encompass everything, every possible object of awareness or aspiration. So I, too, am perfectly free and undetermined, and I can realize this. To realize it is salvation.

What am I to be saved from? The answer in one word is *finitude*. Insofar as I am this person, distinguished by name and form, I am alienated from the infinite Being. Salvation consists in being united with Brahman, in realizing this union and getting beyond consciousness of distinction from Brahman; hence the opposite of salvation is ignorance of the saving truth, it is concern about myself as this person, attention to my interests as a finite person or to the interests of any other person. It is worth while to look about in the *Upanishads* for ways in which such attention to the finite is manifested and for their consequences. This is to look about for the primary modes of finite existence and for the blight upon it.

I pause a moment to note that, different as Plato's doctrine of three ultimate principles is from mystical monism, and different as his conception of God is from that of Brahman, there is remarkable agreement on what is wrong with finitude and on the penalty for that wrong. Individuality and motion enter the world from the material principle; and while God can manage to persuade the material principle to accept a degree of order into motion, He cannot do the best thing of all, viz., remove motion altogether. Circular motion is the best kind of motion because it is most nearly not motion at all. God managed to achieve circularity in the motions of the heavenly bodies. Plato's admiration of the circular courses of the stars, plus his notion that individuality (union of form and material) and movement are inseparable from this world, lead him to say that the rational soul of man, though capable of existing and performing apart from matter and the body, is compelled periodically to return to a corporate state. Thus he comes to explain reincarnation; indeed, all history is cyclical, that of civilizations as much as that of persons.

These same themes occur in the *Upanishads*.

((Prajapati said:))
1. "O Mayhavan, verily, this body (*sarira*) is mortal. It has been appropriated by Death (*Mrtyu*). [But] it is the standing-ground of the deathless, bodiless Self. Verily, he who is incorporate has been appropriated by pleasure and pain. Verily, there is no freedom from pleasure and pain for one while he is incorporate. Verily, while one is bodiless, pleasure and pain do not touch him.
2. ". . . As a draft-animal is yoked in a wagon, even so this spirit (*prana*) is yoked in this body."
Chandogya Upanishad VIII.xii. RM 76

This vigorous and graphic text plainly identifies evil with finitude. While embodied the self is confined in a prison, subjected to the drag of passion; pleasure, too, is evil. The self is alien to the body; with the body come disturbances, partiality of view, passion and blindness, and death at the last. This condition is the opposite of freedom.

7. "Which is the self?" . . .
"The person here who among the senses is made of knowledge, who is the light in the heart.
8. "Verily, this person, by being born and obtaining a body, is joined with evils. When he departs, on dying, he leaves evils behind. . . ."
Brhadaranyaka Upanishad IV.iii. RM 86

This is not the thesis that on balance evil outweighs good; the assessment is not gotten by counting or measurement. My existence as a finite item is itself evil. Wherever one thing differs from another, there is evil: this *is* evil and needs to be overcome.

> By the mind alone is It [the ancient, primeval *Brahman*] to be perceived.
> There is on earth no diversity.
> He gets death after death,
> Who perceives here seeming diversity.
>
> *Brhadaranyaka Upanishad* IV.iv.19. RM 88

In comparison with Brahman, finite items do not exist. Hence there is no diversity.

> In this which vitalizes all things, which appears in all things,
>   the Great —
> In this Brahmā-wheel the self flutters about,
> Thinking that itself and the Actuator are different.
> When favored by Him, it attains immortality.
>
> *Svetasvatara Upanishad* I.6. RM 89

This point, that the finite is lost, is made in several passages in the *Maitri Upanishad*. One of these is a model of its kind and was imitated in early Buddhist preaching.

> 3. . . . in this ill-smelling, unsubstantial body, which is a conglomerate of bone, skin, muscle, marrow, flesh, semen, blood, mucus, tears, rheum, feces, urine, wind, bile, and phlegm, what is the good of enjoyment of desires? In this body, which is afflicted with desire, anger, covetousness, delusion, fear, despondency, envy, separation from the desirable, union with the undesirable, hunger, thirst, senility, death, disease, sorrow, and the like, what is the good of enjoyment of desires?
> 4. And we see that this whole world is decaying as these gnats, mosquitoes, and the like, the grass, and the trees that arise and perish.
>   . . . the drying up of great oceans, the falling away of mountain peaks, the deviation of the pole-star. . . .
>
> *Maitri Upanishad* I. RM 93[7]

Another passage in the same *Upanishad* distinguishes between the self as infinite, one with Brahman, and the self as bound to finitude. The latter is called "the elemental self."

> [Then he said:] "There is indeed another, different self, called 'the elemental self.' . . .
> "Now, he, assuredly, indeed, who is said to be in 'the body' is said

---

[7] There is of course no thesis here. But what language! Tonnze McCobber, Buy Sannsonn!

to be 'the elemental self.' Now, its immortal self is like 'the drop of
water on the lotus leaf.'
((Editor's Note: That is, unaffected by externals.))
"This [elemental self], verily, is overcome by Nature's qualities.
". . . In thinking 'This is I' and 'That is mine,' he binds himself
with his self, as does a bird with a snare. . . ."
Maitri Upanishad III.2. RM 94

1. ". . . What is the rule for this elemental self, whereby, on
   quitting this body, it may come to complete union with the Self?"
4. "Therefore, by knowledge (*vidya*), by austerity (*tapas*), and by
   meditation (*cinta*), *Brahman* is apprehended. . . .
   "So when this chariot-rider is liberated from those things wherewith he was filled full and overcome, then he attains complete
   union with the *Atman*." *Ibid.* IV. RM 95

The lesson here is plain enough. The proper response to this
present life is revulsion. My infinite self is in bondage in this world:
enslaved to individuality, movement, ambition and passion, and all
the hazards and ills of bodily experience.

This lesson is accentuated by the doctrine of rebirth; repetition
is the penalty for finitude. One passage suggests that this notion
should not be propagated.

"Yajnavalkya," said he, "when the voice of a dead man goes into
fire, his breath into wind, his eye into the sun, his mind into the
moon, his hearing into the quarters of heaven, his body into the earth,
his self (*atman*) into space, the hairs of his head into plants, the hairs
of his body into trees, and his blood and semen are placed in water,
what then becomes of this person?"
"Artabhaga, my dear, take my hand. We two only will know of
this. This is not for us two [to speak of] in public."
The two went away and deliberated. What they said was *karma*
(action). What they praised was *karma*. Verily, one becomes good
by good action, bad by bad action.
Brhadaranyaka Upanishad III.ii.13. RM 82-83

. . . According as one acts, according as one conducts himself, so
does he become. . . . *Ibid.* IV.iv.5. RM 87

The conception of *Karma* as applied to my career in this present
life is familiar enough, and though it conflicts with the notions of
divine forgiveness and of the possibility of a new life, it is by itself
not especially depressing or shocking. But it is associated with rebirth, and therefore carries a sting. (The secret was not kept.)

. . . those who are of pleasant conduct here — the prospect is, indeed, that they will enter a pleasant womb, either the womb of a
brahmin, or the womb of a *ksatriya,* or the womb of a *vaisya.* But those
who are of stinking conduct here — the prospect is, indeed, that they

will enter a stinking womb, either the womb of a dog, or the womb
of a swine, or the womb of an outcast (*candala*).

Chandogya Upanishad V.x.7. RM 66-67

These pictures, resembling Plato's, would not frighten me were it not
for the emphasis on the view that finite existence itself is evil. The
rebirth doctrine is galling because it threatens me with failure to
escape, an endless prospect of separation from the divine.

7. He, however, who has not understanding,
    Who is unmindful and impure,
    Reaches not the goal,
    But goes on to transmigration [rebirth].
8. He, however, who has understanding,
    Who is mindful and ever pure,
    Reaches the goal
    From which he is born no more. . . .
15. What is soundless, touchless, formless, imperishable,
    Likewise tasteless, constant, odorless,
    Without beginning, without end, higher than the great, stable —
    By discerning That, one is liberated from the mouth of death.

Katha Upanishad III. RM 46-47

Whatever is here, that is there.
What is there, that again is here.
He obtains death after death
Who seems to see a difference here.

Ibid. IV.10. RM 48

Salvation is loss of form, for Brahman is formless. The goal is
not to be this or that (it is not fellowship or more perfect activation
of certain powers). Desire is striving toward something definite; its
effect is existence — and re-existence, rebirth. According to Buddha,
to exist is misery, and the cause of existence is desire, finite striving.

1. . . . They who, being without desire, worship the Person
    And are wise, pass beyond the seed [of rebirth] here.
2. He who in fancy forms desires,
    Because of his desires is born [again] here and there.
    But of him whose desire is satisfied, who is a perfected self,
    All desires even here on earth vanish away.

Mundaka Upanishad III.ii. RM 54

". . . he who has concentrated all his senses upon the Self; he who
is harmless (*ahimsant*) toward all things elsewhere than at holy places
(*tirtha*) — he, indeed, who lives thus throughout his length of life,
reaches the Brahmā-world and does not return hither again — yea,
he does not return hither again!"

Chandogya Upanishad VIII.xv. RM 77

On this point there is this verse:
    Where one's mind is attached — the inner self
    Goes thereto with action, being attached to it alone.

> Obtaining the end of his action,
> Whatever he does in this world,
> He comes again from that world
> To this world of action.
> — So the man who desires.
>
> *Brhadaranyaka Upanishad* IV.iv.6. RM 87

> . . . *Brahman*-knowers
> Become merged in *Brahman,* intent thereon, liberated from the womb
> [i.e., from rebirth].   *Svetasvatara Upanishad* I.7. RM 90

> . . . "Sir, if thus you describe the greatness of this Self, there is still
> another, different one. Who is he, called self, who, being overcome
> by the bright or dark fruits of action, enters a good or an evil womb,
> so that his course is downward or upward and he wanders around,
> overcome by the pairs of opposites?"
>
> *Maitri Upanishad* III.1. RM 94

This self, which wanders, lost and straying, is my empirical self, concerned about this and that. Being finite is being astray. It is evil to be finite, to be myself; and the penalty is inability to cease. Facing this, I am nauseated. I cry out for an end to this fluttering like a moth.

> And we see that this whole world is decaying, as these gnats, mos-
> quitoes, and the like. . . .
> In this sort of cycle of existence (*samsara*) what is the good of
> enjoyment of desires, when after a man has fed on them there is seen
> repeatedly his return here to earth?
> Be pleased to deliver me. In this cycle of existence I am like a frog
> in a waterless well. . . .   *Maitri Upanishad* I.4. RM 93-94

One ought to feel properly the despair voiced in this outcry. What a gospel! I suggest that it would be profitable to read along-side these passages the portion of Virgil's *Aeneid*, Book VI, that tells of Aeneas' sorrow at the experience of meeting his father in Elysium and at learning the intolerable truth about rebirth. Virgil, like Plato, offers no escape from finite existence. One may have a longer or shorter respite from existing in this world; but eventually the world-age ends, the cosmic clock strikes, and each spirit is reborn into de-filing matter. Aeneas would be better off had he not learned the truth. Now, Hinduism contains many texts teaching the same thing. The saintly person may unite himself with Brahman and so gain immunity from finitude — for the remainder of his world-age; but then Brahman repeats the world process once more. Hindu popular literature, especially the *Puranas*, contains elaborate versions of the theme of world-repetition.[8]

---

[8] A convenient reference is Heinrich Zimmer, *Myths and Symbols in Indian Art and Civilization* (New York, 1946) ; see Chapter One.

Still, it is not correct to say that in the *Upanishads* no way of escape is taught. They do speak of a way, sketching a bit of the technique required and characterizing the personality-set of the saintly person. I shall present a number of relevant passages, without extensive comment.

Begin with one in which a more familiar way of life, that of active participation in the traditional ritual of prayer and sacrifice, is rejected for a new mystical way.

10. Thinking sacrifice and merit is the chiefest thing,
    Naught better do they know — deluded!
    Having had enjoyment on the top of the heaven won by good works,
    They re-enter this world, or a lower.

11. They who practice austerity and faith in the forest,
    The peaceful knowers who live on alms,
    Depart passionless through the door of the sun,
    To where is that immortal Person (*Purusa*), e'en the imperishable Self (*Atman*). . . .

12. Having scrutinized the worlds that are built up by work, *a brahmin*
    Should arrive at indifference. The [world] that was not made is not [won] by what is done.
    For the sake of his knowledge let him go, fuel in hand,
    To a spiritual teacher who is learned in the scriptures and established on *Brahman*.   *Mundaka Upanishad* I.ii. RM 52

This "indifference" is to be understood strictly, exactly in conformity with the mystical denial of the importance of *any* finite aims. *No* desire is worthy of satisfaction, for all desire aims at something finite, at some end selected above other possible ends. And nothing important ever happens in this world.

2. He who in fancy forms desires,
   Because of his desires is born [again], here and there.
   But of him whose desire is satisfied, who is a perfected self,
   All desires even here on earth vanish away.

5. Attaining Him, the seers who are satisfied with knowledge,
   Who are perfected selves, from passion free, tranquil —
   Attaining Him who is the universally omnipresent, those wise,
   Devout selves into the All itself do enter.
                                            Ibid. III.ii. RM 54-55

[Yajnavalkya said:] "He who passes beyond hunger and thirst, beyond sorrow and delusion, beyond old age and death — *brahmins* who know such a Self overcome desire for sons, desire for wealth, desire for worlds, and live the life of mendicants. For desire for sons is desire for wealth, and desire for wealth is desire for worlds, for both these are merely desires. Therefore, let a *brahmin* become disgusted with learning and desire to live as a child. When he has become disgusted both with the state of childhood and with learning,

> then he becomes an ascetic. When he has become disgusted both with
> the non-ascetic state and with the ascetic state, then he becomes a
> *brahmin.*   *Brhadaranyaka Upanishad* III.v. RM 83

This prescription to pass beyond desire for anything that has an
alternative explicitly rules out moral concern.

> Such a one, verily, the thought does not torment: "Why have I
> not done the good? Why have I done the evil?" He who knows this,
> delivers himself from these two [thoughts]. For truly, from both of
> these he delivers himself — he who knows this!
> Such is the mystic doctrine *(upanishad)* !
>   *Taittiriya Upanishad* II.9. RM 61

This point is indeed a mark of mysticism. The consistent mystic
does not regard the good-evil contrast significant for the Absolute
(nor did Hegel) — both good and evil are finite, differential predicates, and hence included in the whole which, as including them,
transcends them. At this point, certainly, theism diverges from mysticism, and for a fundamental reason.

The mystic passion is to have no passion. The truth about existence is bitter, indeed intolerable; one faces it with cultivated indifference. There is some kinship here with the Stoic attitude. Buddhism
is often described as commending compassion: in my judgment, this
compassion or love is love of nothing.

At any rate, the *Upanishads* praise this passionlessness as the way
of salvation, as removing all evils, as bringing one to the goal of
union with the infinite.

> 6.   . . . Now the man who does not desire. — He who is without
> desire, who is freed from desire, whose desire is satisfied, whose desire
> is the Self — his breaths do not depart. Being very *Brahman,* he goes
> to *Brahman.*
> 12. If a person knew the Self *(Atman)*
>   With the thought "I am he!"
>   With what desire, for love of what
>   Would he cling unto the body?
> 13. He who has found and awakened to the Self
>   That has entered this conglomerate abode —
>   He is the maker of everything, for he is the creator of all;
>   The world is his: indeed, he is the world itself.
>   *Brhadaranyaka Upanishad* IV.iv. RM 87

> 10. . . . By meditation upon Him, by union with Him, and by entering
>   into His being
>   More and more, there is finally cessation from every illusion.
> 11. By knowing God there is a falling off of all fetters;
>   With distresses destroyed, there is cessation of birth and death.
>   By meditating upon Him there is a third stage at the dissolution
>   of the body,

Even universal lordship; being absolute, his desire is satisfied.

Svetascatara Upanishad I. RM 90

17.   . . . To the unity of the One goes he who knows this.
   ((*This* is the identity of *Brahman* and *Atman*.))
18.   The precept for effecting this [unity] is this: restraint of the breath, withdrawal of the senses, meditation, concentration, contemplation, absorption. Such is said to be the sixfold *yoga*. . . .
30.   . . . Verily, freedom from desire is like the choicest extract from the choicest treasure. For, a person who is made up of all desires, who has the marks of determination, conception, and self-conceit, is bound. Hence, in being the opposite of that, he is liberated. . . .

Maitri Upanishad VI. RM 96

And now, to close with my study of the mystical monism of the *Upanishads*, I quote a passage worthy of being memorized.

. . . Samsara [cycle of existence] is just one's own thought;
With effort he should cleanse it, then.
What is one's thought, that he becomes;
This is the eternal mystery.

For by tranquillity of thought,
Deeds, good and evil, one destroys.
With self serene, stayed on the Self,
Delight eternal one enjoys.

As firmly as the thought of man
Is fixed within the realm of sense —
If thus on Brahman it were fixed,
Who would not be released from bond? . . .

By making mind all motionless,
From sloth and from distraction freed,
When unto mindlessness one comes,
Then that is the supreme estate! . . .

The mind, in truth, is for mankind
The means of bondage and release;
For bondage, if to objects bound;
From objects free — that's called release! . . .

Maitri Upanishad VI.34. RM 96

4

Necessary Being

ALVIN PLANTINGA, Associate Professor of Philosophy, Wayne State University. A.B., Calvin College; A.M., University of Michigan; Ph.D., Yale University. Articles in *Review of Metaphysics, Philosophical Review, Philosophical Studies, Australasian Journal of Philosophy.*

Necessary Being

BY ALVIN PLANTINGA

IT IS OFTEN SAID THAT THE IMPORTANT PHILOSOPHICAL QUESTIONS ABOUT
religious belief are not questions of proof but questions of meaning.
The skeptic used to insist that "it is wrong always, everywhere, and
for anyone, to believe anything upon insufficient evidence"[1] and
that the evidence for religious or theological teachings is insufficient
indeed; he now claims that the teachings themselves are logically
questionable or out of order or even senseless. A case in point is
the assertion that God is the *necessary being*. Theologians and
religious persons do say in fact that God is the necessary being. In
this respect, they say, God is to be contrasted with all other beings
whatever; these others are merely *contingent*. Some have argued
that from the very concept of God it follows that He is a necessary
being; and a necessary being, they point out, necessarily exists.[2] On
the other hand, it has been argued that God must indeed be a necessary being . . . but since the concept of necessary being is self-contradictory, God necessarily does not exist.[3] And many philosophers
have claimed that the locution "necessary being" is a piece of straight
nonsense; hence if there is a God, He cannot possibly be a necessary

---

[1] W. K. Clifford, "The Ethics of Belief" in *Lectures and Essays* (London, 1901).
[2] Anselm, in one formulation of the ontological argument. Cf. N. Malcolm,
"Anselm's Ontological Arguments," *Philosophical Review*, Jan., 1960.
[3] J. N. Findlay, "Can God's Existence Be Disproved?", *Mind*, 1949. Reprinted
in *New Essays in Philosophical Theology*, edited by Anthony Flew and Alasdair
MacIntyre (London, 1955).

being. The claim that God is the necessary being, then, is trouble-some. My purpose in this paper is to discover whether that claim can be construed in a way which is both logically proper and reli-giously adequate.

What requirements must a "religiously adequate" account of necessary being meet? First, by "religiously adequate" I mean "ade-quate to the demands of the Christian religion." The doctrine that God is the necessary being perhaps occurs in other religions as well, particularly in Judaism and Islam. But whether this is so is not my concern here. So to see what requirements a religiously adequate account of God's necessity must meet, we must see what it is about Christianity that leads the believer to hold this doctrine. The answer is at least twofold. First, there is the pressure in theistic religions to ascribe *unlimited superiority* to God. The object of worship (as opposed to surpassing admiration or limitless respect), God is not merely very great; He is the greatest of all beings. Nor is He merely the greatest of all beings as a matter of fact; God is the greatest possible being; He is "that than which none greater can be conceived." Now mere creatures have, so to speak, a tenuous and uneasy hold upon their existence. They are made by God and can be unmade by Him. They exist only by courtesy and their continued existence depends upon the continued favor of their creator. And God's su-periority to His creatures is manifested, not merely in the fact that this dependence is not reciprocal, but in the fact that He alone has always existed, will always exist, cannot cease to exist. "From ever-lasting to everlasting, thou art."[4]

A second feature of Christian theism leads to the same conclu-sion. For the believer, God is the being in whom *absolute trust* may be placed; He is an invincible and utterly reliable ally. Earthly fathers, in spite of good intentions, may fail in various ways; but the Heavenly Father cannot be defeated by any eventuality whatever. Earthly parents are sometimes thwarted in their efforts, and as the child discovers to his dismay, parents are subject to death. But God differs from any earthly parent in just this respect; nothing can thwart His purposes, and the threat of non-existence does not con-front Him. Hence, the believer claims, God exists in some necessary manner; He *cannot* cease to exist. These two features of Christian theism (and perhaps others as well) lead the believer to assert that God is the necessary being. A religiously adequate account of God's

---

4 See Findlay's article mentioned above. Findlay puts this very well.

necessity, therefore, must allow the believer to say, in some non-Pickwickian sense of "cannot," that God cannot cease existing.

An example of an account of God's necessity that does not seem to meet this requirement is to be found in J. J. C. Smart's "The Existence of God."[5] After asserting that the existence of God cannot be *logically* necessary, Smart makes the following suggestion:

> I think I can see roughly what sort of necessity theological necessity might be. Let me give an analogy from physics. It is not a logical necessity that the velocity of light in a vacuum should be constant. It would, however, upset physical theory considerably if we denied it. Similarly it is not a logical necessity that God exists. But it would clearly upset the structure of our religious attitudes in the most violent way if we denied it or even entertained the possibility of its falsehood.[6]

It is indeed true that the believer's attitude of worship would be upset in the most violent way if he denied or were doubtful of the existence of God. Engaging in Christian worship without believing in God is like admitting that Pegasus is a mere myth while eagerly scanning the heavens for a glimpse of him. The belief that God exists is a presupposition of the Christian's entire religious enterprise. But contrary to the apparent intent of Smart's suggestion, when the believer says that God is the necessary being he is not, surely, uttering the mere truism that his religious attitudes would be upset if he ceased to believe in God. For it is quite in accord with theism to admit the possibility of persons who believe that God is the necessary being and yet have no religious attitudes at all. "The devils also believe, and they tremble."[7] And one of the things the devils might well believe is that God is the necessary being; but, of course, there is no question of *their* religious attitudes being upset. More importantly, on Smart's account the assertion of God's necessity becomes an assertion about believers and their religious attitudes rather than an assertion about God. His account does not allow the believer to assert straightforwardly that God cannot cease to exist; and it thereby fails to do justice to the concept of necessary existence.

I

If Smart's explanation won't do, how *are* we to construe the assertion that God is the necessary being?

It has been argued that to speak of necessary *beings* (or for that

---

5 *Church Quarterly Review*, 1955. Reprinted in Flew and MacIntyre, *op. cit.*
6 In Flew and MacIntyre, *op. cit.*, p. 40.
7 James 2:19.

matter of contingent beings) is to talk egregious nonsense. Locutions such as "necessary" and "contingent," so the claim goes, apply properly to statements or propositions only; to speak of a necessary being is like speaking of an unpunctual triangle. Argument for this view is distressingly scarce, however, and it is accordingly difficult to evaluate. But even if the proscription upon the phrase "necessary being" is correct, the theist will be happy to oblige, presumably, by holding instead that the statement "God exists" is necessary. We may begin by examining that claim.

A fashionable view has it that a statement or proposition is necessary if and only if it is analytic. Whether that view is correct is a matter of controversy; but at any rate it is clear that all analytic propositions are necessary. We shall first inquire, therefore, whether the proposition "God exists" is analytic. And for present purposes a proposition is analytic if and only if its denial is self-contradictory. Now our proposition does not, at first glance anyway, seem to be analytic, for the proposition "God does not exist" does not seem to be contradictory. Indeed, many philosophers and even some theologians have cheerfully accepted the proposition that God does not exist. And this apparently leads J. N. Findlay to believe that "God exists" is not analytic, on the grounds, presumably, that if it were, no one who seriously considered it would deny it.[8] But, of course, often there *is* sensible disagreement as to whether a given proposition is analytic. Leaving aside such cases as complicated mathematical and logical propositions, we might note the controversy as to whether one can consistently assert the existence of a logically private language. Hence the fact that "God exists" does not prima facie appear analytic by no means settles the question. What is needed is some sort of argument to *show* that it is not analytic.

And such argument, I think, can be provided. Let us begin by recognizing a class of statements which assert or entail the existence of a thing or things of some specified kind, e.g., "There are female cab-drivers," or "Some children are very noisy." We may refer to statements of this sort as "existential statements" and to their contradictories as "contra-existential statements." In making an existential statement, I assert that there is at least one thing which satisfies a certain description. Now it often happens that the description in question is complex in the sense that it comprises several logically

8 *Op. cit.* See especially pp. 48 and 54. See also G. B. Hughes' comments on Findlay's paper, in Flew and MacIntyre, *op. cit.,* pp. 61, 62.

independent properties or characteristics.[9] And if it is complex (as is, e.g., the description implied by "centaur"), then my assertion that at least one thing satisfies that description entails that at least one thing has all of the properties included in the description. If I say, "There are some centaurs," I am saying that there is at least one thing which has each of the properties included in the connotation of "centaur." My statement, therefore, entails that certain statements of the form "A has F" are true where what replaces "A" refers to some specific individual which in fact has all of the properties comprising the connotation of "centaur" and where "F" may be replaced by the names of those properties. Some of these statements would be the following: "A has a human head," "A has a human chest," "A has an equine lower body," etc. Some existential statements, therefore, are complex in the sense that they entail several logically independent propositions of the above form.

It is for this reason, of course, that existential statements may be self-contradictory. For our purposes, a self-contradictory statement may be characterized as one which entails two statements such that one of the entailed statements is the denial of the other. "Jones is a married bachelor," for example, entails that Jones is married and also that Jones is not married; similarly such existential statements as "There are round squares" or "There are octogenarians under fifty years of age" are contradictory.

Contra-existential statements, on the other hand, are not in this sense complex. Suppose the connotation of "centaur" is comprised by properties A, B, C, D. In asserting that there are no centaurs I am not, of course, asserting that there are no individuals with the property A. I am not, for example, asserting that nothing has the head of a man, or an equine lower body. What I am asserting is only that no individual satisfies the description in question by having *all* the properties comprising the connotation of "centaur"; I am saying that there is nothing which is ABCD. But that statement is not complex. For it may be regarded as asserting, of each individual, that either it is non-A or non-B or non-C or non-D (where "X is non-A" is to mean the same as "X is not A"). And the truth of any instantiation of such a statement requires only that *one* of its disjuncts be true. But if so, the statement in question does not and cannot entail *two* statements one of which is the denial of the other; hence it cannot be contradictory. And of course the point may be put

9 Properties A and B are logically independent if the statement that X has A neither entails nor is entailed by the statement that X has B.

more generally; to deny that there are any X's is to assert that no individual has all of the properties comprising the connotation of "X." But such an assertion is not complex in the above sense and cannot, therefore, be contradictory. And if no contra-existential statement is contradictory, no existential statement is analytic; accordingly, "God exists" is not analytic.

An objection might be directed against the *specific* thesis that the statement "God exists" is not analytic: if "is a man" is one of the properties included in the connotation of "bachelor," to deny that bachelors are men would be contradictory. So, if "is existent" is one of the properties included in the connotation of the term "God," it would be contradictory to deny that God exists. And, the argument might proceed, existence *is* one of the properties included in the concept of God. This line has been familiar since Anselm. And the answer, traditional since Kant, is that existence is not a property; it cannot, therefore, be one of the properties included in the connotation of "God." Kant's answer, someone might say, takes too short a way with Anselm's argument. For when I say "This chair exists," I am surely saying something that might not have been true; since what I say *is* true, I am saying something about *something;* and if not about this chair, then about what? But if I can say something about a chair by saying that it exists, there is good reason to hold that existence *is* a property or predicate.[10]

This argument is wrong on more than one count. But even if existence *is* a property, it is a property of a very special sort, and the features that distinguish it from other properties are just what make it impossible that existential statements be analytic. That this is the case may be suggested in the following way: Any synthetic non-existential statement of subject predicate form may be turned into an analytic statement by the simple expedient of redefining the subject term in such a way that the property mentioned in the predicate is annexed to the connotation of the subject term. For example, the statement, "All crows are black" (taken non-existentially), can be made analytic simply by annexing "black" to the normal connotation of "crow"; the proposition then says what "All black crows are black" says when the terms involved have their usual meanings. In like fashion we can convert "All potatoes are edible" into an analytic statement by adding "edible" to the normal connotation of potato.

10 Cf. G. E. Moore, "Is Existence a Predicate?", *Proceedings of the Aristotelian Society,* Supplementary Volume XV, 1936. Reprinted in *Logic and Language, Second Series,* edited by A. Flew (Oxford, 1953), pp. 92-93.

(A similar procedure can be specified for statements that do not yield to subject predicate analysis.) But existential statements cannot be made analytic by redefinition in this way. Consider, for example, the statement, "There are centaurs." Can this statement be rendered analytic by redefinition? Let's try. Presumably the thing to do is to annex the property of existence, ascribed to centaurs by the statement in question, to the connotation of "centaur." "Centaur" in our redefined sense means what "existent centaur" ordinarily means. "There are centaurs" then comes to "There are existent centaurs." Is that proposition analytic? It does not seem so. For the difference between a centaur and an existent centaur is far from clear. It might be argued that to say "Centaurs exist" and to say "Existent centaurs exist" is to say the same thing. And if so, of course there would be no contradiction in denying that there are existent centaurs. But even if there is a difference between centaurs and existent centaurs, even if the adjective "existent" marks off some special class of centaurs (e.g., existent centaurs as opposed to merely imaginary ones), we can still deny that there are existent centaurs without contradiction, for we can consistently deny that there are any centaurs at all. And if there are no centaurs at all, of course there are no existent ones. So the fact that existential propositions cannot be made analytic by redefinition indicates a crucial difference between existence, if it is a property at all, and other properties. It is in virtue of that difference, I suggest, that non-contradictory existential statements are all synthetic. It follows, then, that "God exists" is not analytic.

And if not analytic, it may be asked, in what sense necessary? Some philosophers hold that propositions expressing the incompatibility of certain colors, or the relational properties of certain tones, or certain spatial and temporal relations are necessary though not analytic. The proposition, "Nothing can be green and red all over at the same time," e.g., is sometimes said to be both synthetic and necessary. Is the assertion that God exists necessary in the way that such propositions are said to be? Surely not. For the distinguishing characteristic of synthetic necessary propositions, as explained by their defenders, is that their denials, while logically quite consistent, are nonetheless inconceivable. And the best evidence that "God exists" does not enjoy this characteristic is just that reasonable and intelligent people do in fact conceive its denial. This answer would be inappropriate to the suggestion that the proposition is analytic, for reasonable people do sometimes appear to hold beliefs revealed contradictory by subsequent investigation. But it is the best and only conclusive reply to the claim that though the statement in question is synthetic, its denial is nonetheless inconceivable. A secondary count against the claim is that all other propositions said to enjoy this status describe or report relationships between possible instances of two or more properties; none of them assert that any property *has* instances or that some description actually applies to anything. "Whatever is colored is extended" has been held to be both necessary and synthetic; that claim is not made for "There are colored objects." Hence, the claim that "God exists" is a synthetic necessary proposition is implausible.

The above discussion raises most acutely the question whether any meaning at all can be given to the assertion that God is the necessary being. In what follows, I shall try to explain the proposition that God is a necessary being in a way which is faithful to the conceptual scheme of theism but avoids the paradoxical conclusion that "God exists" is logically necessary.

II

We may begin by considering two somewhat peculiar questions. Suppose someone asked, "Why is it that all vacuums are empty?" The question is puzzling. It is indeed true and necessarily true that all vacuums are empty. But if the phrase, "Why is it that . . .," is taken to have the same role here that it does in, say, "Why is it that there are craters on the moon?", then the question seems senseless, for there seems to be no sensible way of answering it. "They just are" won't do; that suggests that perhaps they might not have been. "I don't know" won't do as a reply either, for there is nothing here we don't know — there is no room for some unknown fact which would serve as an answer to the question. One might possibly use this sentence to ask why we use the word "vacuum" to designate spaces entirely devoid of matter; presumably many other sequences of letters would do as well. But that question is about speakers and language habits; it is not about vacuums at all. Again, the question might be a misleading way of asking for the conditions under which vacuums occur. And other reinterpretations could be suggested. But one who repudiated all such reinterpretations and insisted that he meant the question in a perfectly straightforward manner would betray misunderstanding of one or another of the concepts involved. For in the case of any analytic statement A, the words "Why is it that A?" do not express a genuine query; since there is no room for an answer (since nothing *could* serve as an answer), nothing is being asked.

Now let us consider a different sort of question. Suppose someone, struck by the fact that his desk might not have existed, asks, "Why is it that this desk exists?" Perhaps there are several sorts of reply we could give him. One answer might be that the desk exists because a certain carpenter made it. But suppose our questioner is still puzzled; the carpenter, he says, also might not have existed, so why did *he* exist? We could answer again by referring to some other beings or states of affairs which were causally sufficient for the existence of the carpenter; but of course, the same question will arise about these beings, and about the causes of these beings, and so indefinitely. No matter how far back we push this series of questions and answers, our questioner may remain dissatisfied. It may appear to us that he is looking for a *final* answer, one which allows no further questions of the same sort. He seems to be seeking an answer which shares with the analytic statement above the characteristic that it leaves no room for a question of the form, "Why is it that p?" And in order to put an end to the series of questions and answers which, as he claims, never will be able to satisfy him, he may ask, "But why does anything exist at all?"

This is the second unusual question I wish to consider. It *is* an unusual question both in the sense that it is asked by some people only, and then only in certain uncommon moods, and in the sense that it is not easy to see what kind of answer is required. Now the context in which the question arises might suggest that the questioner would be satisfied only with an answer referring to some being that never could fail to exist. And such a being would be a necessary being. But if the kind of necessity involved is *logical* necessity, then (if my previous argument is correct) there *could be* no such being and hence no answer to the question. J. J. C. Smart so interprets the question: ". . . now let us ask, 'Why should anything exist at all?' Logic seems to tell us that the only answer which is not absurd is to say, 'Why shouldn't it?' "[11] But, of course, that retort is a way of rejecting the question altogether; and Smart's argument that the question ought on logical grounds to be rejected rests upon the supposition that the question is "an absurd request for the nonsensical postulation of a logically necessary being."[12] But it need not be interpreted that way.

[11] *Op. cit.,* p. 46.
[12] *Ibid.*

How then *is* it to be interpreted? Let us return to the context of the question. In asking "Why is there anything at all?" the questioner attempts to put an end to the indefinitely long series of questions and answers where the answer to each question mentions a being or state of affairs about which precisely the same question again may be asked. In seeking a *final* answer, he is seeking a statement which puts an end to the series of questions and answers. A necessary being, therefore, may be characterized as (a) a being such that some statement referring to it can serve as a final answer in this sort of question and answer series, an answer which puts an end to the series. But a final answer in the series would refer to a being of an unusual sort; such a being must be one about which the question "Why does it exist?" *does not arise* or cannot sensibly be asked. A necessary being, therefore, may be further characterized as (b) a being about which one cannot sensibly ask why it exists. But of course these two descriptions are not independent. For if a being satisfies description (a) it must also satisfy (b); the statement that a being satisfies (a) entails the statement that it satisfies (b). But similarly if the question "Why does X exist?" cannot sensibly be asked, then quite obviously some statement mentioning X can serve to put an end to the series of questions and answers under consideration. The entailment holds the other way as well. When the theist, therefore, asserts that God is the necessary being, we may construe his remark in the following way. He is pointing out that we cannot sensibly ask, "Why is it that God exists?" And he is holding that some assertion about God is the final answer in the series of questions and answers we have been considering.

Next, we should note that the question "Why does God exist?" never does, in fact, arise. Those who do not believe that God exists will not, of course, ask *why* He exists. But neither do believers ask that question. Outside of theism, so to speak, the question is nonsensical, and inside of theism, the question is never asked. But it is not that the religious person fails to ask why God exists through inadvertence or because of lack of interest. There may be many beings about which the question "Why do they exist?" is never *in fact* asked; and not all such beings are necessary in the sense in question. "Why does God exist?" is never in fact asked (either by religious or non-religious people) because it is a bogus question. If a believer were asked why God exists, he might take it as a request for his reasons for believing in God; but if it is agreed that God exists, then it is less than sensible to ask why He does. And the explanation is not hard to find. Essential to theism is an assertion to the effect that there is a connection between God and all other beings, a connection in virtue of which these others are causally dependent upon God. And this proposition is analytic; it is part of the Hebraic-Christian concept of God that He is "Maker of heaven and earth." But it is also a necessary truth that if God exists, He is Himself uncreated and in no way causally dependent upon anything else. God is a causally necessary condition of the existence of anything else, whereas His existence has no necessary conditions. Now the absence of a necessary condition of the existence of anything is a sufficient condition of the non-existence of that thing; and if a being has no causally necessary conditions, then its non-existence has no causally sufficient conditions. And hence if God does exist, His going out of existence could have no causally sufficient conditions and is therefore causally impossible. If God has no necessary conditions, then it is analytic that His going out of existence, if it occurred, would be an uncaused event; for it is analytic that there can be no causally sufficient conditions of its occurrence. Similarly, His beginning to exist is causally impossible, for since it is analytic that God is not dependent upon anything, He has no cause; and hence His coming into existence would be an event which could have no causally sufficient conditions. So if God does exist, He cannot cease to exist; nor could He have begun to exist.

Now it becomes clear that it is absurd to ask why God exists. To ask that question is to presuppose that God does exist; but it is a necessary truth that if He does, He has no cause. And it is also a necessary truth that if He has no cause, then there is no answer to a question asking for His causal conditions. The question "Why does God exist?" is, therefore, an absurdity. And in this respect there is an important analogy between the statement that God exists and any analytic statement such as "All vacuums are empty." In each case, the question "Why is it that . . .?" cannot arise. A person who seriously asked why all vacuums are empty would betray failure to understand; in the same way someone who seriously asked why God exists would betray misapprehension of the concept of God. And this characteristic is one which the statement "God exists" or "There is a God" shares with necessary statements alone; it is in point to ask, with respect to any contingent assertion p, "Why is it that p?" That this is so may tempt one to conclude, misleadingly, that the proposition "God exists" is necessary though synthetic. This conclusion, though misleading, would serve to focus attention upon the unique role played by the assertion of God's existence in the conceptual scheme of theism. And if we bear in mind that such a conclusion could be no more than a summary way of indicating that role, perhaps no harm would result.

This account raises further questions. In particular, it leaves unexplained such notions as "dependence" and "causally necessary condition" as applied to God. And consideration of these would lead to an interesting and difficult constellation of questions regarding the Christian concepts of creation and divine omnipotence and timelessness. And so it is with any adequate explanation of any aspect of the conceptual system involved in Christianity. One aspect of it leads to and terminates in others. But to say this is only to say that the conceptual system involved in Christianity is a conceptual *system*.

5

The Ethics of Jonathan Edwards

HENRY STOB, Professor of Ethics and Apologetics, Calvin Theological Seminary. A.B., Calvin College; B.D., Calvin Theological Seminary; Th.M., Hartford Theological Seminary; Ph.D., University of Göttingen. Author of *The Christian Concept of Freedom, Principle and Practice;* essays in *The Word of God and the Reformed Faith* (ed. C. Bouma), *Basic Christian Doctrines* (ed. C. F. H. Henry); articles in *The Reformed Journal, The Calvin Forum, The Banner, The Westminster Theological Journal, Revue Reformeé, Christianity Today.*

The Ethics of Jonathan Edwards

BY HENRY STOB

WHEN JONATHAN EDWARDS WAS FOURTEEN YEARS OLD, AND A JUNIOR
at Yale College,[1] Locke's *Essay on the Human Understanding* fell
into his hands and exerted a powerful influence upon him. He says
of the book that he found greater enjoyment in it "than the most
greedy miser finds when gathering up handfuls of silver and gold,
from some newly discovered treasure."[2] Stimulated by the volume
to more or less systematic thinking on philosophical themes, he began about this time a series of what he called "Notes on the Mind,"[3]
a collection of observations which reveal at once his indebtedness to
Locke and the strength and originality of his own thinking.[4] The
scattered notes are little more than philosophical fragments jotted
down "at the happy moment a thought opened spontaneously on
his mind,"[5] but it cannot be doubted that he seriously contemplated

[1] Yale College was founded at New Haven, Connecticut, in 1701, two years
before Edwards' birth, with the purpose of providing training in the liberal arts
and languages, and preparing young men for the Congregational ministry.

[2] Sereno E. Dwight, *The Life of President Edwards*, in *Works*, I, 30.

[3] *Works*, I, 664-702. It "was commenced either during, or soon after, his
perusal of Locke's *Essay*. It contains nine leaves of foolscap, folded separately,
and a few more, obviously written at a later period. . . . " Dwight, *Life*, in
Works, I, 34.

[4] "Even when a boy, he began to study *with his pen in his hand*: not for the
purpose of copying off the thoughts of others, but for the purpose of writing
down and preserving the thoughts suggested to his own mind, from the course
of study which he was pursuing." *Ibid.*, p. 33.

[5] *Ibid.*, p. 33.

a systematic treatise of considerable scope on the themes here com-
mented upon. This is evident from the broad title he prefixed to his
observations: "The Natural History of the Mental World, or of
the Internal World, being a Particular Enquiry into the nature of
the Human Mind, with respect to both its Faculties — the Understanding and the Will — and its various Instincts, and Active and
Passive powers."[6] He proposed to distinguish in the introductory
chapter between two worlds — "the external and the internal: the
external, the subject of Natural Philosophy; the Internal, our own
minds" — and above all to show "how the Knowledge of the latter,
is, in many respects, the most important."[7]

The choice of subject and statement of purpose clearly reveal
where Edwards' interest lay. It was spirit, not nature, that intrigued
him. What is especially to be observed is that his preoccupation
with the spiritual and invisible world was as much due to a profound
conviction of its superiority as to any aptitude and consequent inclination he may have had for abstract thinking. He did not lack
scientific talent. At the age of 12 he wrote an essay on the habits
of spiders, based on his own observations, which reveals an inductive
and empirical genius of the first rank. Dr. McCook, the author of
a monograph on American spiders and their spinningwork, tells of
his chagrin upon learning that "Master Jonathan Edwards" had one
hundred and sixty years before described spinning processes of
which he (Dr. McCook) had thought himself the discoverer,[8] and
Professor Benjamin Silliman, in speaking of Edwards, expresses the
opinion that "had he devoted himself to physical science, he might
have added another Newton to the extraordinary age in which he
commenced his career."[9] However that may be, it can hardly be
doubted that he refused to devote himself to physical science less
from a sense of incapacity for such studies than from a profound
conviction that the physical and external is of little weight as compared with the inner and spiritual. On this conviction, expressed

6 *Works*, I, 664. There also appears as an appendix to the "Notes" a list of
"Subjects to be handled in the Treatise on the Mind."

7 *Ibid.*

8 Henry C. McCook, D.D., "Jonathan Edwards as a Naturalist," *Presbyterian
and Reformed Review*, I, 393.

9 *Ibid.* Sereno Dwight, in commenting on Edwards' *Notes on Natural Science*,
observes: "Had his life been devoted to these pursuits, in a country where he
could at once have availed himself of the discoveries of others, and, the necessary
instruments, he would have met with no ordinary success, in extending the bounds
of human knowledge in the most important and interesting fields of Physical
Science." *Works*, I, 54.

in the proposition that "the things which are seen are temporal and the things which are not seen are eternal," he built his imposing philosophy of inwardness.

It is largely on the series of remarks entitled "The Mind" that Edwards' fame as a philosopher rests. They contain materials for a type of Idealism which, in the history of thought, has usually been associated with Berkeley. This fact, combined with the circumstance that the English Bishop was an older contemporary of Edwards and a resident for a time of Rhode Island, caused the question to be long agitated whether Edwards was in any way dependent upon him.[10] Sereno Dwight had affirmed as early as 1830 that "each wrote independently of the other,"[11] but grounds were supposed to exist which entitled one to call the truth of this remark in question. The investigations of Egbert C. Smyth seem, however, to vindicate Dwight's judgment completely and decisively,[12] and Prof. Schneider sums up the controversy by saying, "It has been proved beyond doubt that Edwards could not have known Berkeley's writings."[13] The philosophies of the two men bear, indeed, a merely superficial resemblance to each other.

Like Berkeley, however, Edwards takes his departure from Locke. Locke, building on the Cartesian dualism between spirit and matter, had added solidity to extension as the primary qualities of matter, but had recognized with Descartes the subjective character of secondary qualities, such as heat, color, and taste. He supposed that the secondary qualities arise within us by the impact of the primary qualities upon our sense organs, and had relegated the latter qualities to some external substance in which in some manner they inhered. This substance he held to be independent of mind and co-ordinate with it. This view Edwards now rejects. Agreeing that secondary qualities exist only in mind, he proves that the same is true of the material substance that had been called in to account for them. The universe, he insists, is qualitatively one. Not mind *and* matter, but mind *alone* is ultimately real. Matter, substance, and body are seen on a closer view to be in no other case than heat, taste, and color. All are merely mental. All turn out in strict

10 For the discussion, see: A. Allen, *Jonathan Edwards* (New York, 1889), pp. 141ff., 309; G. Lyon, *L'idealisme en Angleterre au XVIIIe Siecle* (Paris, 1888), pp. 431ff.
11 *Works*, I, 40.
12 Egbert C. Smyth, "Some Early Writings of Jonathan Edwards," in *American Antiquarian Society Proceedings*, New Series, Vol. X.
13 H. W. Schneider, *The Puritan Mind* (New York, 1930), p. 137.

analysis to be no more than ideas, objects of mind. As such they enjoy a merely derivative reality. They presuppose a thinker.

That, he points out, which we call by the name of body is clearly "nothing but Colour and Figure, which is the termination of this Colour, together with some powers, such as the power of resisting, and motion, etc."[14] But "it is now agreed upon by every knowing philosopher that Colours are not really in the things, no more than Pain is in a needle; but strictly nowhere else but in the mind." Hence, "if Colours exist not out of the mind, then nothing belonging to Body exists out of the mind but Resistance, which is Solidity; and the termination of this Resistance, with its relations, which is Figure; and the communication of this Resistance from space to space, which is Motion; though the latter are nothing but modes of the former. Therefore there is nothing out of the mind but Resistance." But even resistance does not exist out of the mind. "Let us suppose two globes only existing, and no mind. There is nothing there, *ex confesso,* but Resistance. That is, there is such a Law, that the space within the globular figure shall resist. Therefore there is nothing there but a power, or an establishment." If resistance, however, be only a power or establishment, it cannot really exist out of mind, for in such case "one power and establishment must resist another establishment and law of resistance, which is exceedingly ridiculous." It can only be conceived, therefore, as existing "in some mind, in idea." From the phrase "in some mind," however, one is not to infer that mind is a place, or that it can properly be spoken of as having an in and outside. "Place itself is mental, and Within and Without are mere mental conceptions." What is meant when the material universe is said to exist only in mind is "that it is absolutely dependent on the mind for its existence, and does not exist as spirits do, whose existence does not consist in, nor in dependence on, the conception of other minds."[15]

But on whose mind is the material universe dependent for its existence? Not, Edwards answers, on the mind of man. Man is not the measure of things. There are things actually existing of which no created mind is conscious. Such are, for example, the chairs in a locked room, which nobody sees. "The existence of these things is in God's supposing them."[16] That on which the physical world ultimately depends is the eternally existing, all-comprehending,

14 *Works,* I, 668-9.
15 *Ibid.,* p. 671.
16 *Ibid.*

divine mind. "That which truly is the Substance of all bodies, is the infinitely exact, and precise, and perfectly stable Idea, in God's mind, together with his stable Will that the same shall gradually be communicated to us and to other minds according to certain fixed and exact established Methods and Laws."[17]   All nature points, thus, beyond itself to God, in whom and through whom alone it exists. "God, in the beginning, created such a certain number of atoms, of such a determinate bulk and figure, which they yet maintain and always will, and gave them such a motion, of such a direction, and of such a degree of velocity; from whence arise all the natural changes in the Universe, forever, in a continued series."[18]   True, all these bodies and movements are properly and finally only ideas, and hence do not exist anywhere perfectly but in the divine mind; yet, they exist there after such a fashion that "his determination, his care, and his design" insures "that Ideas shall be united forever, just so, and in such a manner, as is agreeable to such a series." Corresponding to this series of ideas which go to make up the things which are vulgarly supposed to be non-ideal, is another series of ideas which God arouses in finite minds; and this correspondence of ideas constitutes human knowledge. "All the ideas that ever were, or ever shall be to all eternity, in any created mind, are answerable to the existence of such a peculiar atom in the beginning of the Creation, of such a determinative figure and size and motion. . . . God causes all changes to arise, as if all these things had actually existed in such a series, in some created mind, and as if created minds had comprehended all things perfectly. And, although created minds do not; yet, the Divine Mind doth; and he orders all things according to his mind, and his ideas."[19]

Edwards is eager to point out that these representations do not involve an emptying of natures, an invalidation of science, or a denial of the real and objective existence of physical objects. "We would not therefore be understood to deny that things are where they seem to be. For the principles we lay down, if they are narrowly looked into, do not infer that. Nor will it be found that they at all make void Natural Philosophy, or the science of the causes or reasons of corporeal changes."[20]   The question at issue concerns the nature of ultimate reality, and this Edwards describes as spiritual, intelligent, voluntary, and personal Being.   Being, he points out, far

17 *Ibid.,* p. 674.
18 *Ibid.,* p. 670.
19 *Ibid.*
20 *Ibid.,* p. 669.

from implying the non-existence of physical things, is precisely that which constitutes their reality and validates their existence. The worth and meaning of things is guaranteed by God Himself. Edwards insists, therefore, that "though we suppose the existence of the whole material universe [to be] absolutely dependent on Idea, yet we may speak in the old way, and as properly, and truly as ever. . . . For to find out the reasons of things in Natural Philosophy is only to find out the proportion of God's acting. And the case is the same, as to such proportions, whether we suppose the world only mental in our sense, or no."[21]

Edwards does not wish to deny solidity any more than does Locke. He wants merely to understand and account for it. Locke supposed it to be a mode of substance. Edwards holds it to be an action of an agent. Locke appeals for its explanation to a something. Edwards appeals to a someone. Of bodies, he says, "Their falling is the action we call Gravity: their stopping upon the surface of the earth, the action whence we gain the idea of solidity. . . . We get the idea and apprehension of solidity, only and entirely, from the observation we make of the ceasing of motion at the limits of some parts of space."[22] But "there is no reason in the nature of the thing itself, why a body, when set in motion, should stop at such limits more than at any other. It must therefore be some arbitrary, active, and voluntary Being that determines it."[23] Solidity is interpretable, therefore, only in terms of an intelligent and voluntary agent. Locke had defined solidity in terms of substance. Edwards has no objection to the word. He, too, will use it, provided it is understood to designate spirit and not matter. He, too, believes in substance, but for him it is personal, not physical. "The reason why it is so exceedingly natural to men to suppose that there is some latent Substance, or something that is altogether hid, that upholds the properties of bodies, is, because all see at first sight that the properties of bodies are such as need some Cause, that shall every moment have influence to their continuance, as well as a cause of their first existence. All therefore agree that there is something that is there, and upholds these properties. And it is most true, there undoubtedly is; but men are wont to content themselves in saying merely, that it is something; but that Something is He 'by whom all things consist.' "[24]

21 *Ibid.*
22 *Ibid.*, p. 674.
23 *Ibid.*, p. 675.
24 *Ibid.*, p. 676.

This, that there is Someone "by whom all things consist," is the primary faith of Edwards. It not only controls his view of nature; it is the foundation of his ethics. Beneath the immediate appearance of things he discerned a personal and eternal reality. The world, in his view, was spiritually constituted. Of much that is immature and passing in his "school-boy compositions," this is permanent. He never came to write the treatise he so early projected, less, it would seem, from lack of time and opportunity than from lack of inclination, his maturer thought operating with an entirely different set of categories. Yet he always held fast to the centrality of God. As a Calvinist, born in a Calvinistic home, the idea was not strange to him. It had, indeed, troubled him at first. "From my childhood up," he says, "my mind has been full of objections against the doctrine of God's sovereignty. It used to appear like a horrible doctrine to me."[25] But later, before he wrote down his observations on the mind, he had attained another insight. It was mediated through the ringing words of I Timothy 1:17, "Now unto the King eternal, immortal, invisible, the only wise God, be honour and glory forever and ever, Amen"; and in commenting on the experience, he says: "As I read the words there came into my soul, and was as it were diffused through it, a sense of the glory of the Divine Being; a new sense quite different from anything I ever experienced before . . . and there has been a wonderful alteration in my mind, with respect to the doctrine of God's sovereignty, from that day to this. . . . I have often since had not only a conviction, but a delightful conviction. The doctrine has very often appeared exceedingly pleasant, bright, and sweet. Absolute sovereignty is what I love to ascribe to God."[26]

His "notes" reflect his deep interest in this truth, and his early Idealism is a real but ill-conceived application of it to the world of nature. One's philosophy is never divorced from one's faith, and this finds particular illustration in Edwards. His belief in the sovereignty of God was not a mere religious sentiment; it was, as well, a determinative intellectual conviction. God's sovereignty he regarded as an undeniable and all-important cosmic fact. Behind the changing appearances of the world, he believed, is the eternal and omnipresent life of God, in whom all things exist and from whom alone they get their meaning. The stars owe their structure to Him, the planets their orbits, and the flakes of snow their crystalline beauty. What

---

25 *Ibid.,* p. 60.
26 *Ibid.*

is particularly significant is the fact that Edwards invariably defines
this sovereignty in ethical terms. Sovereignty, in his view, is not an
abstract quality existing in splendid isolation. By so much less is it
the hypostatization of some soulless force or arbitrary fate. It desig-
nates a moral quality, and reveals God as in the strictest sense good.
It is, indeed, but another word for God's infinite excellence. It is
because God is truly sovereign, because the harmonious system of
things finds its highest term in Him, that there is beauty and excellence in the world at all. Morality owes its very existence to Him,
and the moral life its objectivity and worth. As God stands behind
the world of nature, so He stands behind and validates the life of
spirit. God is not merely the substance of "things" or the cause of
physical changes; He is pre-eminently the ultimate and absolute
moral reality, the supreme ground of moral obligation, and the final
guarantor of virtue. He is the real that makes our ideals significant,
the "is" that gives meaning to our "oughts."

It is this faith in the essentially moral nature of the universe that
underlies all Edwards' utterances on ethics. He regarded it as the one
fact of infinite importance for human conduct. We are not surprised,
therefore, to find him, in his earliest reflections, attempting to render an
intelligible account of it to himself and others. In the "Notes on Mind"
he devotes a number of paragraphs to a consideration of the meaning of
"Excellence," and in these he lays bare the grounds of his faith and indicates at the same time the source of his own moral energy. Excellence,
he says, is "what we are more concerned with than anything else whatsoever: yea, we are concerned with nothing else. But what is this excellency?"[27] What is its nature and ground? In what does it consist, and
what is its validity?

In answering his own question, Edwards chooses first to consider
that in which the excellence of figures and motions consists. It consists by common consent in a certain equality or proportion among
parts. This means that excellence has to do with relations. If the
relation is one of "similarness or identity,"[28] of agreement and
correspondence, then the thing standing in that relation partakes of
excellence. "So the beauty of figures and motions is when one part
has such consonant proportion with the rest, as represents a general
agreeing and consenting together."[29] If, however, the relation is one

27 *Ibid.*, p. 693.
28 *Ibid.*, p. 695.
29 *Ibid.*, p. 697.

of disagreement, discord, and disproportion, the result is imperfection
and want of beauty. "So if there are two bodies of different shapes,
having no similarness of relation between the parts of the extremi-
ties; this, considered by itself, is a deformity."[30] What we mean,
therefore, when we say a thing is inexcellent or deformed, is that its
relations are awry. It does not occupy the right place in the totality
of things. It disrupts the harmony of existence. It does not conform to the whole. It is out of step and off balance. It disagrees
with and is contrary to being-in-general. It is in collision with
reality. This means, however, that reality or being-in-general, is the
very opposite of inexcellence, and this is precisely what Edwards
holds. "Entity," he says, "is the greatest and only good."[31] It is
that because it is, "if we examine narrowly, nothing else but Proportion."[32] It is a universal order, an infinite harmony of parts, a whole
that constitutes a perfectly proportioned one; and by that token it
is the very seat and archetype of excellence. Being and excellence
are one. The obverse is just as true. Inexcellency is contrariety to
being. It is "an approach to Nothing, or a degree of Nothing; . . .
and the greatest and only evil."[33] This does not mean that inexcellence or evil does not exist; it means that they have a merely negative
existence. Sin is not a positive entity, it is a lack and want. It has
no ontological validity and is not metaphysically real. Goodness
and excellence alone are ultimate.

The identity of being with excellence leads Edwards to correlate
degrees of excellence with degrees of being or existence. The notion
that when a thing is it simply is, was not that of Edwards. Existence,
like excellence, consists in relations. It is, therefore, greater or less, depending upon the number and intensity of those relations. "An Arch-
angel must be supposed to have more existence, and to be every way
further removed from nonentity, than a worm."[34] It is but the obverse
of this fact to say that the degree of excellence anything possesses is in
direct proportion to the degree of its being, considered simply as such.
Excellence is measured not only by the number of equalities (which in
complex beauty may be legion), but also by "intenseness, according to
the quantity of being"; for "by how much more perfect Entity is, that
is without mixture of Nothing, by so much the more Excellency."[35]

30 *Ibid.,* p. 695.
31 *Ibid.*
32 *Ibid.,* p. 696.
33 *Ibid.,* p. 695.
34 *Ibid.,* III, 98.
35 *Ibid.,* I, 695.

Implicit in these assertions is Edwards' belief in the merely external and secondary excellence of figures and motions, the relative excellence of finite spirits, and the absolute excellence of God.

That figures and motions are beautiful and possess a kind of excellency Edwards nowhere denies. He recognizes that subtle balancing of part with part that makes for beauty in architecture, and that complex symmetry which constitutes the excellence of a rose. There is a similar beauty in that vast complex of cause and effect which gives regularity and order to the physical universe, and which in Edwards' day deistic Newtonians loved to contemplate. But this is an inferior kind of excellence. It is as nothing compared to that spiritual beauty which consists in the consent of minds to minds. It is, indeed, only a shadow of that. He who, enthralled by the excellencies of nature, does not see beyond it to that superior excellence which explains it, understands neither nature nor beauty. "As nothing else has a proper being but Spirits, and as bodies are but the shadow of being, therefore the consent of bodies one to another and the harmony that is among them is but the shadow of excellence. The highest excellence must be the consent of Spirits one to another."[36]

There is, therefore, beyond the physical world, in which it is faintly mirrored, another and spiritual world. Behind the natural is the moral order. Here, too, there is a consent of part to part, a harmonious togetherness in the unity of excellence. But the cohesive force that binds mind to mind is not the physical law of cause and effect. It is the spiritual law of love. "When we spoke of Excellence in Bodies, we were obliged to borrow the word, *Consent*, from spiritual things; but Excellence in and among spirits is in its prime and proper sense, Being's consent to Being. There is no other proper consent but that of *Minds*, even of their Will; which, when it is of Minds towards Minds, it is *Love*, and when of Minds toward other things, it is *choice*. Wherefore all the Primary and Original beauty or excellence, that is among Minds, is love; and into this may all be resolved that is found among them."[37] But even this finite kingdom of love is not self-sufficient or self-explanatory. Behind the moral world lies the religious; behind man is God. Moral excellence or the excellence of finite spirits is therefore merely relative. It is relative because the existence of moral agents is merely relative,

36 *Ibid.*, p. 697.
37 *Ibid.*, p. 699.

being dependent upon that of the creator; and it is relative because their excellence is definable only in terms of Being-in-general, or God.

It follows that God alone is absolutely excellent. "He is . . . infinitely excellent and all excellence and beauty is derived from him."[38] This is inextricably bound up with His being. In God goodness and excellence become truly ontological. God is the prime and original Being, the first and the last, and the pattern of all. He is infinite, universal, and all-comprehending existence, and as such the sum of all perfection. "God has infinitely the greatest share of existence, so that all other being, even the whole universe, is as nothing in comparison with the Divine Being . . . and as God is infinitely the greatest Being, so he is allowed to be infinitely the most beautiful and excellent; and all the beauty to be found throughout the whole creation is but the reflection of the diffused beams of that Being who hath an infinite fulness of brightness and glory. . . . God is not only infinitely greater or more excellent than all other beings, but he is the head of the universal system of existence; the foundation and fountain of all being and all beauty; from whom all is perfectly derived, and on whom all is most absolutely and perfectly dependent; of whom, and through whom, and to whom is all being and all perfection; and whose being and beauty are, as it were, the sum and comprehension of all existence and all excellence."[39] In God, therefore, ethics and metaphysics meet. He is the absolute goodness that renders morality meaningful and valid. Combining in Himself the "is" and the "ought to be," He is at once the ground and archetype of all true virtue.

One may be inclined to question at this point the consistency of Edwards' thinking. He had previously defined excellence as the consent of being to being. He regarded it, therefore, as having to do with relations. This means that goodness is relative. But if goodness is relative there is obviously no warrant for absolutizing it in God. How is God, the absolute, compatible with excellence, which consists only in relations? Are we not forced here to the disjunction: either God is good, and consequently relative; or He is absolute, and consequently beyond good and evil? Of these alternatives, however, Edwards accepts neither. God, he says, is love, and that in the strictest moral sense. In setting this forth he begins by reaffirming the necessary connection between excellency

---

38 *Ibid.*, p. 700.
39 *Ibid.*, III, 103.

and relation. "One alone, without any reference to any more, cannot be excellent: for in such case there can be no manner of relation
no way, and therefore no such thing as consent."[40]   In other words,
both existence and morality are fundamentally social.   A being that
should exist in utter isolation would not be a being at all.   He would
be simply a mental abstraction.   Nor could he be described as moral,
since beings, and not abstractions, are the proper and only subjects
of morality.   An individual, therefore, considered simply as such,
is neither real nor virtuous.   This is true of finite spirits, but it is
equally true of God.   He, too, is good only by virtue of His relations; but, unlike those of finite spirits, these relations are not external.   God does indeed *exercise* His goodness in relation to His
creatures, but it does not consist in this exercise.   "He was as excellent before he created the universe as he is now."[41]   The relations
that determine God's goodness are internal.   He is Himself a society.
"'Tis peculiar to God, that he has beauty within himself, consisting
in Being's consenting with his own Being, or the love of himself, in
his Holy Spirit."[42]   If God were what the Deists suppose He is, a
simple being without metaphysical distinctions, then indeed it were
folly to speak of Him as good.   "In a being that is absolutely without any plurality, there cannot be Excellency, for there can be no
such thing as consent or agreement."[43]   But God is not "without
consent of parts."[44]   He is at once absolute and social, for He is
triune.

Edwards' Trinitarian doctrine is a combination of the traditional Christian teaching and the psychological views current in
his day.   Along with his contemporaries, he had distinguished two
faculties in the human mind — understanding and will.[45]   Understanding he had defined as that by which the soul "is capable of perception and speculation, or by which it discerns and judges of things";
and will, "that by which the soul is some way inclined with respect
to the things it views or considers."[46]   Both go to make up what
the older psychology had denominated the rational soul, in distinc-

40 *Ibid.*, I, 697.
41 *Ibid.*, p. 700.
42 *Ibid.*, p. 701.
43 *Ibid.*, p. 697.
44 *Ibid.*, p. 697.
45 Calvin, Shepard, Hobbes, Malebranche, Cumberland, Watts, Locke, and others
had made the same distinction.
46 *Works,* V, 10.

tion from the vegetable and sensible. Understanding, moreover, is further analyzable into the four subordinate faculties of sensation, imagination, memory, and judgment.

Sensation, in Edwards' view, provides all the materials with which the mind operates. "All ideas begin from thence; and there never can be any idea, thought, or act of the mind, unless the mind first received some ideas from sensation, or some other way equivalent, wherein the mind is wholly passive in receiving them."[47] In this he was in complete agreement with Locke, who had allowed the conception to control the views he set down in his *Essay*. The two thinkers parted company only when they described the nature of the objects stimulating the sense impressions, Locke describing them as physical and Edwards as ideal. Edwards, however, never abandoned the view that simple ideas are altogether dependent upon the senses. It appears again, for example, in his description of the thoughts and attitudes of the saints as being due to a "new sense" imparted by the Holy Spirit.[48]

Imagination and memory Edwards regarded as particular modes of perception. The first he defines as "that power of the mind by which one has an image of the things which are the objects of sense when those things are not actually present to be perceived by the senses"; and the second, or memory, as "the identity, in some degree, of Ideas that we formerly had in our minds, with a consciousness that we formerly had them, and a supposition that their former being in the mind is the cause of their being in us at present."[49] The materials of both are provided by sensation, and the mind in both is predominately passive.

Reason or judgment is the *active* principle in the understanding. There is something of the will in it. In judgment the mind not only receives; it reacts. It reflects upon the ideas provided by sensation — sorts, arranges, classifies, and combines them. It is this faculty of the understanding that distinguishes man from beasts, and constitutes him most like God. "A very great difference between men and beasts is, that Beasts have no voluntary actions about their own thoughts; for it is in this only that reasoning differs from mere perception and memory. It is the act of the Will, in bringing its ideas into contemplation, and ranging and comparing of them in reflection and abstraction. The minds of Beasts, if I may call them minds, are

---

47 *Ibid.*, I, 666.
48 *Ibid.*, V, 155.
49 *Ibid.*, I, 680.

purely passive with respect to all their ideas. The minds of men are not only passive, but abundantly active."[50]

The second faculty of the mind is will. Edwards did not conceive of it as a separate organ in man's soul. He regarded it simply as a mode of the soul's existence, or, in other words, as an affective and therefore energetic attitude of the soul toward the things perceived by the understanding. "It is the faculty by which the soul beholds things — not as an unaffected spectator, but — either as liking or disliking, pleased or displeased, approving or rejecting."[51] It is therefore indissolubly connected with the passions or affections. It is, in fact, identical with these. "The will and the affections of the soul are not two faculties; the affections are not essentially distinct from the will."[52] It is, for example, correct to say that the will is the soul in action, but this is only to observe that the affections are the moving springs in all the affairs of life. "Such is man's nature that he is very inactive any otherwise than he is influenced by either love or hatred, desire, hope, fear, or some other affection. . . . Take away all love and hatred, all hope and fear, all anger, zeal, and affectionate desire, and the world would be in a great measure motionless and dead; there would be no such thing as activity among mankind, or any earnest pursuit whatsoever."[53] The moving, activating, energizing principle in the soul is, therefore, the will, or which is the same thing, the soul's inclination to, or affection for, the thing toward which it moves.

It is with this psychology that Edwards approached the Christian doctrine of the Trinity. His interest in it was more than casual. As he saw in the Nicaean Formula more than a curious example of high Greek speculation, so his attachment to it was more than conservative loyalty to Christian tradition. He accepted it as a profound truth to which not only as a believer in divine revelation but also as a teacher of morality he was necessarily committed. He is brought to consider it now by the exigencies of his ethical theory.[54]

[50] *Ibid.*, p. 682.
[51] *Ibid.*, V, 10.
[52] *Ibid.*
[53] *Ibid.*, p. 14.
[54] Besides the fugitive and incidental references that are to be found throughout his writings, there are especially three sources for our knowledge of Edwards' Trinitarian views. The first is his *Treatise on Grace*, edited by Alexander B. Grosart, and published in 1865, along with other items, in a volume entitled *Selections from the Unpublished Writings of Jonathan Edwards,* and printed privately in Edinburgh. The second is his *Observations Concerning the Scripture*

Edwards had previously defined God as the eternal, all-comprehending mind. This definition serves him now as a point of departure. Being mind, God has both understanding and will. Since
He is divine and incorporeal mind, there are, of course, "no such
distinctions to be admitted as in ours between Perception or Idea,
and Reasoning and Judgment."[55] Yet the manner of the divine understanding, "if it be anything that can be any way signified by that
word of ours,"[56] must be by idea. It must be supposed, accordingly,
that God "perpetually and eternally has a most perfect idea of
himself, as it were an exact Image of and representation of himself
ever before him and in actual view."[57] It is in the unvaried presence
of this infinitely perfect idea that God's understanding or wisdom
consists. He knows all things and has all wisdom, because He has
an idea of Himself, who is "the all-comprehending being — he that
is, and there is none else."[58] But if God beholds Himself, He must
become His own object. There must be a duality. The idea that
God has of Himself is a perfect idea, that is, it accords precisely
with His being; there is nothing in the thinker that is not found in
the idea. Hence God is in a real sense repeated. The case could
be illustrated from our own thinking. If we had a perfect idea, for
example, of love, that idea would be identical with the thing itself,
and if we had a perfect idea of all that went on within us, we would
have a double existence. God has such an idea of Himself, and the
Deity is, accordingly, truly and properly repeated. "Therefore as
God with perfect clearness, fulness, and strength, understands himself, views his own essence, . . . that idea which God hath of himself
is absolutely himself. This representation of the divine nature and
essence is the divine nature and essence again. . . . Hereby there is
another person begotten . . . and this person is the second Person in
the Trinity, the Only begotten and dearly beloved Son of God."[59]

The Holy Spirit, or the Divine Love, is generated in a similar

---

Oeconomy of the Trinity and Covenant of Redemption, published in New York
in 1880, with an introduction and appendix by Egbert C. Smyth. The third,
and most important, is a publication of George P. Fisher entitled, *An Unpublished
Essay of Edwards on the Trinity, with Remarks on Edwards and His Theology,*
New York, 1903.

55 Edwards, *An Essay on the Trinity,* in *Representative Selections,* edited by
Clarence H. Faust and Thomas H. Johnson (New York, 1935), p. 375.

56 *Ibid.*

57 *Ibid.*

58 *Ibid.,* p. 376.

59 *Ibid.,* pp. 376-7.

fashion. Love in man, Edwards observes, is "scarcely distinguish-able from the complacence he has in any idea."[60] That is, love is the highest degree of inclination to or affection for an idea presented to the mind. Love therefore is a movement, act, or energy; it is the highest expression of will. Love and will are in fact indistinguish-able in God. "As the sum of God's understanding consists in his having an Idea of himself, so the sum of his Will or Inclination con-sists in his loving himself."[61] This Will, or Love, is the third per-son in the Trinity. It is God in act, or God in tension between Him-self, absolutely considered, and His idea of Himself. It is God con-sidered as an affective and energetic attitude toward His own idea. Edwards puts it this way: "The Godhead being thus begotten by God's loving an idea of himself and showing forth in a distinct subsistence or person in that Idea, there proceeds a most pure act, and an in-finitely holy and sacred energy arises between the Father and Son in mutually loving and delighting in each other. . . . This is the eternal and most perfect and essential act of the divine nature, wherein the Godhead acts to an infinite degree in the most perfect manner possible. The deity becomes all act, the divine essence it-self flows out and is as it were breathed forth in love and joy. So the Godhead therein stands forth in yet another manner of sub-sistence, and there proceeds the third person in the Trinity, viz., the Deity in act, for there is no other act but the act of the Will."[62]

In the Godhead, therefore, are three persons or subsistences — the Father, or He who loves and acts; the Son, or He who is loved and acted upon; and the Holy Spirit, or He who is the Divine Love Himself and the Deity in act. All are eternal and necessary, and all are dependent on each of the others. So close is their independence and communion that the Godhead must be said to have only one will and one understanding. Yet each divine subsistence is truly personal; each has both understanding and will; and they form to-gether a most perfect society. "There is such a wonderful union between them that they are, after an ineffable and inconceivable manner, one in another, so that one hath another and they have communion in one another, and are as it were predicable one of another."[63]

60 *Ibid.,* p. 376.
61 *Ibid.,* p. 379.
62 *Ibid.,* p. 377.
63 *Ibid.,* p. 380.

Our primary interest in these representations is not their theological accuracy or want of it.[64] Edwards himself was fully aware of their inadequacy and never supposed that he had given a scientific explanation or a logical demonstration of what must always remain an article of faith. "I am far from pretending to explaining the Trinity so as to render it no longer a mystery. I think it to be the highest and deepest of all divine mysteries still, notwithstanding anything that I have said or conceived about it."[65] The *Essay* must be regarded as nothing more or less than an attempt to enter more deeply into this mystery and so to set forth its meaning for both theology and ethics. Our interest lies in its moral significance.

Edwards' doctrine is ethically significant first because of the fact, already mentioned, that, since God is not a stark one, as the Deists and their Unitarian children supposed, but rather a Trinity of persons constituting in some mysterious and ultimately inexplicable way a oneness of being and a unity of perfection, he can with strict accuracy be regarded as both moral and absolute. Morality is essentially social and as such presupposes relations. Since these relations exist pure and perfect within the very Godhead, apart from all and every relation to any other being or existence, the conditions are fully met which enable one to ascribe supreme excellence to God while maintaining His absolute sovereignty.

A second point of interest is Edwards' emphasis on love as the bond of unity in the Godhead. Love, he says, is so "essential and necessary to the Deity that his nature consists in it."[66] This may strike those as strange who are wont to regard Edwards solely as the grim determinist who preached sulphurous sermons on the wrath of angry and arbitrary Deity. Yet it remains true that there is nothing of Scotus and everything of St. John in Edwards. God, he echoes, is light and God is love, and "whatsoever else can be mentioned in God are nothing but mere modes or relations of Existence."[67] His will, for example, is "not really distinguished from

---

64 It was long believed that Edwards' heirs thought the *Essay* heretical and that they had suppressed it in order to safeguard the reputation of its author. His views have been variously called Orthodox, Sabellian, and Tritheistic. For the controversy itself cf. the articles of Edward A. Park in *Bibliotheca Sacra*, Vol. 38, 1881; Smyth's Introduction to the *Observations;* Fisher's Preface to the *Essay;* and Alexander Allen's *Jonathan Edwards*, pp. 341ff. For a masterful analysis and criticism of Edwards' Trinitarian views, cf. Jan Ridderbos, *De Theologie van Jonathan Edwards* (Amsterdam, 1907), pp. 258-280.

65 *Essay on the Trinity*, p. 381.

66 *Ibid.*, p. 376.

67 *Ibid.*, p. 379.

his Love, but is the same only with a different relation."[68] This
accords, of course, with his entire psychology. Edwards never conceived of will as some imperious and irresponsible power; it was
merely the name he gave to that inclination of the soul which was
the soul's movement toward the object of its affection. That inclination depended wholly on the nature of the soul whose inclination it was. What is primary in any being is his quality, not his
energy, and this is supremely true of God. Not will, but love, is
prior. It is God's character that determines His acts, not His will
that defines His character. God exercises His will, but He is not
Himself will, any more than He is immutability or omnipresence.
On the other hand, He not only has and exercises love; He is Himself love. Will is but the instrument of love, or love-in-operation.
God is indeed to be obeyed, since His will is inviolable, but obedience is not the highest virtue. Even Satan and the damned shall
ultimately obey Him. True blessedness consists in the enjoyment
of God, and of enjoyment the proper and only object is God's character and perfection.[69] That the sum of this perfection is love,
Edwards never tires of reiterating. His elucidation of the Trinitarian formula is one deliberate attempt to show that divine love is
not a mere sentiment that may at any moment be supplanted by
hate, nor merely one attribute among others, nor merely a mode of
God's existence, but that it is His existence itself. Love is the very
Spirit of God, the third person in the blessed Trinity. It is the mark
and sign of the divine society.[70]

A third thing to be noted is the fact that since the Godhead is
in very essence a community of persons, it contains in principle all
the materials of the social life and thus portrays in broad outline
the whole complicated scheme of virtue. Plato had in his *Republic*
proposed a consideration of the state in order that by a contemplation of that large society one might see morality writ large and thus
the better discern its true nature and scope. Edwards proposed a
similar inquiry but appealed beyond the state to the divine community, for what appears in human society in shades and half-tints exists
there clearly and perfectly. It is in this kingdom beyond the stars

---

68 Ibid.

69 Cf. the *Westminster Confession* — "to know and enjoy Him forever."

70 Edwards does frequently speak, of course, of God's hating, being angry, displeased, etc. But he does not regard these as being positive affections in God.
God acts from no other principle than love. Love is the sole source of all His
affections. Out of love for Himself as the sum of all good flows hatred for all
that is contrary and opposite. Hatred, like sin, has only a negative existence.

that we first see, for example, what love is. Here love is shown to be spiritual, disinterested, and unifying. In the light of this ideal we can recognize the actual. This, the eternally real, interprets that which on earth is only in the process of becoming. It is the same with happiness. In God it consists "in the infinite love he has to and delight he has in himself."[71] Happiness is seen, therefore, to be inseparable from love, and totally independent of what Aristotle called "the furniture of fortune." Happiness is in no sense a reward of virtue. That would be to conceive of it externally. It *consists in* virtue, since love, the sum of virtue, is itself delight or happiness.

What is especially to be observed, however, is the steadfast hope and unconquerable optimism that Edwards derived from such representations as these. His was an ethics of the infinite. Ideals spoke to him with a compelling objectivity and importunateness. He knew himself under obligation not merely to the dictates of conscience but through these to the inviolable imperatives of God. This made life serious and morals strenuous, but it gave life its strength and morals its dignity. Behind the human society Edwards discerned the divine. Existing unchangeable in the eternal heavens he saw a goodness of which every earthly good was but the shadow and witness. Behind the society of men stood God, the absolute standard for all relationships between beings. The rules of right, the laws of conduct, and the principles of spiritual intercourse are not, he saw, provincialisms of this planet. They reign beyond the stars. Their seat and fountain is in God Himself. Here lies the root of optimism. Whatever else the Puritan philosophy of life may have been it was neither petty nor pessimistic. The Puritan strode two worlds like a Colossus. He lived under the controlling conviction that the moral life had its source and issue in the eternal, and he was unafraid. The good man, in his view, did not stand alone, but had the universe to back him. He was partner in a venture whose success was assured, for God Himself was in the enterprise. Hence he never feared the future. He knew that the ideal, though ever recessive here, will not always be in flight. Utopia is no idle dream. It most certainly lies ahead because it certainly lies behind. What ought to be will be, for in God it already is.

Edwards' view of the world consists with his view of God. We have already noticed the distinction he made in finite existences

---

[71] *Treatise on Grace*, in A. Grosart, *op. cit.*, p. 48.

between physical objects and human spirits. He makes a corresponding distinction in God between His natural and moral attributes. What intrigues him in each case is the spiritual and ethical. The fact is significant. He lived in an age when the scientific temper was pressing to the fore. Men were turning with a new and intense interest to the study of the measurable and the ponderable. Astronomic physics had opened up amazing vistas, and in the vastness of the universe it revealed, man seemed puny and insignificant. Nature, accordingly, was taking man's place in the center of things. Men stood enraptured around the impressive Newtonian world-machine, fascinated by its laws and revolutions. With measure and rule and mathematical formulae they set about to see how it worked. They learned in the process to be objective, that is, to suppress the personal element in investigations. Men became spectators and observers, not agents. In short, the physical overshadowed the spiritual, and nature dominated mind. Edwards' early idealism was a protest against all this. It was, to be sure, not a protest against science as such. Edwards recognized both the legitimacy and usefulness of nature studies. What he could not tolerate was what he regarded as the usurpation by nature of the place that rightfully belonged to man. Many of his contemporaries seemed willing to lay down their title to the central position in creation. Edwards steadfastly refused to abdicate. The physical, he said, exists but on the outskirts of the universe; on the verge, so to speak, of nothingness. Its existence is dependent, and its value instrumental. It exists in the interest of man. Not to matter, but to spirit, belongs the ascendency. The clue to reality, he was convinced, lay in personality. The ultimate forces in the universe are not those of motion and gravity. They are more refined than that, subtler, and more mysterious. Physical categories will never render the universe intelligible because the universe is built on other and vaster lines than physical science supposes. It rests on a spiritual foundation and has a spiritual goal. It exists in the interest of holiness and virtue. It was because the science of the times was obscuring this truth that Edwards protested against it. Men were raising the principles of physics and mathematics to the dignity of principles of life. As a consequence of being mechanically conceived life became fixed, stable, and static. Religion, as an expression of that life, tended to be shorn of its mysteries and to become formal and moralistic. Ethics became prudential, conduct being guided simply by the dictates of a cool and calculating reason. The emotional side of life was ruthlessly suppressed. For the moods of awe and reverence, for worship and soul-stirring affections there was little or no place. It was a spiritually barren age, drab and uninspiring, and Edwards set his face against it.

As he opposed his age on the human front, so he opposed it on the divine. There were few atheists in Edwards' day. The Deists believed in God and had constructed a definite theology. But it bore all the earmarks of contemporary science. It ignored or obscured the personal and moral qualities of God, and gave prominence to what Edwards called His "natural attributes" — His wisdom and His power. Deists recognized Him as the maker and designer of the world, as the ingenious engineer who had fashioned the complex world machine whose laws it was man's chief business to discover. But they had emptied Him of His fulness. God became a formal first cause or prime mover; something distant, awful, and impersonal. Himself absent, He operated in the world only by proxy — through accurate and inviolable mechanical laws. All this amounted, in Edwards' view, to an intolerable depreciation of Divinity. That God was to be honored for His wisdom and power he never thought of contesting. It is what he repeatedly affirms. Nor did he deny that these attributes stood revealed in the processes of nature. Edwards was as sensitive to its grandeurs as any of his contemporaries. What he insisted on was that God is infinitely more than nature is able to mirror. To see Him there, or to recognize His power, is but to touch the hem of His garment. It is to see Him partially and therefore falsely. God is indeed infinitely wise and infinitely mighty, but this bare admission says nothing really significant about Him. He might for all of that be a destructive power and a malignant mind. It is not, therefore, God's natural attributes that make Him God. He is God because of His moral qualities. The divinity of Divinity lies in holiness and love. Without these "God himself (if that were possible) would be an infinite evil, we ourselves had better never have been; and there had better have been no being."[72] To truly know God is to know Him as a person, as moral, as excellent, and as good. It is to know Him concretely and materially, not abstractly and formally. To know Him in His fulness is to recognize His wisdom and His power operating in complete subservience to His holiness and love.

[72] *Works*, V, 158.

That means that all things in which His wisdom and power are revealed exist in the interest of a purpose dictated by holiness and love. That purpose is not far to seek. Both the superiority of men to things, and of God's moral attributes to the natural, combine to indicate it. Both attest the spiritual character of the universe, and the ethico-religious purpose of creation. This thesis, implicit in his view of God and man, Edwards now elaborates in *A Dissertation Concerning the End for Which God Created the World*.[73] His discussion of the subject proceeds on the assumption that God did indeed create the world. The fact was granted by all parties and needed no defense. The question was: Why did God create the world? What end did He seek?

The question is perhaps best understood when formulated hypothetically on the supposition that the world is non-existent. One might then ask: If God were to create a world, what would be His object in so doing? What ultimate end could and would He have in view? To this question, as Edwards saw it, there could be only one answer. God could have only Himself in view. He certainly could not act in the interest of His creatures. These are, *ex confesso*, non-existent, and it is absurd to suppose that that which does not exist, not even in idea, is the ground of its own existence. But even if we were to suppose the existence of other beings resident somewhere in the primeval void, we would still have to acknowledge God as having respect only to Himself in any act of His will. He is the perfect moral agent. As such He has "respect to things according to their nature and proportions."[74] His moral rectitude "consists in his having the highest regard to that which is in itself highest and best."[75] But since He is Himself the highest and best, in possession of "all possible existence, perfection, and excellence,"[76] He must Himself be the object of all possible regard. He must, if He is to create a world, do it in His own interest. This is what His greatness and holiness demand. If then, as is the case, the world does actually exist, we are bound to recognize it as existing *for* God, as well as *from* Him. "As all things are from God . . .; so all things

---

[73] The dissertation was written in the spring and summer of 1755, at which time Edwards also began his *Dissertation Concerning the Nature of True Virtue*. The works were published for the first time in 1788, in one volume.

[74] *Works*, III, 14.

[75] *Ibid.*, p. 14.

[76] *Ibid.*, p. 16.

tend to him."[77] He is the origin and end of all, the Alpha and the Omega, the efficient and the final cause. He is the "final term to which all things tend in their ultimate issue."[78] This does not mean that He made His existence the end of creation. That "cannot be supposed without great absurdity. His existence cannot be conceived of but as prior to any of God's designs."[79] Nor did He have an extension or growth of His being in view. That is eternally full, beyond all power to add or detract. What He seeks is His honor or praise. "God's glory is the last end of creation."[80] This is what He regards as being "good, valuable, and excellent in itself."[81] This, therefore, is what He aims at, and this is what all His providential dispensations are designed and calculated to achieve.

From this it is seen that the world has a religious goal. One might say with equal truth, however, that its end is moral. In seeking Himself, God seeks His creatures. In aiming at His glory, He aims at their holiness. Distinguishable in thought these aims are identical in fact.[82] "God and the creature, in the emanation of the divine fulness, are not properly set in opposition, or made the opposite parts of a disjunction. Nor ought God's glory and the creature's good, to be viewed as if they were properly and entirely distinct . . . God in seeking their glory and happiness seeks himself; and in seeking himself . . . he seeks their glory and happiness."[83]

There are times when Edwards explains this pantheistically. God, he says, comprehends all entity. "The eternal and infinite Being is, in effect, Being in General."[84] He is identical with universal existence. Love to Himself is therefore identical with love to His creatures, and to seek His own welfare and glory is, by that token, to seek the welfare and happiness of men. Yet such explanations are not characteristic. It is not from the existence of God, but from

---

[77] *Ibid.*, p. 26.
[78] *Ibid.*, p. 40.
[79] *Ibid.*, p. 41.
[80] *Ibid.*, p. 50.
[81] *Ibid.*, p. 51.
[82] Edwards' son and successor regarded this as one of his father's most noteworthy contributions to theological and ethical thought. He says: "For ages it had been disputed whether the end of creation was the happiness of creatures themselves, or the declarative glory of the Creator . . . Mr. Edwards was the first who clearly showed that both these were the ultimate end of creation, that they are only one end, and that they are really one and the same thing." Dr. Edwards, Jr., in Dwight, *Life*, I, 613.
[83] *Works*, III, 97.
[84] *Ibid.*, p. 38.

His love or will, that Edwards would have the matter understood.[85]
He speaks repeatedly in this connection of God's fulness, by which
he understands "all the good which is in God natural and moral."[86]
It is another word for God's love, or the sum of His excellency.
This love is mobile, energetic, and communicative. Its very nature
is to seek an object on which it can spend its beneficent force.

Edwards describes this tendency of love to impart itself, as
a disposition in God "to communicate himself or diffuse his own
fulness."[87] Here lies the reason for the world's existence. God,
driven by the power of His love, created the world to be the object
of His affection and the recipient of that communication of Himself, the disposition to which is an "original property of his nature."[88]
In God there is an infinite fountain of light. It was His pleasure
"that this light should shine forth in beams of communicated knowledge and understanding."[89] God is an infinite fountain of moral
excellence and beauty. It was His desire that this virtue "should flow
out in communicated holiness."[90] In God is an infinite fulness of
joy and happiness. It was His will that these "should have an emanation and become a fountain flowing out in abundant streams, as
beams from the sun."[91] To that end He created man, giving him
existence in order that he might be the "object of his benevolence."[92]

In all this, of course, God manifested a supreme and ultimate
regard to Himself. He had regard to Himself diffused, or "to his
own glory existing in its emanation."[93] Yet, since "himself diffused"
is nothing more or less than the communication of His knowledge,
holiness, and happiness to the creatures He has made, He must be

---

[85] Alexander Allen, *op. cit.*, pp. 331ff., is of the opinion that the *Dissertation*
breathes a Gnostic and Neo-Platonic spirit. It is true that Edwards' language
frequently lays him open to the charge of Pantheism. He speaks of diffusion,
emanation, increase, repetition; and on occasion compares God and the world to the
sun and its rays, a fountain and its stream, a tree and its sap, etc. But these unhappy
modes of expression are misleading. The emanation that Edwards repeatedly speaks
of is that of God's fulness or love, not of His essence. He emphasizes, moreover, that
(1) God's existence is prior to that of the world (*Works,* III, 41); that (2) His creatures
can contribute nothing to His fulness (*ibid.,* p. 15); that (3) the world is a product
of the will, thus the effect of a choice (*ibid.,* p. 30); and that (4) those views are to be
rejected which imply that man in any way shows the divine essence (*ibid.*).
[86] *Works,* I, p. 20.
[87] *Ibid.*
[88] *Ibid.,* p. 21.
[89] *Ibid.,* p. 20.
[90] *Ibid.*
[91] *Ibid.*
[92] *Ibid.,* p. 38.
[93] *Ibid.,* p. 23.

said to have had an ultimate regard also to them. "Here God acting for himself, or making himself his last end, and his acting for their sake, are not to be set in opposition; they are rather to be considered as coinciding one with the other, and implied one in the other."[94]

Edwards never supposed that these goals, once projected, would be automatically achieved through the operation of resident laws, forces, or tendencies. They are moral and religious ends, and thus demand the activity of personal agents. The world is not a machine moving insensibly and relentlessly. It is a sphere in which minds posit ideals and wills undertake to effectuate them. The governing will is God Himself. He is actively and immanently directing all things to moral ends. Edwards could never understand the "strange disposition that men have to thrust God out of the world, or to put him as far out of sight as they can."[95] He saw God everywhere — in every natural phenomenon and in every event of life. The universe is His chariot, and in it He "rides and makes progress toward the last end of all things on the wheels of his providence."[96]

It is the strength of this conception that explains the Puritan's attitude toward nature. There is a sense in which he was indifferent to it. He was no physical scientist. The scientist lives in abstractions. He is forced to isolate. At the very beginning of his studies he takes pains to insulate his investigations from all appreciatory attitudes. In so doing he separates man and the world. The latter he regards as a datum. He approaches it as an object existing independently, and as significant in itself, apart from all considerations of value. When he has laid bare the physical causes of a natural phenomenon he has done with it. Description, not interpretation, is his task. Goals and final causes lie quite without his purview. It was different with the Puritan. He approached nature religiously. For him it was not a datum to be investigated, but a voice to be heard. He did not regard it as an independently significant magnitude. It was a finger pointing beyond itself to its creator, whose instrument it was. Study of it was, therefore, not an inherently valuable enterprise. It was valuable only in so far as it enabled one the better to see Him who uses

---

94 *Ibid.,* p. 24. This does not, in Edwards' view, argue God's dependence on the creature. The delight God has in His creatures' happiness cannot properly be said to be what He receives from the creature. "It is only the effect of his own work in and communication to the creature . . . . The sun receives nothing from the jewel that receives its light." *Ibid.,* p. 28.

95 *Treatise on Grace* in A. Grosart, *op. cit.,* p. 40.

96 *Miscellaneous Observations,* edited by A. Grosart, p. 100.

it for the moral and religious ends in whose interest the world exists.
Nature was not so much a thing to be conquered as a teacher to be
heard. So conceived it was of absorbing interest. Every event had
its meaning. Let their physical antecedents be what they may, all
natural phenomena are events in a vast moral government. All that
happens, happens to the end that the society of love, happiness, and
holiness may be firmly established upon earth.

It is important to observe that these providential dispensations,
in Edwards' view, were pedagogical, not judicial in character. He
did not look for a balancing of moral accounts in this life. This
is the day of grace. The Judgment, with its distribution of rewards
and punishments, is to come in the future, when all men will be
called to give an account of the improvement they made of God's
dealing with them. Edwards did not distinguish, therefore, between
good and bad providences. All God's providential dealings with men
are in intention good. Be they pleasant or unpleasant, all are whole-
some and gracious in design. Whether they are that in fact and
ultimately, depends on man's attitude toward them. If in bright
days men grow proud and complacent, and in dark days impatient
and rebellious, God's beneficent dispensations turn out to be savours
of death unto death. If, on the other hand, men, moved by love
to God, are thankful in prosperity, and submissive in adversity, all
things work together for their benefit. The good man, therefore,
is not to be defined in terms of the particular providences that cross
his path, but rather in terms of the attitude he takes toward them.
Wealth, success, and ease are no more a mark of virtue than ill-fortune
is of vice. These things are in themselves indifferent. They are
weighty only as they effect the dispositions of the heart. The Puritan therefore learned to face life bravely and to taste the whole of it.
The bitter was as nourishing to him as the sweet. In both he saw
the dispensation of a gracious Father, who, whether with a smile or
with a rod, was disciplining him for membership in the perfect
kingdom. This kept him from courting the sweet as a sign that he
stood high in God's favor. He knew that God did not traffic in
such signs. Love, either that of man to God or that of God to man,
is not deducible from things external. It is altogether a matter of
the heart and has its evidence in itself. If it is bound to express itself
in action, its validation is outside that action's consequences. "I may
pursue knowledge, religion, the glory of God, and the good of mankind with the utmost vigour, but am to leave the honour of it entirely at God's disposal, as a thing with which I have no immediate

concern."[97] It might, here and now, be dishonour, defeat, and morti-
fication. Even so it is a means of grace. "Great instances of morti-
fication are deep wounds given to the body of sin; hard blows,
which make him stagger and reel. We thereby get strong ground
and footing against him and he is the weaker ever after."[98] To the
good therefore all things are good, and to the evil all things are evil.
As for the saints, "the wheels of the chariot of the universe move
for them; and the progress that God makes therein on his throne
above the firmament, the pavement of his chariot, is for them; and
every event in the universe is in subserviency to their help and
benefit."[99]

---

[97] *Works,* I, p. 86.
[98] *Ibid.,* p. 80.
[99] *Miscellaneous Observations,* p. 100.

6

For a Renewal of an Old Departure in Ethics

HENRY B. VEATCH, Distinguished Service Professor of Philosophy, Indiana University. A.B., A.M., Ph.D., Harvard University. Author of *Intentional Logic, Realism and Nominalism Revisited, Logic as a Human Instrument* (with Francis H. Parker), *Rational Man;* articles in *Philosophy and Phenomenological Research, Review of Metaphysics, Journal of Philosophy, The New Scholasticism, The Thomist.*

For a Renewal of an Old Departure in Ethics

BY HENRY B. VEATCH

NOT INFREQUENTLY NOWADAYS ONE HEARS BITTER COMPLAINTS DIRECTED against ethics of the current academic variety: "Why, it isn't ethics at all. It never even gets around to properly ethical questions. So far from telling us what we ought to do, or how we ought to live, it trails off in endless discussions of the meaning of the word 'good,' or in countless arguments about whether expressions containing words like 'ought' and 'ought not' are used in the same way as ordinary imperatives, whether they admit of being contradicted, whether they can be true or false, etc." Moreover, what all these charges seem to boil down to is that questions as to the meaning and use of ethical terms just aren't the substantive questions of ethics: this may all be meta-ethics, but it certainly isn't ethics!

Very well, then, suppose that one wants to do ethics and not just meta-ethics. Suppose, further, that in doing ethics one proposes to do the very sort of thing that Charles Stevenson in his influential book, *Ethics and Language*, expressly refrained from doing — i.e., suppose one proposes to do ethics and not merely an analysis of the language of ethics[1] — just how is one to go about doing it? What is one to say? Where is one to begin? After all, the enterprise has lately become so unfashionable that one scarcely knows how to get started.

Perhaps, though, the best way to start when one does not know

[1] Cf. *Ethics and Language* (New Haven, 1944), p. 1.

141

how to get started is just to start. Indeed, the least that can be said
for fools is that they do rush in where angels fear to tread. So let us
plunge *in medias res* with two quotations, the one from Jane Austen
and the other from C. P. Snow.

> Sir Walter Elliott, of Kellynch Hall, in Somersetshire, was a man
> who, for his own amusement, never took up any book but the Ba-
> ronetage; there he found occupation for an idle hour, and consola-
> tion in a distressed one; . . .
> Vanity was the beginning and end of Sir Walter Elliott's character:
> vanity of person and of situation. He had been remarkably handsome
> in his youth, and at fifty-four was still a very fine man. Few women
> could think more of their personal appearance than he did, nor
> would the valet of any new made lord be more delighted with the
> place he held in society. He considered the blessing of beauty as in-
> ferior only to the blessing of baronetcy; and the Sir Walter Elliott,
> who united these gifts, was the constant object of his warmest respect
> and devotion.[2]

> I looked round Nightingale's sitting-room. It was without feature,
> it was the room of a man concentrated into himself, so that he had
> nothing to spend outside; it showed nothing of the rich, solid comfort
> which Brown had given to his, or the eccentric picturesqueness of Roy
> Calvert's. Nightingale was a man drawn into himself. Suspicion and
> envy lived in him; they were part of his nature. But he had been
> unlucky, he had been frustrated in his most cherished hope, and now
> envy never left him alone.
> He was forty-three, and a bachelor. Why he had not married, I did
> not know: there was nothing unmasculine about him. That was
> not, however, his abiding disappointment. He had once possessed
> great promise. He had known what it was to hold creative dreams:
> and they had not come off. That was his bitterness. As a very
> young man he had shown a spark of real talent. He was one of the
> earliest theoretical chemists. By twenty-three he had written two
> good papers on molecular structure. He had, so I was told, anticipated
> Heitler-London and the orbital theory; he was ten years ahead of
> his time. The college had elected him, everything seemed easy. But
> the spark burnt out. The years passed. Often he had new concep-
> tions; but the power to execute them had escaped from him.
> It would have been bitter to the most generous heart. In Night-
> ingale's, it made him fester with envy. He longed in compensation
> for every job within reach, in reason and out of reason. It was mor-
> bid that he should have fancied his chances of the tutorship before
> Brown, his senior and a man made for the job; but it rankled in him
> after a dozen years. Each job in the college for which he was passed
> over, he saw with suspicion as a sign of the conspiracy directed against
> him.

2 *Persuasion*, Ch. 1.

His reputation in his subject was already gone. He would not get into the Royal Society now. But, as March came round each year, he waited for the announcement of the Royal elections in expectation, in anguish, in bitter suspiciousness, at moments in the knowledge of what he might have been.[3]

Now, surely, no one could read either of these accounts without readily recognizing Sir Walter Elliott to be an ass, and Nightingale to be a man whose whole life has become infected, twisted, and miserable as a result of the kind of creeping consumption that is so often brought on by envy, resentment, and self-pity. Indeed, one has only to hear accounts of the actions and behavior of men like this, and one finds oneself most naturally and almost inevitably passing moral or ethical judgments upon them. Oh, it is true that in making such judgments, we would, any of us, recognize that in given instances, perhaps even in most instances, our judgments might be mistaken; and yet we would none of us doubt for a moment — at least not in our everyday lives and outside of such academic poses as we may strike in lectures and learned articles — that such judgments are in general quite as warranted and quite as reliable as the judgment that the tree outside my window is a maple and not an elm, or that the noise which I hear in the street is that of a motorbike and not an automobile.

But just what is it that is implied by the fact that we do seem to make moral judgments so readily and so naturally and with such confidence as to their being in the main sound and warranted? Must not the implication be that there really is a difference between living well and living foolishly, between making something of our lives and making a mess of them? Oh, it's true that if you put a rhetorical question such as this to a professor of philosophy, he might prove a bit stuffy and pedantic and refuse to give the expected affirmative answer. He would doubtless mutter something about logical entailments and then go on to observe that the mere fact that all men everywhere tend to make certain kinds of judgment certainly does not entail that such judgments are either true or warranted.

Still, philosophy professors notwithstanding, one cannot help thinking of Lincoln's dictum that while you can perhaps fool all of the people some of the time, and some of the people all of the time, you can't fool all of the people all of the time. And certainly, there is no denying the fact that human beings generally do seem to recognize that the living of their lives is something that they may do

---

3 *The Masters* (New York, 1959), Ch. 5, pp. 44-45 (Anchor edition).

either well or badly. And perhaps when pressed further, they might even acknowledge that there presumably must be a kind of art, or "know-how," so far as the living of one's life is concerned, much as there is an art or know-how when it comes to performing such more specialized activities as practicing medicine, running a farm, driving a car, or playing the fiddle. Indeed, just as there is a real distinction between a good doctor and a poor one, or between a good driver and a bad, why would there not also be a real distinction between a good man and a bad?

But alas, driving out meta-ethics is much like driving out the devil: it escapes through the door, only to slip back in through the window. For no sooner does one try to get on with the business of ethics, as if it were nothing more nor less than a sort of art of living, comparable to and yet in its own way different from such other arts as those of medicine, engineering, gardening or what not, than one immediately finds one's way blocked at the outset by a number of difficulties which are like so many roadblocks that meta-ethics would appear to have placed in the way of further progress in ethics itself. For how can one get very far with investigations regarding the right way to live as over against the wrong way, if distinctions between right and wrong, and good and bad, etc., are a purely relative matter? Or how can one intelligently go about trying to discover what the good life for a human being is, if the very idea of trying to learn about goodness from studying man's nature and the conditions and circumstances in which he finds himself — if the very idea of this sort of thing involves one in the so-called naturalistic fallacy?

Very well, then, suppose these roadblocks exist and that they are a real bar to anyone's getting on with ethics proper, cannot we get busy and clear them away? At least, that is the sort of task that I would like to set for myself in this paper, that of removing at least two of these roadblocks, viz., that of relativism on the one hand and that of the naturalistic fallacy on the other.

First, then, as to relativism. Now surely in this day and age it is hardly necessary to elaborate either on the evidence in support of ethical relativism, or on how, if relativism is true, there just would not be any objective basis for the moral judgments that we make concerning our own and other men's behavior. For as to the former, is it not simply the case that moral values and moral judgments are in fact relative to class, to culture, to locality, to age, to civilization, to psychological and physiological make-up, etc.? And as to the latter, is it not equally true that from the fact of such a relativity of moral standards we are apt to conclude — not too cogently perhaps,[4] but with complete conviction nonetheless — that moral and ethical judgments just as such have no basis in fact whatever?

But now to all such relativistic and skeptical considerations in regard to morals and ethics, I would make bold to offer a simple and straightforward rejoinder. relativism in ethics simply cannot be maintained without inconsistency; or better, anyone who undertakes to deny the possibility of moral or ethical knowledge cannot avoid being inconsistent. But how so?

Well, if I mistake not, the sort of inconsistency to which the denial of ethical knowledge leads is one to which contemporary ethical writers and philosophers generally have perhaps paid but too little attention. For the relevant inconsistency here is not an inconsistency of the more usual type. Indeed, it is not like the more familiar kind of inconsistency that is involved in attempts to formulate a position of general philosophical skepticism. For example, "I know that there is no knowledge," or "It is true that there is no truth." Clearly, in the very formulation of such statements one contradicts oneself.[5] And yet in the formulation of a position of skepticism in regard to ethical knowledge, there is no such inconsistency involved. For instance, "I know that there is no knowledge in matters of ethics," or "It's true that ethical judgments cannot be true in the usual sense" — such statements are not self-contradictory at all.

Where, then, does the inconsistency arise? I suggest that it arises not in any properly theoretical context, but solely in what I would call the practical or, if you will, the existential context of the skeptic's own being and existence. Thus, suppose a man asserts that all ethical judgments, or all value judgments, are without any real warrant or foundation. Still having made the statement, the

---

[4] The point here is that the mere fact that all men, or at least most men, tend to disagree in their moral or ethical judgments — this fact as such does not entail the conclusion that there is no truth in matters of ethics and that ethics is a purely relative matter. But once again, the mere absence of logical entailment hardly suffices to convince any one that he does not have good reason to suspect the very possibility of a genuine knowledge in matters of ethics, considering that it is disagreement rather than agreement that is the rule when it comes to ethical judgments.

[5] It is well known that the possibility of such self-contradiction might be denied, supposing that one were operating with a system of logic having some such thing as a theory of types or its equivalent as one of the built-in features of the system. But this difficulty can simply be disregarded in the present context.

man cannot just cease to exist. He must go on living, which is to say he must go on making choices. But to make a choice is to make at least an implicit value judgment to the effect that what he does finally choose is somehow better or preferable or superior to the alternatives he rejects. And yet by hypothesis, our ethical skeptic has already declared that no value judgment has any legitimate foundation. What, then, of his own value judgments, which he cannot help making and which, in making, he cannot help supposing to be in some sense warranted and true?

Now when caught in a predicament of this nature, the ethical skeptic tends, I believe, almost invariably, albeit usually quite unwittingly, to resort to a most curious device. He tends to adduce his own very skepticism concerning the warrant for any value judgment as being itself the warrant for the value judgments that he himself makes. It is as if he were more or less unconsciously trying to justify himself along some such lines as these: "Since all judgments as to the better course of action for one to follow, or the course one ought to follow, are without foundation, it therefore would seem that the only sensible thing for me to do (sc. the better thing for me to do, or the thing that I ought to do) is thus and so."

Indeed, I believe I can even document this curious kind of inconsistency that attaches to ethical skepticism by means of two examples that may not be altogether unfamiliar. Thus, for one, consider the interesting and excellently written little book entitled *Patterns of Culture*, by the distinguished American anthropologist Ruth Benedict. In that book Professor Benedict is strong in her advocacy of what might be called an ethical relativism: all of our value judgments, she says in effect, all judgments as to what we ought or ought not to do, are relative to the particular culture of which we are a part, and hence are quite without warrant in the nature of things. And yet curiously enough, having thus made her case for the utter relativity of morals, Professor Benedict then proceeds to point a moral of her own. It is the moral of tolerance. And, apparently, her argument seems to be to this effect: since all judgments as to how men ought to act are purely relative to their culture, and so are without foundation, therefore what men ought to do under the circumstances is to cultivate an attitude of greater tolerance to people of other cultures than their own. In other words, the judgment that there is no basis for ethical judgments becomes itself the basis of an ethical judgment.

And by way of a second example I can cite the less distinguished,

but rather more notorious, case of the late unlamented Benito Mussolini. For unlike Professor Benedict, Mussolini did not use his ethical
skepticism as a ground for justifying an ethics of tolerance. No, as
he himself put it in his *Autobiography*:

> There is nothing more relativistic than Fascist attitudes and ac-
> tivity. . . . From the fact that all ideologies are of equal value, that
> all ideologies are mere fictions, the modern relativist infers that every-
> body has the right to create for himself his own ideology and to at-
> tempt to enforce it with all the energy of which he is capable.[6]

Once again we see how the characteristic inconsistency of the ethical
relativist is clearly exhibited: for it is Mussolini's utter skepticism
in regard to all rights and wrongs that supposedly provides him with
what he apparently thinks is a justification for the swaggering assertion of his own right to enforce his way on everyone else.

Very well, then, suppose that such arguments are convincing
and that one cannot very well deny the possibility of ethical knowledge and remain consistent with oneself, still where does that get us?
Certainly in one sense it does not get us very far. For merely to
expose the inconsistencies involved in a position of ethical skepticism
does not as such serve to rebut the specific difficulties that have given
rise to such a position in the first place. Just the same, to recognize
that one cannot consistently deny the possibility of a genuine knowledge of values, of oughts and such like, may at least give us reason
to suppose that by diligently looking about us we can perhaps eventually achieve something on the order of a genuine knowledge of what
is best for us as human beings, and of what we as human beings
ought to be doing in the way of ordering and disposing our lives as
intelligently and wisely as possible.

But, alas, no sooner does one make a statement such as the one
just preceding, than one finds oneself right smack up against the
second roadblock, that of the naturalistic fallacy. For consider the
suggestion that "by diligently looking about us we can perhaps
eventually achieve something on the order of a genuine knowledge
of what is best for us as human beings, and of what we as human
beings ought to be doing in the way of ordering and disposing our
lives as intelligently and wisely as possible." The mistake here is
all too obvious. Indeed, it is the sort of mistake that in the new
fashion of philosophical parlance might be called a "category mistake": for in the very nature of the case, looking about us can only

---

6 Quoted from Helmut Kuhn, *Freedom Forgotten and Remembered* (Chapel
Hill, 1943), p. 18.

acquaint us with what is so in fact; it cannot possibly acquaint us with what ought to be.

For that matter, the same sort of mistake would appear to attach to the entire proposal which I put forward earlier, that we might try regarding ethics as a sort of art or know-how with respect to the living of our lives. For any such proposal presupposes that there is a natural perfection or completion of human life, a natural end or goal, a naturally determined fullness of human existence, toward which human beings are naturally oriented or directed, whether they ever actually attain it or not, and even whether they be actually conscious of it or not, much as an acorn just is naturally ordered to the attainment of its complete development in the healthy, full-grown oak tree. Yes, it is only in the light of such a natural standard of human perfection that one can determine what are the naturally right and intelligent courses for men to follow if they are ever to achieve such a goal.

Clearly, though, in the light of the naturalistic fallacy, Aristotelian-inspired rhetoric of this sort may now be seen to be quite beside the point. For even if it were true that there were such a natural goal or natural perfection, so far as human life is concerned, that still would not have any bearing on ethics. Indeed, where could one find a more glaring case of the naturalistic fallacy than in just such an attempted equation of the natural with the ethical!

Yes, suppose that one were to play along with Aristotle and entertain for a time his definition of the good as that at which all things aim, or as simply the natural perfection of a thing; or, perhaps more metaphysically, as the natural completion or activity or ἐνέργεια of any potency or δύναμις whatever. Once more, would not the "fallacy" here or the "category mistake" be all too patent? For even supposing that there are natural tendencies in things, or potentialities that are naturally ordered to their characteristic perfections and fulfillments — and further, that we can to a certain extent come to know what these are — still, what possible grounds does all this give us for supposing these natural ends or objectives to be good or to be the sort of thing we ought to strive for? To infer that merely because a thing is natural, it is therefore good, is surely fallacious; it is the naturalistic fallacy in short.

Still, we need to be more specific if we are to sense the full import for ethics of this so-called naturalistic fallacy. Reduced to its simplest terms, the notion of such a fallacy derives its original force and plausibility, as I see it, from the quite obvious truth that in attempting to define anything or to state what it is, we must assert the thing in question to be what it is and not anything else. "Everything is what it is, and not another thing." Such, it will be remembered, was the celebrated dictum of Bishop Butler which Moore chose as the epigraph of *Principia Ethica*. Nor can it very well be denied that such a dictum is unexceptionable.

Nevertheless, in order to render such a principle, which seems true enough in itself, at the same time applicable to actual, concrete claimants to the title of being no less than the defining characteristics of "good," Moore proposed his open question test. Thus, suppose that with Aristotle one were to claim that the good is that at which all things aim, or with the hedonists that the good is simply the pleasant, or with R. B. Perry that the good is just the desired, then Moore's open question test could be applied and each of these respective claims could be shown to be invalid. For suppose in a given instance that something is aimed at, or is pleasant, or is desired, is it not always meaningful to ask whether the thing in question is, after all, good?

Moreover, if such a question is thus meaningful, if it is an open question in other words, then there is no possibility of merely equating the goodness of a thing with its being aimed at, or its being pleasant, or its being desired. And the reason is that any definition of good can only take the form of an analytic truth; and an analytic truth must needs be a truth the opposite of which would be simply inconceivable and self-contradictory. In contrast, a synthetic truth is a truth which, though true, is only contingently true, or a truth the opposite of which is at least conceivable and not self-contradictory. Consequently, if, on the application of the open question test, it turns out that it is meaningful to raise the question as to the correctness of the proposed definition of "good" as being that at which something aims or that toward which it tends, then such a definition turns out not to be a definition at all, because it is not an analytic truth. At best, it is but a synthetic truth.

Such, then, is the character of the fallacy. But just what is its import for ethics? Well, the story is almost too well known to bear repeating of how Moore, when he started applying his open question test, found it served to rule out not merely such proposed defining properties of goodness as "pleasant," "desired," etc., but any and all natural properties as well. And not only any and every natural property, but any and every metaphysical property, too. Hence Moore concluded that goodness could only be a "non-natural" property. But, unfortunately, save for the intuitionists, it seemed that God alone could ever know a non-natural property, considering that it could not be anything that one would ever encounter either in the world of nature, or in that of supernature, or even in that of being generally. Yes, in the face of such sweeping eliminations, one might begin to wonder whether even the divine capacity would be adequate for the discernment of these mysterious, non-natural properties. And in fact, ever since Moore, the consensus has tended to be that goodness just is not any kind of a property at all, natural or non-natural. And by saying that goodness is not a property, what apparently is meant is that when one asserts that something is good, one is not describing it, so much as commending it, or recommending it, or grading it, or trying to get someone else to approve of it, or manifesting some sort of pro-attitude toward it, or what not. Moreover, the upshot of all this would seem to be that goodness, to say nothing of all the various other moral and ethical notions like rightness, wrongness, oughtness, etc., either have come to be deprived of any status in reality at all, or at least their status in the real world has been so seriously compromised, as to render it exceedingly difficult to determine in just what sense a thing may be said to be good really and in fact, or to be right or wrong or what ought to be or what not.

Thus once again, and just as in the case of relativism, it would appear to be a set of meta-ethical considerations that have had the effect of undermining any such thing as a science of ethics. It is as if the very idea of an objectively grounded and warranted knowledge in regard to matters of ethics had been rendered dubious, if not impossible. How, indeed, can I or anyone else be said to know that Sir Walter Elliott was an ass, or that Nightingale had ruined and wasted his life? In so far as these are moral judgments, can they be said to reflect what is really the case as regards Elliott or Nightingale, or do they only reflect our own feelings or attitudes toward them, or our attempts at warning others not to be like them?

But now granted that the naturalistic fallacy has thus turned out to be a device which recent practitioners of meta-ethics have employed in such a way as to discredit the very possibility of an ethical or moral knowledge, or at least to compromise and severely restrict the knowledge claims of the traditional discipline of ethics — granted all this, is there any way in which this roadblock of the naturalistic fallacy can be cleared away from the path of ethics? I think there is. And to this end I should like first of all to make use of certain criticisms which Professor Frankena made against the notion of the naturalistic fallacy several years ago.[7] For it does seem to me that these criticisms are patient of an interpretation which would quite effectively dispose of the naturalistic fallacy as a meta-ethical device.

In effect, Professor Frankena seems willing enough to accept Moore's notion that any definition would in the nature of the case have to be an instance of analytic truth, and he also seems to go along with Moore's open question test as a means of determining whether any proposed definition is in fact a definition or not. However, moving to the question of a possible definition of "good," Frankena suggests that a convinced hedonist or a convinced adherent of the interest theory of value might each propound as a definition of "good" either " 'Good' means simply 'pleasant,' " or "For anything to be good means for it to be desired." Moreover, when the open question test is applied to these definitions, the hedonist or the advocate of the interest theory could perfectly well insist that their definitions had passed the test perfectly. After all, to a convinced hedonist "good" does mean "pleasant" and nothing else; nor need he admit for an instant that there is meaning to the question of whether a given experience might be pleasant and yet at the same time not be good.

To be sure, Frankena himself seems to imply that, so far as he can determine, goodness is not a natural property like being pleasant or being desired. And yet the difference between goodness and such natural properties is not anything that can be established by the argument of the naturalistic fallacy. Rather, supposing that *on other grounds* one can establish that goodness is not a natural property, *then*, Frankena feels, one could show that it would be committing the naturalistic fallacy to define goodness in terms of a natural property: one would be declaring goodness to be something that it was not. But the point of Frankena's criticism is that the argument of the naturalistic fallacy, so far from being a meta-ethical device that rules out *a priori* the very possibility of trying to find out by means of ethical enquiry what goodness is, is, instead, an argument that becomes applicable only as a result of ethical enquiry and only after one has already determined in one way or another what goodness is, in contrast to what it is not.

So much for the one criticism. But there is, I believe, an even more far-reaching criticism of the naturalistic fallacy argument than

[7] W. K. Frankena, "The Naturalistic Fallacy," *Mind*, XLVIII (N. S., No. 192), 464-477.

Frankena's. For Frankena, it will be remembered, seemed to acquiesce in Moore's understanding of definition as analytic truth and in his suggestion of the open question test as a criterion of such definition. And yet when these two latter points are rather more closely scrutinized, I wonder if they will not turn out to be strangely self-destructive, not merely with respect to Moore's own efforts to understand goodness, but also with respect to any and every effort to understand anything whatever for what it is.

Once more, be it remembered that Moore chose as the motto for his own undertaking Butler's dictum, "Everything is what it is and not another thing," and that the task which he set himself was the specific one of finding out what goodness is. Moreover, he construed this task as meaning that his primary quest would be for a definition of "good." And yet no proposed definition of good seemed to meet the criteria of definition. On the contrary, all such definitions as "The good is that at which all things aim," or "The good is simply the pleasant," or "The good is any object of any interest" — all of these definitions seemed to commit the naturalistic fallacy. And why? Simply because, Moore thought, it is always meaningful to ask whether the pleasant is, after all, necessarily good, or whether it is not at least conceivable that something might be an object of interest and still not be good, or whether, just because something is naturally aimed at, that necessarily makes it good. And as long as it is meaningful to ask these questions, as long as such questions are at least significant, then the proposed definitions cannot possibly be definitions. For a definition can only be an analytic truth and an analytic truth, it would seem, must be one the opposite of which would be self-contradictory and hence literally inconceivable. Accordingly, if a proposed definition of "good" might conceivably be false, if its opposite is at least meaningful and conceivable, and hence not self-contradictory, then one just does not have a definition of "good."

Now what could be more cogent than this? And yet note that the upshot of it all is to make of definitions little more than tautologies.[8] For clearly, if a truth is such that its opposite is simply inconceivable and patently self-contradictory, in the manner of "A is non-A," then that truth itself can be no other than a mere tautology of the form "A is A."

---

8 It should be apparent from the context that this word is being used in its everyday sense, rather than in the technical sense of "true by the truth-table test."

Surely, though, whatever may be its cogency or its currency, is not this a rather fantastic notion of definition? For is it really the case that there can be no talk of our defining anything — i.e., no talk of our coming to understand anything for what it is, no talk of our recognizing what pertains to the very nature of anything — without our being compelled to acknowledge that the definition in which such knowledge and understanding of what a thing is comes to be expressed and formulated, can be no more than a tautology which does not really tell us anything at all?

Now we all know it to be one of the key contentions of modern logic and semantics that a tautology is uninformative, that it tells us nothing about the world, that it does not even tell us anything about the very things which it itself is at least ostensibly a statement about. Thus, to use Professor Hospers' apt illustrations, "All black cats bring bad luck" is certainly a statement about black cats; but "All black cats are black," strictly speaking, does not say anything about black cats at all. And the reason, presumably, is that the truth of such a statement does not depend upon the content of the statement at all, but only upon its form. That is to say, the truth of "All black cats are black" does not depend upon anything that is distinctive and peculiar about black cats, but simply on the form of the proposition in which such an assertion is made. In other words, any statement of the form, "Anything that is an 'a' as well as a 'b' is an 'a,'" or "Every A is A" will be necessarily true, regardless of whether the statement happens to be about black cats, green dragons, the property "good," or even, for that matter, the non-property "good." For as Wittgenstein remarked — to cite the *locus classicus* — "I know, e.g., nothing about the weather when I know that it rains or does not rain."[9] In short, all such tautologies, and all such statements the opposite of which are self-contradictory — all such truths are no more than formal truths, or logical truths, or, if you will, linguistic truths. In any case, they give no information about the world, or even about their own subject matter.

But now it would appear that if we follow Moore in construing definitions as no more than analytic truths such that their opposites are simply inconceivable and self-contradictory, then we find ourselves confronted with a curiously ironical and even paradoxical result. For if definitions be no more than analytic truths, and analytic truths no more than tautologies, then a definition will be constitution-

9 *Tractatus*, 4.610.

ally debarred, so to speak, not merely from telling us what anything is, but even from ever telling us anything about anything.

Indeed, to return to the case of Moore, we might even say that on this basis the very epigraph of his book, so far from being illuminating, turns out to be self-defeating and even systematically frustrating. For granted that everything is what it is, and not another thing, then unhappily, no sooner will one wish to know, or undertake to find out, concerning anything, just what it is, than his wish and his undertaking must needs be doomed *a priori* to failure and frustration. For presumably, the only proper and allowable answer to a question of the form "What is x?" has to be of the form "x is x." But any statement of this form will be no more than a tautology, and, as such, will not tell one anything about x at all, much less what it is.

Yes, we could even set up the paradox in this way: granted that everything is what it is and not another thing, then the necessary consequences, so far as knowledge is concerned, would be that no one could ever *know* concerning anything, what it is, simply because the form in which the statement of one's knowledge would have to be couched would be a form such as to render this very sort of knowledge impossible.

Apparently, then, the only way Moore was able to make his conception of the naturalistic fallacy a telling one was to base it on a notion of definition that could have no other effect than to render futile his, Moore's, own undertaking of trying to understand what goodness is and not to confuse it with anything else.

Not only that, but it would also seem to be a notion of definition that is quite implausible and untenable in itself. For just consider: Is it not perfectly reasonable for anyone of us, say, to be somewhat puzzled as to just what it means to say of something that it is good, much as we might be puzzled to know just what it is to be human, or to be an electron, or to be spatially extended, or to be religious, or to be in potency with respect to something, or what not else? Moreover, not only is it perfectly reasonable to ask such questions, but it is also perfectly reasonable to suppose that we might very well succeed in reaching informative and illuminating answers to such questions. In other words, that our conception of definition should be such that the very possibility of answers in such cases should be ruled out *a priori* is nothing short of fantastic.

To take but one example, suppose that with respect to human beings we ask just what it means to be human. Now surely human nature is what it is and not anything else. Further, to suppose that being human is in any respect other than what it is would certainly involve one in self-contradiction. And yet does it follow from this that any statement as to what it means to be human, or what is involved in being human, is bound to be no more than a tautology which tells us nothing at all? For instance, suppose we say that man is a rational animal, and suppose that by our definition we intend no mere verbal definition of the word "man," but a real definition, then we would seem thereby to have ruled out all sorts of other accounts of human nature and other ways of characterizing human beings — other ways and accounts which might have occurred to us, but which now, by our present definition, are excluded as being false and erroneous.

Not only that, but we must also recognize that the definition we have thus finally arrived at may still be mistaken. That is to say, although we might be firmly convinced that it pertained to the very nature of man, or was a necessary part of the meaning of man to be rational, still, in all honesty and perhaps in all sanity, we can and should recognize that we might be wrong. Indeed, further experience may very well lead us to see that being rational is not a necessary feature of human nature after all.

In other words, our definition, both in virtue of what it rules out, as well as in virtue of the possibility that it might be wrong, is clearly informative. At the same time, for all of its informativeness and for all of its being more than any mere tautology or formal truth, our definition of man as a rational animal we must nonetheless consider to be such that it does no more than assert or declare, with respect to human beings, what they are. Hence to suppose human beings not to be this, but something else, would, on the basis of this definition, be to suppose them to be other than what they are. In other words, it would be a self-contradictory supposition.

But this is to say no more than that any definition, if it be a true definition of its definiendum, must be self-evidently true, or, in the rather more precise terminology of the Scholastics, it must be *per se notum* — i.e., the thing that is being defined can come to be known only through itself and not through another. And yet this in no wise implies that such a definition can be no more than a linguistic or formal truth, a mere tautology, which, in stating what the definiendum is, turns out not to inform us of what it is at all. No, the precise purport of the definition is to inform us of what the thing we are defining really is.

Now, admittedly, this is by no means a complete and adequate account of the nature of definition. And yet it surely suffices to show the untenability of that alternative notion of definition upon which the argument of the naturalistic fallacy rests. Moreover, once this latter and curiously far-fetched notion of definition is exposed for what it is, then the naturalistic fallacy itself turns out to be not so much a roadblock in the path of ethics, as a mere red herring. Further, the whole chain of meta-ethical consequences that has come to be suspended from the naturalistic fallacy as being the fixed point of nearly all modern English ethical theory — this chain simply collapses.

Suppose, indeed, that we briefly run over some of these consequences once again. As we saw, Moore himself started out determined to find out what good is. But confounded by his own device of the naturalistic fallacy, he concluded that one could not find out about goodness through any sort of investigation and inquiry concerning things in the real world. Rather, goodness is something that one can know only by intuiting it. For that matter, it is not even a property of things in the ordinary sense at all, but rather a "non-natural" property, as he called it. Little wonder, then, that thinkers who followed Moore carried this argument one step further and insisted that goodness is not a property at all. And though different ones meant different things by this, they all seemed to agree pretty much that when we call things "good," we are not thereby attributing to these same things any sort of feature or characteristic that may be taken to be actually present in them as they are in themselves and in reality. But if goodness is thus not to be found in the real things of the world, then it becomes difficult to see just how ethics can ever make good its claims to being a legitimate body of knowledge. Not only that, but there would not seem to be any real warrant or basis in fact for those everyday moral judgments which we pass on people of the like of Sir Walter Elliott or Nightingale.

Eliminate the naturalistic fallacy, though, and all these consequences that are so embarrassing and provide so many difficulties for present-day ethics just disappear altogether. And while, so far as the argument of this present paper goes, we are still far from having established what the good is, much less that it is that at which all things aim, still may we not hope that at least some of the barriers to carrying out such a properly ethical investigation have been removed? Perhaps it may once more be possible to do ethics in the rather more classical mode of a properly and genuinely cognitive

enterprise directed toward discovering and learning what the differences between good and bad, and right and wrong, really are. Exit
meta-ethics, and re-enter ethics!

7

Motives and Obligations

DEWEY J. HOITENGA, JR., Associate Professor of Philosophy, Juniata College. A.B., Calvin College; B.D., Calvin Theological Seminary; A.M., Ph.D., Harvard University. Articles in *The Reformed Journal*.

Motives and Obligations

BY DEWEY J. HOITENGA, JR.

To what kind of motive should a moralist appeal — whether he is a parent, a guidance counsellor, a friend, or a preacher? Moralists themselves, and we who observe them and evaluate their task, tend often to answer this question by insisting that their appeal should be different from that of the furniture salesman, the social club organizer, or professional entertainer. While all these, it is felt, may legitimately appeal to our comfort, our interest, or our sense of humor — our natural motives — the moralists ought to appeal to something more noble, something peculiarly moral in us, namely, our sense of duty or obligation.

Now any tendency to think of the moralist's appeal in this fashion is itself moralistic, prescribing as it does what the moralist should do. As such, however, the tendency embraces two assumptions, and perhaps a third, which provide the topic for the present essay. The first assumption is an empirical one to the effect that obligations can, as a matter of fact, function in the role of motivation. The second one is a moral one, namely, that obligations ought, as a condition of the moral character of the appeal, to constitute the motivational appeal, while the natural motives ought not to. With respect to the first of these assumptions, I will support the view that obligations can be motivational, but will call attention to the fact that, so far, philosophers have not proved a still further assumption often present, namely, that obligations must be motivational as a matter of logical necessity. As for the second assumption, I will take for granted that right acts can have natural motives, and will argue that it cannot be proved that, in order to preserve the moral character of a motivational appeal, such motives ought not be addressed. I shall also be correlating some recent theological discussion of the topic with that of the philosophers, not so much because it throws any additional light on the empirical assumption or the logical one, but because it points up a feature of motivation within a religious context that is relevant to the moral assumption that natural motives ought not to be the concern of the moralist. I hope throughout to entertain, in an admittedly sketchy and exploratory manner, a doubt about the easy separation that frequently exists between our thoughts of what is "natural" on the one hand, and of what is "moral" on the other.

I

In a critical summary of some important contributions to the subject over the past several decades, Professor William K. Frankena focusses the two opposing views with regard to the logical assumption that obligations must be motives as follows:

> Internalists hold that motivation must be provided for because it is involved in the analysis of moral judgments and so is essential for an action's being or being shown to be obligatory. Externalists insist that motivation is not part of the analysis of moral judgments or of the justification of moral claims; for them motivation is an important problem, but only because it is necessary to persuade people to act in accordance with their obligations.[1]

On the basis of his analysis of numerous contributions to the discussion Frankena reaches two conclusions with respect to its present status: (1) Internalists have not been able to disprove externalism,[2] and (2) Internalists have not been able conclusively to prove internalism.[3] There are two further conclusions that Frankena is ready to accept, thereby giving a more complete account of the status of the controversy than emerges from his detailed analysis alone: (3) Externalists will not be able to disprove internalism either: "We might now go on to consider corresponding arguments against internalism. It is, however, difficult to find such arguments explicitly set forth in recent literature, and perhaps we may assume

---

[1] William K. Frankena, "Obligation and Motivation in Recent Moral Philosophy," in *Essays in Moral Philosophy*, edited by I. A. Melden, (Seattle, 1958), p. 41.
[2] *Ibid.*, Sections II-V.
[3] *Ibid.*, Sections VI-X.

that they too would turn out to be inconclusive."[4] (4) Nor, finally, can externalists conclusively prove externalism. This I infer from the fact that Frankena regards the force of his arguments as enabling him only to maintain externalism against the arguments of the internalist, not as a conclusive disproof of the internalist thesis; from his increasing uncertainty of the externalist thesis;[5] and from his main general conclusion: "The main result yielded by our discussion, then, is that the opposition we are studying cannot be resolved, as so many seem to think, by such relatively small-scale logical or semi-logical arguments as we have been dealing with."[6]

Professor Frankena then goes on to make a proposal regarding any future discussion of the topic which is as important as his critical analysis of the discussion in the past. In the absence of any decisive logical refutations of one view by the other, we shall have to look for telling arguments on another level, a "macroscopic" level requiring "not only small-scale analytical inquiries but also studies in the history of ethics and morality, in the relation of morality to society and of society to the individual, as well as in epistemology and in the psychology of human motivation."[7] I agree with this, and would affirm that the broader level of inquiry extends not only to those important areas which Frankena refers to but also to those of religion, metaphysics, and theology. The problem here suggested, however, is itself one of motivation: how are we going to motivate moral philosophers to get their investigations beyond their small-scale analytical inquiries? On the basis of Frankena's analysis we may conclude that the logical arguments available at the present time are insufficient to resolve the opposition, but that is all. An invitation to despair over already existing arguments will not, however, be enough to prevent ambitious moral philosophers from continuing to search for new ones. What further would be needed is an argument to the effect that a resolution of the issue is impossible. Such an argument I wish now to set forth.

But first we must be very clear as to what the opposition really is. According to the description given above, the internalist's claim is that "if anything is an obligation, it is also a motivation"; while the externalist's is that "if anything is an obligation, it is excluded from being a motivation." It is important to understand what the

---

4 *Ibid.*, p. 72.
5 *Ibid.*, pp. 42f.
6 *Ibid.*, p. 73.
7 *Ibid.*, p. 80; cf. pp. 74-181.

traditional issue is because it must be sharply distinguished from a *new* issue that Frankena wishes to propose (and rightly, I think) on the basis of some distinctions and concessions he wishes externalists and internalists to adopt. The new issue, as will presently be explained, is an empirical, psychological issue, by contrast with the present one, which is an issue between total, categorical views.

We can begin the argument, now, by appreciating a logical feature of the opposition between the two traditional views that seems to have escaped notice. It has been noticed, of course, that the two views cannot both be true. What has been overlooked is that they can perfectly well both be false. They are related to each other, that is, not as logical contradictories, but as logical contraries. And that we should explore the possibility that they may both be false seems to be the obvious import of the impasse that has arisen in the attempts to establish either one of them true. The recognition that both theories cannot be true is an obvious temptation for philosophers to plunge into arguments to show which one is false by proving one of them true. But the recognition that both may be false ought to be at least an invitation to abandon the issue as it has been construed and look for another. And both theories will be false if the disconfirming double proposition is true that obligations sometimes motivate and sometimes do not. If this proposition can be supported, and granted by both parties to the traditional dispute, then these parties will no longer find themselves in the total, categorical opposition that has been implicit or explicit in their discussion to the present; they will find themselves with a new issue: not a logical one, but an empirical and psychological one, namely, why do obligations sometimes motivate and sometimes fail?

But is this double proposition true? Prima facie evidence that it is may be found in the intensity with which philosophers try to maintain either half of the proposition in its universal and logically necessary form. But their efforts, if they are meant to illuminate moral experience for us, must in turn be grounded in that experience. Moral experience, it would appear, must contain two elementary types of data, namely, that obligations sometimes move us, and sometimes do not. If both of these can be supported, then clearly what has led the conventional theorists astray is their hasty generalization on the basis of only one type of obligation experience. As an alternative to such generalization on the basis of an incomplete appreciation of moral experience, with its concomitant attempts to provide logically conclusive defenses of the result, it would appear more fruitful to face the complexity of moral experience (if that can be established) — and if we do this, we shall be unable to avoid, I think, the macroscopic investigations referred to.

Since the examination of moral experience and the consequent support of the disconfirming proposition require a basic distinction which Frankena insists upon in his own attempts to defend externalism against the extreme internalist claim, while at the same time giving a responsive ear to that claim, we should first set forth that distinction. The tendency, referred to at the beginning of this paper, to require the appeal of the moralist to be unique, would probably adopt, on first thought, the internalist point of view. That it need not do so, however, Frankena argues by means of developing within the externalist view what may be called a "moderate" externalist position, by contrast with the extreme, categorical position so far envisaged. According to Frankena, such a moderate externalist

> can admit that there is a nonmoral obligation and even a "subjective" moral obligation that logically entails motivation. He can accept any statement that says that having an obligation, assenting to one, or being said to have one causally or *psychologically* involves the existence of a corresponding motivation. He may also agree that assenting to an obligation *logically* entails the existence of motivation for acting accordingly.[8]

These concessions of the moderate externalist (and the first one mentioned is the important one) depend upon the validity of the distinction between a "subjective" and an "objective" obligation. If the distinction is valid, however, the externalist accomplishes two important things: first, by being able to recognize at least the possibility of a uniquely moral appeal, he succeeds in avoiding the harshness of the extreme externalist's position in which it is not open in any way to appeal motivationally to obligation, since motivation is, in that position, regarded as strictly independent, both logically and psychologically, of it; second, by allowing the possible objectivity of the obligation, he preserves the distinction between the motivation and the obligation (if, at any rate, by "motive" is meant something subjective, i.e., *in* an agent, and by "objective" is meant something not in an agent).

But in accomplishing these two things, what the moderate externalist has really achieved, it appears to me, is a resolution of the categorical issue between externalism and internalism — although Frankena, if I understand him correctly, does not wish to press the

8 *Ibid.*, p. 73.

importance of the distinction that far. He limits its significance to
providing "some clarity about the exact points at issue."[9] That the
distinction does provide such clarification is indeed true, and important. The clarification consists essentially in this, that the internalist-externalist debate must be focussed only on "subjective
obligations," that is, only on obligations in so far as they have become part of an agent, either by awareness, recognition, assent or
acceptance — whatever degree of connection happens best to describe the relationship. And this clearly changes the issue from being a logical analysis of an abstract concept, obligation, to being a
psychological inquiry into what actually occurs when obligations
enter into the mind, heart, or soul of the agent. The issue cannot
intelligently concern obligations in their exclusively "objective"
sense, since these are excluded from a motivational role by definition. Yet Frankena seems to think that it does, for, having elaborated
the concessions, he still summarizes the issue as follows:

> What he [the externalist] must deny, and the internalist assert, is that
> having objectively a certain moral obligation logically entails having
> some motivation for fulfilling it, that justifying a judgment of ob-
> jective moral obligation logically implies establishing or producing a
> motivational buttress, and that it is logically impossible that there
> should be a state of apprehending a moral obligation of one's own
> which is not accompanied by such a buttress (even if this "mere in-
> tellectual apprehension" is never actual and does not amount to what
> is called "assenting to" or "acknowledging" an obligation) .[10]

This summary, however, confuses the (senseless) issue over objective obligations with the (rightful) issue over obligations in so far
as they have entered into the "subjectivity" of the agent. This happens, I think, because Frankena, while concerned to moderate his
own externalism, appears to stop short of requiring the internalist
to moderate his internalism. And this may be due to the fact
that it is probably more difficult to persuade an internalist of the
need for an objective sense of obligation than to convince an externalist of the need to connect obligation with motivation in the agent.
If these concessions are to function, however, toward a resolution
of the controversy, as I am contending they should, not only must
the externalist admit the possibility of an important connection sometimes occurring between obligation and motivation; the internalist
also must admit the possibility of an important separation between
them. What the externalist must abandon is the extreme thesis of

---

9 *Ibid.*
10 *Ibid.,* pp. 73f.

the logical necessity of the separation; the internalist, the extreme thesis of the logical necessity of their connection.

We have seen that the externalist is able to abandon his extreme thesis and yet retain as a possibility, at least, what was the point of his case, namely, that obligations need not entail motivation. We should now supply an argument from moral experience which shows that he must abandon his extreme thesis of the logically universal and necessary separation between obligation and motivation by finding evidence for that half of the disconfirming proposition which asserts that obligations can sometimes function as motives. An experience on which such an argument can rest is that of the conflict[11] between "duty" and "interest." If such an experience is genuine, it is evidence that at least sometimes an obligation can function in a motivational role, for it is with a motive itself (some interest) that it competes (and presumably often checks), and it would seem that the only thing that could compete with a motive as a motive would be another motive. An instance like this should compel the externalist to recognize the internalist thesis that obligations at least sometimes do function motivationally (though of course the internalist could not use the example to support an extreme claim that they are required to do so). It also compels the externalist to recognize that this motivational function of an obligation, in the conflict situation at least, presupposes its being assented to, felt, or at least apprehended (therefore its being subjective); for otherwise the conflict would not be one of *experience*. But this will in turn move the externalist to distinguish between the subjective and objective senses of obligation that we have already pointed up, in order to preserve the possibility of obligations also failing to play a motivational role (though no ground is here available for the claim that an obligation must be able to occur in the objective way envisaged by the externalist).

It is, however, precisely such ground that is needed to compel the internalist to moderate his extreme thesis of the logically universal and necessary connection between an obligation and a motivation, and to support therefore the second half of the disconfirming proposition that obligations sometimes do not motivate at all; for convincing support of a non-motivational view of obligation seems clearly tied up with demonstrating the objectivity of the obligation. Now it may seem that to require an internalist to admit the objectivity of obligation is demanding more of him than to require an externalist

11 This will be discussed more fully in a different connection below.

to admit its subjectivity, since for the externalist that admission did not require giving up his belief in the externality of obligation, while to admit the objectivity of obligation does require the internalist to give up his belief in the internality of motivation to obligation — his whole thesis. Of course he must give up something of his belief if the moderation of his position is to mean anything at all. But he should be content that he can still maintain his logical case about obligations in their subjective sense, which the externalist also finds it possible (only not necessary, as does the internalist) to accept.

To what kind of experience can we appeal in support of the claim that obligations must be able to occur, at least sometimes, in an objective, and consequently non-motivational, way? Frankena supports the claim by citing the experience of "thinking something" as an obligation and the experience of "asking what" an obligation may be:

> In fact, when a man thinks that something is his duty, what he thinks is that it is a duty independently of his thinking so (and independently of his wanting to do it); and when he asks what his duty is, he implies that he has a duty that he does not yet recognize, and what he is seeking to know, as it were, is what it would have been his duty to do even if he had not discovered it.[12]

The former type of experience is not as convincing as the latter. A man may of course think of his duty as independent of his thinking it, but merely thinking so does not make it so. When, however, a man asks what his duty is in a given situation, the presuppositions are that such a duty exists and that, as existent, it is nevertheless not yet subjective in any way (let alone motivational). Now the only condition that can make these presuppositions possible is the objectivity (externality to the agent) of the obligation in question. And that these presuppositions are true, at least sometimes, is seen from the fact that otherwise we could never discover an obligation or be informed of one, which is contrary to experience.

If these arguments, and perhaps others like them, from moral experience are acceptable, we may conclude that there can be no issue between internalism and externalism as total theoretical views of obligation — simply because both are false. This conclusion does not seem to be opened up by Frankena's discussion, though much of that discussion seems at least to suggest it. He writes, indeed:

> Personally, it seems to me that the choice must in practice be between an externalism that makes such concessions and an internalism that

12 Frankena, *op. cit.*, p. 63.

recognizes such a distinction [between exciting and justifying reasons] . . . . It is the internalists rather than the externalists who have failed to notice the ambiguity and . . . this failure vitiates much of their argument.[13]

But if all this is so, it implies that the categorical issue which fails to observe the important distinction concerned must be distinguished from the psychological issue which is bound to observe it. And if this is done, then, as I hope to have shown, contrary to Frankena: (1) the internalist need not assert that having *objectively* a moral obligation logically entails having some motivation for fulfilling it;[14] (2) there is a level (the traditional, categorical level) on which internalism and externalism can be refuted, if not by each other, then by the complexity of moral experience;[15] and (3) the issue on which the macroscopic considerations must be brought to bear is no longer this old opposition of total, theoretical viewpoints, but a new, psychological question: Do subjective moral obligations move us, and if so, how? and if not, why not?[16] And as a truly psychological question, it cannot be restricted, furthermore, to a question of "our intentions in the use of moral language," as W. D. Falk proposes; it must involve the question, ultimately, of the moral ability of human nature itself.[17]

II

Christian theologians, though usually preoccupied with the peculiar foundations and implications of Christian ethics, nevertheless occasionally engage in an independent discussion of the issue of duty versus advantage[18] as motives for doing the will of God. Some recent theological discussion exhibits no more agreement than that of the philosophers either on the empirical adequacy or moral neces-

---

13 *Ibid.*, pp. 74f.

14 *Ibid.*, p. 73; cf. footnote 10 above.

15 Cf. *ibid.*, p. 74: "It does follow that neither kind of moral philosophy can be decisively refuted by the other, and that we must give up the quest for certainty in the sense of no longer hoping for such refutations." Cf. also p. 72, quoted above in footnote 4.

16 But cf. *ibid.*, p. 74, continuing: "But it does not follow that nothing can be said for one view as against the other. What does follow is that the whole discussion must consciously move to another level." What I have argued is that not only must the discussion move to a new level, but also face a new and different type question.

17 This is implicit, I think, in Frankena's discussion of Falk, *ibid.*, pp. 76-80.

18 Self-interest is not the only natural motive, if Hume, Butler, Mill, *et al.*, are correct in their proposal of the social feeling of sympathy or benevolence. It constantly appears, however, in theological, and in some philosophical, discussion as the model natural motive.

sity of obligations as motives. Because the Bible, however, seems to contain appeals to both motivations — that of sheer obedience,[19] suggestive of the internalist point of view, and that of divine reward,[20] suggestive of externalism, the positions taken by theologians are not so categorically opposed as those taken by philosophers who have sought to maintain their respective positions with the rigor and exclusivism of logical necessity. The theologians do indicate their varying sympathies, however, by the manner of their reaction to the Biblical data. Some appear to depreciate the reward side of the Biblical combination and may be correlated, therefore, with the "internalists" among the philosophers. Others welcome both sides of the combination and may be regarded as "moderate externalists."

The former — internalists — are observed toning down the emphasis on reward that they find on the pages of Scripture. Professor A. N. Wilder, for example, writes:

> It is important at this point to emphasize and illustrate how much Jesus relied upon the sheer validity of his truth and on the native discernment of his hearers. . . . This confidence of Jesus in the persuasive power of the truth and in the ultimate moral discernment of common men seems to have taken precedence with him over other enforcing features. . . . We do not wish to rule out entirely the place of such [eschatological] sanction in the teaching. . . . But these formal sanctions should be looked upon as supplementary rather than as compromising the fundamental sanctions.[21]

Rudolph Bultmann is more unfriendly toward the Biblical appeals to reward. Commenting also on the sayings of Jesus, he says:

> The thought of reward stands in a peculiarly paradoxical, perhaps contradictory, relation to the demand for obedience. But it is absolutely clear that Jesus demanded obedience without any secondary motive. . . . But Jesus is wholly certain that man *does* receive reward or punishment from God. . . . These consequences cannot serve as the motive in the exact sense, where the idea of obedience is completely carried through.[22]

The latter — moderate externalists — are observed to welcome the Biblical combination, to defend its integrity, and to question any undue eminence accorded to the duty-appeal. K. E. Kirk, in the Bampton Lectures for 1928, had this to say:

---

[19] E.g., Matt. 5:39-42, 8:22, 16:24, 25; Luke 14:26-33.

[20] E.g., Matt. 5:3-9, 22, 29, 6:14, 22:39; Mark 10:28-31.

[21] *Eschatology and Ethics in the Teaching of Jesus* (New York, 1939), pp. 116f., 141.

[22] *Jesus and the Word* (New York, 1958), p. 79. Cf. also *Theology of the New Testament,* (New York, 1951-55), I, 14f.

To *refuse* to think of reward, to set oneself deliberately to *ignore* the idea of reward, is as unevangelical, though not as immoral, as to practice virtue for the sake of reward. . . . *As a practical maxim for life*, the phrase, "The first concern of ethical thought should be for the purity of moral motive," is a profoundly dangerous guide. . . . Our Lord's method of expressing the truth was at once appropriate, original, and inspiring. He gave the thought of reward a baffling prominence in His teaching that men should learn not to be afraid of it. They were not to make reward their goal; but neither were they to be so shocked at the idea, if and when it presented itself, as to immerse themselves in studied attempts at forgetfulness. Leaving behind thoughts both of reward and of disinterestedness as equally self-centered, they were to look forward to that true self-forgetfulness which cannot be acquired by human effort, but comes only to those whose hearts are set on God.[23]

And Editor Carl F. H. Henry, in a recent book, writes:

The notion that the admission of reward as a motivation for ethics leads necessarily to the deterioration of the ethical ideal is erroneous. The secular denial of the validity of reward must be repudiated. . . . Christian ethics is not destructive of self-interest, but rather promotes an enlightened self-interest which finds its own welfare in the conformity of creaturely life to the creator's will.[24]

Henry agrees with writers like Wilder and Bultmann that "Jesus never makes the expectation of reward the chief motive of the Christian life." But he differs in emphasis from them when he goes on to say:

Yet it is an overstatement to contend that only duty which is performed without expectation of reward will be rewarded. Only what is done from love will be rewarded, but there is no reason to exclude the expectation of reward from what is so done.[25]

Now each of the two theological approaches above has its task: the internalistically oriented theologian who is embarrassed by the Biblical combination must justify exegetically (not just morally) to the externalist his tendency to eliminate the prominent eschatological rewards offered in Scripture as an acceptable aspect of Christian motivation. This he often tries to do, in contemporary theology, by regarding the eschatological aspects of the Biblical message as myth, apparently on the assumption that this hermeneutical type excludes a relevance to motivation. I shall presently suggest a defense which places these eschatological aspects in proper focus and thereby tempers the objections which moralists bring against them. The ex-

---

23 *The Vision of God* (London, 1947), pp. 75f. (abridged edition).
24 *Christian Personal Ethics* (Grand Rapids, Michigan, 1957), p. 540.
25 *Ibid.*, pp. 544f.

ternalist, on the other hand, who welcomes the combination, must vindicate morally (not just exegetically) to the internalist the acceptability of the eschatological motivation for conduct. This he often tries to do either by insisting that man is a purposive creature whose moral performance cannot be motivationally abstracted from his whole dynamic toward self-realization in the cosmic scheme of things viewed in final relationship to God; or, as Kirk may be seen doing above, by warning of the dangers accompanying the desire for a pure moral motive.

If the classic Protestant conviction of salvation by grace indicates a motive for conduct, it is certainly that of gratitude.[26] Though gratitude cannot, as will become evident, escape the philosophic issue with which this essay began, it does appear on first sight to offer something of a solution to the impasse created by the more extreme theological protagonists in that controversy. An internalist, in a conceding mood, could adopt the motive of gratitude to alleviate his embarrassment in the presence of the Biblical offer of rewards for the fulfillment of duty, in such a way that he need not, for the sake of this issue, even raise the question of the mythical or non-mythical status of the eschatological events. For the whole point of the doctrine of salvation by grace is that the reward, eternal life, is realized not only eschatologically but also in the present time.[27] The reward has in essence been already received, and without the performance of any good deeds at all (indeed, in spite of their non-performance). So that if there is in the believer the present experience (as well as the future hope) of eternal life, he has already obtained the advantage before he hears the divine imperative for good works. And then the advantage no longer figures as a motive for doing these works in the morally suspect sense of a reward to be calculated and gained; it is a gift.

Nevertheless, while gratitude thus seems to rescue Christian motivation from the charge of calculating self-interest, it does not deliver it completely from a necessary relation to self-interest. For whether the motive of an act be some advantage to be gained or some advantage already received, the motive appears to remain a natural one, lacking that peculiarly morally "pure" quality which the internalist in his more rigorous moods so diligently seeks. If gratitude is the primary motivation of Christian living, that is, there is no escaping

26 Cf. *The Heidelberg Catechism,* Questions and Answers 2, 86, 87.
27 Compare on this question Wilder, *op. cit.,* Chs. 3-7 with Henry, *op. cit.,* Ch. 24.

the recognition that the springs of such living lie in self-interest. And since self-interest is in itself no moral problem for Carl Henry, he has no difficulty regarding gratitude explicitly as the "primary motive for Christian obedience."[28]

This involvement in advantage, as it is natural but not obviously moral, is precisely what disturbs the purist who seeks a disinterested motive for the performance of moral acts. Characteristically, therefore, A. N. Wilder, by contrast with Henry, tends to drop gratitude, after mentioning it as a more laudable motive than reward, from his explicit analysis of motivation, in favor of the compelling divine authority of the commands, as the essentially moving power of a believer's life.[29] St. Bernard of Clairvaux, with eloquence, did something like this long ago:

> First, therefore, man loves himself for his own sake. . . . And when he sees that he cannot subsist of himself he begins to seek God through faith as something, as it were, necessary for him, and to love Him. Thus he loves God according to the second degree, but for his own sake, not for Himself. But when, . . . little by little God becomes known to him through experience . . . and consequently He grows sweet; and thus by tasting how sweet is the Lord he passes to the third degree so that he loves God now, not for his own sake but for Himself.[30]

But an internalist need not fear the loss of his whole cause by accepting gratitude as the primary motive and thereby remaining somewhere within St. Bernard's "second degree" of love. For while the externalist sets up gratitude as a natural but not obviously moral motive, he, the internalist, can counter by setting it up as a moral, because a not obviously natural one. He can, that is, simply remind the externalist that gratitude is a natural motive only when it occurs, but that often it fails to occur, thereby becoming subject to the category of obligation. Indeed, according to St. Paul, ingratitude is as natural a response to the knowledge of God and His benefits as gratitude appeared, at first sight, to be.[31] And thus gratitude, which was first proposed as a natural motive, has become subject also to the category of obligation, suggesting an examination of the question: Can natural motives be obligations?

[28] Henry, *op. cit.*, p. 529.
[29] Wilder, *op. cit.*, pp. 93; 120ff.
[30] Bernard of Clairvaux, *On the Love of God*, anthologized in *Christian Ethics: Sources of the Living Tradition*, edited by W. Beach and H. R. Niebuhr (New York, 1955), p. 192.
[31] Romans 1:21.

The proposition that motives themselves can be obligations must deal with the objection, presented vigorously in recent philosophy by Sir W. D. Ross, that for a motive to be an obligation is a self-contradiction, since an obligation implies possibility and it is impossible to bring about motives at will.[32] Now it does seem necessary to hold that no *act* can be obligatory upon an agent unless it is possible in some sense[33] for him to perform it — regardless of what the motive may be, and it is with the obligatory character of acts that many moral philosophers (unfortunately) have been preoccupied. But what if the moral consciousness includes, in addition to the sense of what I ought to do, a sense of what I ought to be, and if the latter cannot be reduced to the former? This would introduce a reference for obligation to which the premise of its requiring possibility is less obviously applicable, for what an agent ought to be involves not only his motives, but all his traits, habits, dispositions and past experiences — indeed, his whole character, what he has *already* come to *be*. But the present state of one's character, what a man is at the moment, is less apparently subject, if at all, to the requirement moralists call freedom of moral choice than an act which a man may presently be deliberating. But does recognition of this (very serious) complication logically entail that there can be no responsibility, no obligation, with regard to the character that is already possessed? I think not; and that such obligation can exist can be seen from the incredibility of restricting the extent of moral obligation simply to the acts about to be performed — not including, that is, how (because of some condition in the agent) they are to be performed. For then a man never could be morally acquitted for having performed a wrong act (which nevertheless rightly occurs); nor could a man himself ever be blamed for his wrong act, since his act alone could be bad; nor could he ever be blamed for doing a right act (which nevertheless rightly occurs when he is said to have done what was right, but "in the wrong way"); that is, there could be no obligation ever to act morally in the *full* sense of the term — in a word, there would never exist an obligation to *be* a good man. But this obligation I take to be as essential to our moral consciousness as the obligation to perform certain "right" acts.

The theological discussion that we have considered does not

---

32 *The Right and the Good,* Ch. 1, anthologized in *Readings in Ethical Theory,* edited by W. Sellars and J. Hospers (New York, 1952), pp. 165ff. Cf. also on the problem H. J. Paton, *The Categorical Imperative* (Chicago, 1948), pp. 117f.
33 Cf. Frankena's analysis of this possibility in *op. cit.,* p. 60.

provide any further light on the problem of resolving the internalist-externalist debate among the philosophers. The resolution of this would require, as I have tried to indicate, an argument supporting an objective sense of obligation that will be as convincing to the internalist as the need for the subjective sense of obligation appeared to the concession-minded externalist. Protestant theology, however, in so far as it sets forth gratitude as the primary motive for "good works," does give us occasion to ask a second question: Why does a natural motive for doing right acts sometimes occur and sometimes not? It would appear that any full-scale psychological inquiry into the first question (why do subjective obligations sometimes motivate and sometimes fail?) should consider this question as well. Its importance for the problem of the motivational appeal of the moralist must now be made clear.

It might be thought that the motivational conflict that often exists between duty and interest will support any tendency we may have to discredit the role of natural motives in the performance of moral acts. Reflection upon this conflict does not, however, so much support this tendency as assume it; and this is the assumption that must be opened to question in the face of those who insist that moral appeals must, to be moral, be unique. According to H. A. Prichard, it is reflection on this type of experience that gives rise to moral philosophy itself:

> Anyone who, stimulated by education, has come to feel the force of the various obligations in life, at some time or other comes to feel the irksomeness of carrying them out, and to recognize the sacrifice of interest involved; and, if thoughtful, he inevitably puts to himself the question, "Is there really a reason why I should act in the ways in which hitherto I have thought I ought to act?" . . . and his and other people's moral philosophizing is an attempt to supply the answer . . . .[34]

Prichard's analysis of some answers that have been given to this question reveals the ambiguity of it.[35] One may be asking, that is, for the moral ground of the obligation that irks him; or he may be asking for an additional incentive that will motivate him to carry it out in spite of its irksomeness. Prichard's own view is that the first question is mistaken and the second one irrelevant. The first question is

---

[34] "Does Moral Philosophy Rest Upon a Mistake?" in Sellars and Hospers, *op. cit.*, p. 149.

[35] Cf. Frankena, *op. cit.*, pp. 45f. St. Bernard of Clairvaux also saw it long ago: "Indeed, when the question is asked why God should be loved, it may have one of two meanings: whether it is God's title to our love or our own advantage in loving Him." *Op. cit.*, p. 183.

mistaken, he holds, because the ground of something's being obligatory cannot be logically distinguished from its obligatory character itself, and if this character is recognized, one already has the answer to his question. The second question is irrelevant, he claims, because "the rightness or wrongness of an act has nothing to do with any question of motives at all."[36] I will be concerned here not with his rejection of the first question as a mistake but with his rejection of the second question as irrelevant.

Even if it can be shown that natural incentives cannot be relied upon to guarantee the rightness of acts (and no doubt it can), such incentives are not thereby morally irrelevant if, as I would maintain, the moral consciousness of man provides him not only with a sense of what he ought to do, but also with a sense of what he ought to be.[37] The question, that is, as to whether or not a man can *be* good is as much a part of moral philosophy as what makes the acts he ought to do *right* acts. But if this is so, the role of natural incentives for moral acts is not utterly irrelevant; it is instead at least consistent with morality, if not actually supported by it.

To what, then, is the distrust of such motives, so frequently encountered in some moral philosophers, due? Though clearly suggested by the fact that such motives often conflict with moral obligations, the distrust cannot be based on this conflict; for it is not the case that anything that conflicts with a moral obligation is thereby morally suspect, as the situation that arises when two moral obligations themselves conflict will testify. Nor can it be based on any failure to recognize such natural motives as obligatory in those instances where they might have been possible but were actually nonexistent, for this would presuppose the infallibility of the moral faculty, which has not been proved. Nor is there any proof from the dictum that "the rightness or wrongness of an act has nothing to do with any question of the motives at all," for this, if it should be true, proves too much for the purpose of deriving from it a distrust of those motives. For this dictum asserts only the complete independence of the obligatoriness of an act from its motives, and from this it follows not that motives are to be distrusted, but that whether they are to be trusted or not is undetermined.

The distrust or moral disapproval of natural motives must there-

---

36 Prichard, *op. cit.,* pp. 153f.
37 And still further, I would hold, with a sense of what the universe ought to be. Cf. Bernard of Clairvaux: "True love asks no reward but *deserves* one." *Op. cit.,* p. 185 (emphasis mine) .

fore be derived from the mere fact that they are natural, and not consequently obviously moral. Now on one level of reflection, the fact that something is natural and also actually existent makes it logically odd to propose it as an obligation; for that "it ought" seems to be completely obviated by the fact that "it is." But the difficulty is more deep-seated than this: logical oddness would hardly lead to moral distrust, and that is what must be accounted for. But that it cannot be accounted for in this way is evident from the recognition that any distrust so grounded would be analogous to a distrust of the rightness of an act on the basis of its actually having been performed. But the sheer performance or non-performance of human acts is never regarded by the faculty of moral judgment as the ground for their being judged either right or wrong. No more, then, does the occurrence or non-occurrence of natural motives offer any basis for their being judged right or wrong. To exclude anything natural from the possibility of its being subject to the category of moral obligation, on the basis of its actual occurrence, involves an assumption that begs the whole question as to whether natural entities are exclusively natural or not.[38] The whole point of Plato's theory, it may be said in his defense against Prichard's objection,[39] is that human self-realization, regardless of how advantageous to natural incentives it may be made to appear, presents itself to man also as an unfulfilled (and even inadequately understood) ideal, therefore as an obligation: an obligation which not only determines what acts he ought to perform, but in addition is certainly not indifferent to what interests and inclinations he possesses. There can be no argument, therefore, from an analysis of the duty-interest conflict, or from the actual occurrence of natural motives, to the conclusion that such motives are morally suspect.

I conclude that the extreme internalist has no grounds, through his insistence on a "pure" moral motive, offhand morally to disapprove the natural motives of man; even though the externalist, through his insistence that these motives may, with no moral objection, bring about right acts without the help of the sense that

38 Compare this formulation of the assumption with that exposed by Frankena in his article, "The Naturalistic Fallacy," in Sellars and Hospers, *op, cit.* Cf. p. 111: "To assume that the ethical characteristic is exclusively ethical is to beg precisely the question which is at issue when the definition is offered [by some "naturalist" in ethics]."

39 Cf. *op. cit.,* pp. 149f., also his *Duty and Interest,* anthologized in Sellars and Hospers, *op. cit.,* pp. 470ff.

these acts are obligations, has nevertheless no grounds thereby uncritically to approve them.

To what kind of motive, then, should a moralist appeal? He may appeal, it would appear, either to obligations or to natural motives with no logical or moral impropriety. Of course, the most striking practical feature is that he often proves ineffective either way. Obligations may or may not motivate; natural motives for doing right acts may or may not be present. Either way of accounting for the moralist's failures points up the most important problem of all: Why are men sometimes, and sometimes not, good men? The very existence of moralistic appeals, as well as the failures of these appeals, indicates that sometimes, at least, men are not good. Is there any promise that men can ever be good in a way that is free from this indication arising within the perspective of moralists and their appeals? It will be at this point that the Christian theologian makes his most important contribution: preachers, whatever of moralists they may be when they try to get us to act, are not preachers until they declare to us what act God, in Jesus Christ, has done. Preachers, that is, are nothing but moralists until they become *heralds*. This contribution to the whole topic of motives and obligations will raise macroscopic considerations indeed.

8

A Restricted Motive Theory of Ethics

FRED E. BROUWER, Assistant Professor of Philosophy, Washington and Jefferson College. A.B., Calvin College; A.M., University of Michigan; Ph.D., Yale University. Articles in *Review of Metaphysics, Gordon Review.*

A Restricted Motive Theory of Ethics

BY FRED E. BROUWER

IN THIS PAPER I WANT TO CONSIDER A NORMATIVE ETHICAL THEORY which has not been very fully explored. In general, the theory is an attempt to base the rightness of actions upon the goodness of motives. Of course, there have been a number of moral philosophers who have proposed motive theories of ethics. For the most part, however, these theories face a crucial difficulty. The view to be presented here has, I believe, certain affinities with the views of Jonathan Edwards, Butler, Hutcheson, Kant, Martineau, L. A. Reid, G. C. Field, and Joseph, among others. Furthermore, I think that it most fully represents the ethical teachings of Jesus in so far as He implicitly presented an ethical theory at all. My main concern, however, will not be to show that this view represents the teaching of Jesus,[1] nor to trace historical affinities in any detail.

In this essay I would like to develop a motive theory by way of contrast with other normative theories. To this purpose, I will first present a schema as a means for analyzing moral action, and in terms of this schema sketch some main normative theories. Then after viewing some typical criticisms of motive theories, I shall out-

---

[1] Perhaps Professor Blanshard's discussion of the attitude theory of ethics may be taken as showing in a general way the ethical position of Jesus. Brand Blanshard, "Personal Ethics," in *Preface to Philosophy: Textbook*, edited by W. E. Hocking *et al.* (New York, 1947), pp. 150-158. Joseph Sittler's little *The Structure of Christian Ethics* (Baton Rouge, 1958) presents a very dynamic interpretation of Biblical ethics.

line what I call a restricted motive theory. I should emphasize that this is a brief outline — a tentative exploration rather than a definitive statement.

In writing this paper I found it convenient to use the ethical writings of Sir W. D. Ross as a springboard, for Ross presented his views in sharp outline, and he has been one of the foremost critics of motive theories.

I

As a means of diagnosing moral action, the following schema proves to be useful. In such and such circumstances, I/he intend(s) to (did) ___#1___ with such and such consequences ___#2___ (actual, probable, foreseeable, or intended consequences as the case may be), which behavior may be described as an action of ___#3___ for the sake of ___#4___ because ___#5___. For each of the five blanks there is a special kind of description. Simply and roughly, in blank No. 1 belongs a morally neutral description of human behavior, of a human proceeding culminating in a terminal state of affairs; in blank No. 2 a description of relevant consequences from a certain perspective; in blank No. 3 a description (or identification) of the behavior as a kind of moral action; in blank No. 4 a description of the end(s), the motive, the intention with which the action was done; in blank No. 5 a description of the motivational influences, "force(s)" — what may be in a sense a "cause" of the action. For a preliminary example, in such and such circumstances, he intends to (did) put a powder (poison) in Mr. Khrushchev's vodka, with such and such consequences, which behavior may be described as an action of killing Khrushchev for the sake of helping his country because he loves his country.[2]

I said above that blank No. 1 calls for a morally neutral description of a human proceeding or behavior that culminates in a terminal state of affairs. The description is one which a not abnormal spectator could make by observing the situation. The observer may have to look carefully or make some tests, but is not to include any

---

[2] Many cautionary comments should be made about this proposed schema. First of all, the schema is rough, tentative, and somewhat artificial. The actual phrasing of the schema I am sure may be improved. As it stands, ordinary English may need to be altered if not sacrificed. The schema is not a transcription from ordinary language. Furthermore, any filled-in schema may say too little or too much: one may have to expand the schema in certain situations; on the other hand, a given filled-in schema may be somewhat redundant. One might also note the difference between a schema filled in by an agent and one filled in by an observer.

words that are, as it were, morally toned. For example, I may see someone handing another person one hundred dollars and not know whether the action may be further described as a bribe, a repayment, a gift, a loan, or possibly a sleep-walker's mistake. The description on this level, as such, need not indicate whether the proceeding is intentional or even voluntary. It may be difficult on this level to make a description without implying that the action is intentional or voluntary, or without using morally toned words. Witness the first example of "putting or dropping a powder (poison) into Mr. Khrushchev's vodka." "Poison," of course, is a suggestive word. But it may not be too far-fetched to imagine a doctor putting what may be described as a poison into the vodka to quiet Khrushchev's nerves. If we knew the circumstances we probably would call the powder a medicine. But an observer might be able to find out that the powder is a poison without knowing that it is used in this case as a medicine.

Human proceedings, of course, have a wide variety of consequences. Some of these may be foreseen by the agent, others not. Not all the foreseen consequences of an action need be intended by the agent, for he may do something in spite of some undesirable but likely consequences. There may be many consequences of an action that the agent cannot reasonably be expected to foresee. For the purposes of analyzing a contemplated action, one may select for blank No. 2 those foreseeable or probable consequences which one considers morally relevant. In analyzing a completed action, one selects the relevant actual consequences and perhaps also some additional anticipated consequences.

An observer may see someone doing or performing some activity and yet ask, "What are you doing?" Among other things he may be asking for a kind of activity or action. He may be asking for a further description of that which he sees the agent doing, for what further the person is doing in doing something we might describe in blank No. 1. Often actions are identified by such participial words as stealing, killing, lying, hurting, harming, helping, truth-telling, promise-keeping, repaying, bribing, etc.[3] These activities (identified in blank No. 3) are regarded as intentional human actions, as doings of something, and are in what Anscombe calls "the description of

---

[3] These actions I say are morally toned. In *Intention* (Oxford, 1957), p. 84, G. E. Anscombe gives in the right hand column a list of actions which are not so morally toned. In certain cases we may want to put action words in blank No. 3 which are not obviously, if at all, morally toned.

intentional actions."[4] It may be the case that the agent acted voluntarily, but that he did not do what is mentioned in blank No. 3 intentionally. A person may do an action which he intends to be of a certain kind (e.g., a helping), but which an observer would want to describe differently (e.g., as a harming). The mother who brings up her child mainly on candy does not intend to, but does in fact, harm her child. Many actions are best described in several ways: an action may be a helping of one person and a hurting of another.

The actions referred to in blank No. 3 may be done with different purposes or ends in view. In blank No. 4 we mention the objective, the reason, the motive, the purpose, the end, the intention with which the action was done.[5] One may see a person doing an action (as in blank No. 3) and yet ask "Why?" or "For what reason are you doing that?" The answer is expected in the form of "in order to" or "for the sake of." I chose "for the sake of" to preserve the participial form. Thus, regarding an action done for its own sake, blanks No. 3 and No. 4 will be similar. But one may have several ends in mind. One may choose one end as a means to a further end. If so, blank No. 4 may have to be expanded by adding an additional "for the sake of" and an appropriate blank in serial form.

In some contexts one may ask, "Why did you have that end or purpose or reason for action?" As a suitable answer we may refer in blank No. 5 to some psychological fact, some fact of the person's motivation, and also possibly to some other facts. The words that go into blank No. 5 (often typical motive words) may refer to a

---

4 *Ibid.*, p. 83. Anscombe also points out that such actions (as offending or hurting) may be done unintentionally but "there would be no such thing if it were never the description of an intentional action."

5 I am not saying that these terms are always equivalent or unequivocal. Aristotle has pointed out that "end" may refer to a future terminal state of affairs, or to an activity itself. "Intention" shows the same ambiguity: one may distinguish the intention with which an action is done from the intention in acting. I am using the word "motive" as equivalent to "the reason for which the action was done" or "the intention with which the action was done." A motive thus indicates that a person in some sense was aware of a certain end and also implies that he had a pro-attitude toward that end. This may appear not to be the most common use of the term "motive," but I believe that many moral philosophers use it in this way. This means that for the most part typical motive words do not belong in blank No. 4 but rather in No. 5. Typical motive words, for example *revenge* and *greed,* classify actions according to why they were done (their intention). To act from revenge is to intend to hurt someone who has done something bad to you. To act from greed is to intend to get a lot of something for oneself. I do not think of motives as psychological entities existing in one's mind, but rather as a person's pro- and con-attitudes, his "set" toward certain objects or experiences.

kind of occurrent feeling, thought, or pro-attitude, or also to dispositional motivational forces. In our common sense thinking we often regard what is mentioned in blank No. 5 as the cause of our action.

Let us take a closer look at my proposed example. I shall use an abbreviated schema in the past tense for reasons of simplicity. He put a powder (poison) in Mr. Khrushchev's vodka, which may be described as an action of killing him for the sake of helping his country because he loves his country (or he is patriotic). Possibly one might describe the action as a helping of one's country, or suggest that killing Mr. Khrushchev is one's (proximate) end. And certainly it is desirable to further explicate "he loves his country" or "he is patriotic." But I think that the usefulness of the schema may be brought out by means of contrast. We may compare the example above (as example 1) with the following, example 2: He put a powder (poison) in Mr. Khrushchev's vodka, which may be described as an action of killing him for the sake of helping his country and (for the sake of) being a hero because his vanity overcame his reluctance to kill. Example 3: He put a powder (poison) in Mr. Khrushchev's vodka, which may be described as an action of killing him for the sake of helping his country and (for the sake of) killing him because he could fulfill his urge to kill someone without appearing dishonorable.

I think we may quite safely regard the action (as an action of killing) as intentional in all three cases. But it may be hard to decide in examples 2 and 3 whether helping his country was or was not properly an end of the person. In some cases we can imagine that the agent regarded helping his country as a means to his further end. But we can imagine other bases where the agent did not at all care about helping his country and possibly did not even think of it. We note that in blank No. 5 several things can be indicated: what kind of person the agent is; the particular feelings he had at the time of the action; whether he killed reluctantly or very eagerly; certain past facts, for example, that his parents were killed by the Russians in Hungary. Also it can be pointed out that regarding example 1 in certain circumstances we might want to substitute for "he loves his country," "he thinks it his duty to help his country," or "he thinks that helping his country is the best thing to do," as example 4. In example 3 we might want to substitute for "it would fulfill his urge to kill someone," "for such and such reasons he thinks that killing Mr. Khrushchev is the right thing, the best thing to do, or is his duty," as example 5.

The schema, in a sense, is a means of indicating what took place or will take place. Blanks No. 2, No. 3, No. 4, and No. 5 are a further specification of blank No. 1. But this does not mean that one is doing entirely different things in filling out blanks No. 2-No. 5, for it must be clear that the blanks are in a way internally related: there is some, as it is called, logical or analytic relation between them. Consider this rather simple example: He gave the man $100 as an act of helping him for the sake of helping him because he felt kindly or benevolently toward him. "He helped him" (he did this as an action of helping him), "his end was to help him," "he acted from benevolence" (he desired to help him) say roughly the same thing. In special contexts these clauses may have different meanings. A man may desire to help a person and not actually help him. But failing to help is to be understood in terms of helping. From No. 4 one is likely to infer No. 3 and No. 2, and possibly No. 1. Of course, there are exceptions. But this is the reason for having the extended schema. It is also true that from No. 3 we may be able to learn something about No. 4, and from No. 4, something about No. 5.

Although the blanks are thus very closely related, it is still useful to distinguish them. Perhaps the blanks may be described, somewhat arbitrarily, in the following way: blank No. 1 — the context of behavior, blank No. 2 — the context of consequences, blank No. 3 — the context of action, blank No. 4 — the context of motive, blank No. 5 — the context of motivating influences.

II

Blanks No. 2, No. 3, and No. 4 of the schema provide in a general way three different contexts for evaluating moral action. Teleologists use primarily the second blank, deontologists the third, and motive theorists the fourth and possibly the fifth. Each of these types of theories emphasizes a certain basic moral concept: the teleologists use "value" or "intrinsic goodness," deontologists "duty" or "obligation," motive theorists "moral goodness." Thus we may call blank No. 2 the context of value, blank No. 3 the context of rightness, and blank No. 4 the context of goodness.

In general, teleologists attempt to evaluate (and often define) the rightness of an action in terms of the sum-total value of its consequences. According to John Stuart Mill, "Actions are right in proportion as they tend to promote happiness. . . . The motive has nothing to do with the morality of the action, though much with the worth of the agent. He who saves a fellow creature from drowning does what is morally right, whether his motive be duty or the hope of being paid for his trouble."[6] It would appear that the value of the foreseeable consequences of the five actions described in section one are unfavorable and that, therefore, all the actions are equally wrong, regardless of the purposes of the agent.

Certainly the utilitarian injunction to seek the greatest happiness of the greatest number carries with it a certain attractiveness. But one soon encounters difficulties in attempting to apply this principle. In the first place, what are to count as the consequences of an action? It would appear that any action has a countless number of consequences. Surely we do not have to wait for these to judge actions. But, the teleologist may reply, we may count the intended, foreseeable, expectable consequences. Just so. Yet it is still problematic whether we can calculate, even roughly, and compare the value of the consequences, actual or foreseeable, of many actions, even if we regard pleasure or anything else as the sole intrinsic value. But, even more important, deontologists like Sir W. D. Ross claim that in our moral deliberations we often do not make use of the teleological principle and that, furthermore, we should not always use it. For, according to Ross, certain actions we regard as wrong are justifiable by the utilitarian standard and others we regard as right are not so justifiable.

Consider these two examples. Example 6: A doctor gave some incorrect information to a very wealthy, miserly patient, which behavior may be described as telling a lie and helping himself for the sake of getting an extra $1000 fee because he thought he might make good use of the money. (We might want to expand the schema and list some good end — say to contribute the $1000 to Calvin College.) Example 7: A doctor gave some incorrect information to a very wealthy, miserly patient, which behavior may be described as telling a lie and saving a patient's life for the sake of saving the patient's life because the doctor believed it his job to save lives. It is likely that both actions may be justified by the utilitarian principle. Yet clearly we regard action 6 as wrong.

---

[6] *Utilitarianism*, Ch. 2.

The ideal utilitarians, like G. E. Moore and H. Rashdall, recognized difficulties in the classical utilitarian position and amended it by recognizing other intrinsic values besides pleasure.[7] They emphasized that one should always strive to produce the greatest good, but they recognized that the greatest good is not necessarily an additive sum of isolable value elements. Moore talked about the value of organic wholes whose value is a toti-resultant product of, and not an additive sum of, incommensurable elements. In elaborating his position, Moore appeals to this principle as self-evident: "If we knew that the effect of a given action really would be to make the world, as a whole, worse than it would have been if we had acted differently, it certainly would be wrong for us to do that action."[8] Moore might say that even though action 6 may be justified hedonistically, yet the resulting state of the universe is really not better but worse. I think it is evident, however, that in making this move the ideal utilitarians give up the teleological principle in any workable, significant form. If values are incommensurate then we cannot calculate them. The principle of Moore that we should not make the world worse, in effect, appears to say no more than that we should do the better action. And everyone may agree with this.

The British deontologists of the twentieth century lodged a quite successful attack on teleological theories. In effect, they denied that the teleological principle was our main ethical criterion for judgments of right and wrong. H. A. Prichard and Ross tried to show that the rightness of actions is not dependent upon, nor definable in terms of, goodness or value of any kind, whether of consequences, motives, or the action itself. Judgments of right and wrong are immediate and ultimate: one can give no further justification for our intuitions of right and wrong.

According to Ross, moral experience is characterized by an awareness of prima facie duties or obligations, such as truth-telling, promise-keeping, promoting valuable consequences. These are not absolute duties in the sense that we should always tell the truth or keep our promises. Rather, action of these types has a tendency to be right. If an act of truth-telling conflicts with no other prima facie obligation, then it is one's duty to tell the truth. The objec-

---

7 One should really say that Moore and Rashdall recognized difficulties in the classical utilitarian position as it is often interpreted. There is evidence for regarding Mill as holding a restricted utilitarian position.

8 *Ethics* (London, 1911), p. 181.

tively right action is that one which "would discharge in the fullest possible measure the various claims or prima facie duties that are involved in this situation."[9]   It should be noted that promoting valuable consequences (the teleological principle) is only one of a number of prima facie obligations.   According to Ross, some right acts (e.g., some truth-tellings) may produce no positive valuable consequences and even, possibly, may produce disvalue.

Ross would say that in both examples 6 and 7 we have a prima facie duty to tell the truth, but that only in example 7 may the prima facie duty of seeking good consequences override that of truth-telling.

By distinguishing between an act and an action, Ross was able sharply to separate rightness and moral goodness.   An act is the thing that is done (in *Foundations of Ethics*, the initiation of change), an action is the doing of it (in *Foundations*, the initiation of change from a certain motive).   Acts are right or wrong, whereas actions may be morally good or bad.   The rightness of acts is independent of the motives which produced them: right acts need have no moral goodness.

It would appear that the deontologists have made some good phenomenological points against the teleologists, but Ross' position is not without its difficulties.   Apart from difficulties in ontology (non-natural qualities) and moral epistemology (intuition of non-natural qualities), many philosophers have questioned Ross' sharp distinctions between consequences, act, and action (motive) and, correspondingly, the sharp distinctions between value, rightness, and moral goodness.

In particular, certain utilitarians question the connection between prima facie duties and valuable consequences.   They admit, for example, that the value of the actual consequences of a particular action of truth-telling is not always immediately evident.   But, they wonder, does not the practice of truth-telling have valuable consequences?   These utilitarians, variously called rule or restricted utilitarians, admit that it is true that we simply do not use the teleological principle in all of our deliberations.   They distinguish between justifying a particular action and justifying a rule, or a practice, or a class of actions.   They agree that we often do and should attempt to justify particular actions by rules (one of which may be to seek

9 *Foundations of Ethics* (London, 1939), p. 190, Ross' other notable work is *The Right and the Good* (Oxford, 1930).

valuable consequences), but that we should justify the rules or practices themselves by the teleological principle.[10]

This position certainly appears to combine many of the merits of
both the teleological and the deontological positions and also to eliminate certain defects of both positions. Critics, however, have raised
questions about this position. Granted that moral rules are often
helpful, do we think of our moral decisions as deductions from or as
following from a set of rules, however ideal they may be? Can
we adequately compare alternative practices or rules in terms of
their valuable consequences? How does one go about making a
decision when conflicting rules are applicable to a situation? How
is one to act if one believes that commonly accepted rules or practices are either bad or worse than a conceivable alternative? The
rule utilitarians have begun to face these questions. Whether they
can fully answer them remains to be seen.

III

Before I state a version of the motive theory, I will first attempt
to suggest some reasons why philosophers are attracted to motive
theories and then view some typical objections, notably those of
Ross, to motive theories.

Lewis Beck characterizes Kant's position in the following way.

> In passing a moral judgment, I do not pass on the success or fail-
> ure of an action in leading to the object of some desire. I need not
> await the issue of an action to decide whether it was good or bad;
> I need only know the motive which led to it. In making a moral
> decision, I do not first need to know whether the action I undertake
> will succeed or not; I do not even need to know whether, in fact, I
> have the power to produce the effect. But in acts of skill and pru-
> dence, success is everything, and motives are of importance only in-
> directly, if at all.
>
> But, even more obviously, I do not morally judge actions themselves
> so much as decisions to act. Though Kant often writes as if an
> action is the object of moral judgment and is itself good or bad, it
> must be remembered that action is not merely an item of external
> behavior (e.g., the emitting of certain sounds) but includes, as its
> definitive component, the motives, intentions, and decisions which
> lead to it. The complex act of making a decision for certain reasons
> and not for others is what we attend to in moral judgment; but in
> matters of skill and prudence, it is the act and its outcome that
> count.[11]

---

10 John Rawls states the rule utilitarian position in a notable essay, "Two
Concepts of Rules," *The Philosophical Review*, 64 (1955), 3-32.

11 *A Commentary on Kant's Critique of Practical Reason* (Chicago, 1960), p. 113.

It appears to be phenomenologically true that, first and foremost, it is human actions that we judge morally and not mere behavior, events or happenings. The Hebrews may have stoned oxen and the Greeks may have tried animals for performing certain "actions," but today we do not judge animals morally. Nor do we regard involuntary or unintentional human behavior as bona fide human actions, as primary subjects of moral judgments. It appears that we individuate human behavior as human actions in terms of intentions, motives, and reasons for action and not in terms of either the consequences of or the "objective qualities" of certain actions.

From the point of view of morality, it seems to be of central importance that men set out to do certain things and that they set out to do these things for certain reasons. If for the most part men did right actions accidentally or unintentionally, moral phenomena would be entirely different. Contrary to some social cynics, it is difficult to imagine a world where right actions are generally done accidentally. It may be true that some right acts are done accidentally; it is not accidental that most right actions, that normally right actions, are not done accidentally.

In addition, although it is important that men set out to do certain things, it is also important that most moral settings-out-to-do are well motivated. It is not accidental that most right actions are done from good reasons and motives, are done with a certain spirit. There seems to be a very close connection between right actions and good motivation.

Ross is happy to admit much of this.

> Yet, as might be expected, goodness of character is the only condition that with even the slightest degree of probability tends for the doing of right acts. If a man is not morally good, it is only by the merest accident that he does what he ought. The act to which he is attracted by one feature of it, itself morally indifferent or bad, may be the act toward which a good man would be attracted by its whole system of morally significant features, but if it is so, the coincidence is accidental.[12]

Yet, Ross would insist that, although it is true that usually right acts are not done accidentally, it need not be true that well-motivated actions are usually right; and he would point out, furthermore, that as a matter of fact a goodly number of well-motivated actions are not right. Although there are some connections between right acts and morally good actions, Ross insists that one should not collapse the distinction between the two.

[12] *Foundations of Ethics*, p. 310.

Ross asks these questions of a motive theory: The same act may be done from different motives — does its rightness vary with the motive? Different kinds of acts may be done from the same motive — are these acts equally right? A person may be well motivated but yet act unintelligently — is his action then right?

In addition to pointing out these difficulties, Ross marshalls two main arguments to show that the rightness of an act is independent of its motive.[13] In the first place, he argues that our desires and motives are not under our immediate control, as we cannot produce some desires at will. Since "ought" implies "can," it cannot be our duty to produce or act from these desires or motives. Our duty is only to do a certain act (or to set ourself to do it).

Secondly, it cannot be our duty to act from the sense of duty. Ross argues that the expression a, "It is my duty to do act A from the sense of duty" means b, "It is my duty to do act A from the sense that it is my duty to do act A." But the latter part of this last sentence implies c, "that what I think is that it is my duty to-do-act-A-simply." But this is in contradiction with b. On the one hand, it is my duty to do act A simply, and on the other hand, to do act A from the sense that it is my duty to do act A. We may add to c, clause d, "from the sense that it is my duty to do act A." But then we would need to add a similar clause to d. It is plain then, according to Ross, that we would need to add an infinite series of such amendments.[14]

If one grants Ross that it cannot be our duty to act from certain motives, then one is likely to concede that the rightness of an action does not depend solely upon the value of the motive from which the action was done. For if the rightness of an action depends upon the motive from which it is done and if we cannot control our motives, then it would appear that we cannot voluntarily do right actions.

IV

Ross, it will be remembered, criticized both the teleological and motive theories on the basis that neither the value of the consequences

---

13 Ross gives these arguments in *The Right and the Good* on pp. 4-6 and in *Foundations of Ethics* on pp. 114-123.

14 These arguments of Ross have produced a number of replies. In general, critics have pointed out that Ross' conception of an act is inadequate. Perhaps the most extended criticisms of Ross on these points have been made by O. A. Johnson in *Rightness and Goodness* (The Hague, 1959). Although I believe that both of Ross' main arguments are misleading, here I will note only that they are not applicable to a restricted motive theory.

of a particular act nor the goodness of the actual motive of an action can serve as the *ground* of its rightness. It seems that Ross makes an important point in his criticisms of each of these theories. But as his criticism of teleological theories does not apply to restricted utilitarianism, so also, I believe, his criticism of motive theories does not apply to a restricted motive theory. Ross' mistake, as I see it, was to look for some *actual* quality as the ground of the rightness of an act. Since some right acts are neither well motivated nor productive of favorable consequences, he concluded, erroneously I believe, that neither motives nor consequences can be the ground of the rightness of the act. His conclusion should have been that neither the *actual* motive nor the *actual* consequences can serve as the ground of the rightness of an act.

We may recall that rule utilitarianism, apparently the most plausible of the teleological positions, maintains that the rightness of an action is seen as justified in terms of the consequences of a class of actions and not necessarily in terms of the consequences of the action itself. In a somewhat similar fashion, I think it possible for a motive theory to escape Ross' criticism. Instead of basing the rightness of an action upon the actual motive of the action (as the ground of its rightness), I think it plausible for a restricted motive theory to justify a particular action in terms of a type or class of motives.

According to a restricted motive theory, then, a right action is typically a good action. That is, an action is right because the well-motivated moral agent in this situation typically would do this kind of action, the action with this description. The goodness of an action centers around its motivation. And the right action is right because it is seen as or interpreted as the good action. In an important sense, however, a particular act, something that is done, may be judged to be right without at the same time being judged as actually a good action. If one knows or suspects that a particular action is badly motivated, it is still possible to judge it as the right act. In a sense the right act is done by an agent if he saves a drowning man, even if he plans to kill or hurt him later.[15] A particular act may be judged to be right and also to be a morally bad action. What is done accidentally may be interpreted by courtesy as a doing, as an action. Such an act may be judged right because it is interpreted by courtesy as a right action. And the right action is

---

[15] Pressed by a critic, Mill in the later editions of *Utilitarianism* is forced to admit that an agent who saves a drowning person in order later to hurt him does a different action than one who saves him because of duty.

interpreted as a good action, that is, it is seen to be the action that the well-motivated man would do. But a right act is untypically a bad action.

A wrong act on the other hand is typically a bad action. But, as a bad action may be a right act, so also a wrong action may in fact be good in the sense that it is well-motivated. One needs to make a distinction between a well-motivated action and a (full-bodied) good action, for the well-motivated person may be either unwise or insensitive. On the one hand, he may be ignorant of some relevant facts in a moral situation or he may miscalculate the means in his attempt to achieve some good end; on the other hand, he might be insensitive to some other motive that might be fitting in this situation — that is, he may not be aware of some other purpose or end that is here relevant. The good action is the well-motivated wise and sensitive action.[16] Even Ross admits that the completely good action is necessarily right.

An action may be wrong if it is poorly motivated, unwise, or insensitive. If an action is badly motivated, unwise, or insensitive, it may as a matter of fact be the right act; but it is right only accidentally, and because it is interpreted as a good action — as what the well-motivated, wise, and sensitive person would do.

Thus it is indeed possible for a restricted motive theory to make a distinction between a subjectively right action (well motivated) and an objectively right action (good). One need not, and indeed should not, agree with those who, according to Ross, hold "a view which amounts to saying that so long as our motive is good it does not matter what we do." The way to hell may be paved with good intentions, although of course one cannot get to heaven without them. In an important sense, it is part of our general obligation to act as wisely and as sensitively as possible. As I have noted, wisdom and sensitivity are not to be minimized.

It must be recognized that the distinction between the subjec-

---

16 I said above that the goodness of an action centers around its motivation. In saying this, however, I do not want to minimize the conditions of wisdom and sensitivity. Even though most right actions are well motivated, who would estimate the wrongs and injustices done by well-intentioned people? Yet it is likely true that the well-motivated agent never knowingly or deliberately acts unwisely or insensitively, whereas informed and sensitive persons may be poorly motivated. An implicit general theory of value may be important to the morally good person in aiding him to act wisely and sensitively. Historically, utilitarianism has done a great service in calling attention to these conditions of wisdom and sensitivity. Especially on the level of social ethics does the condition of the wisdom of actions and policies come to the fore.

tively right action and the objectively right action is not a real one for the moral agent in a practical situation: he never has to make a choice between the two. He may worry whether his envisaged action is the best possible action, but for him the objectively right action is inseparable from what he thinks to be right. He feels he ought to do what he thinks is best.

The moral agent in a practical situation is wondering what to do, is looking for the best action. If he is in a moral frame of mind, he is ready to do the action which he thinks is best. In many such cases, his primary aim as it were is to fill in blank No. 1 of the schema. It would appear that he understands blank No. 1 in terms of blank No. 3. When he recognizes an action as of a certain (moral) kind, he may feel morally justified in, may have a good reason for, doing the action.

If this is so, it seems plausible to argue that before action, the moral agent primarily considers the action he is to do and not his motives. The truth of this, however, need not undercut the motive position. For, I think it may be argued, in such a situation it is pointless or redundant to consider one's motives or to ask what the agent's motives are. In an important sense motives have already been implicitly considered. The agent in some sense is intending to do what he thinks is right and good, what is the best action. If the agent decides that his action should be an action of helping in this case, he is acting (helping) for the sake of helping. The end is implicitly chosen in the choosing of the action. If the agent decides to do what he believes to be right, he is doing the action for its own sake and not for some other reason or end.[17] Thus it still may be true that "helping a person is a good reason for an action's being right" is to be understood in terms of the position that the end of helping a person (benevolence) is a morally good end. It may be true that the reason why certain kinds of actions are right is best understood within this general framework: well-motivated persons, persons in a moral frame of mind, would have the corresponding good ends.[18]

In a given situation a moral agent may or may not decide from a moral point of view. Very often the alternative of deciding or

[17] To ask for the motive of an action is often to discredit an action, to point out that it was not done for its own sake.

[18] For judging particular actions, I think it best to consider blank No. 4 as basic and to regard blank No. 5 as supplemental to blank No. 4. Blank No. 5 may be regarded as giving some additional information that may be relevant.

not deciding from the moral point of view appears to the agent as a conflict of motives or ends of action. Very often the agent is faced with an objective demand, an action which is here fitting, and a subjective demand, an action that he would like to do. The conflict may appear as a conflict between an other-regarding motive and a self-regarding motive, or possibly between a long-range end and a short-range end. There need not be a conflict between duty and interest, however, for the morally good person may have a strong pro-attitude toward the better end.

In reflecting on one of our past actions, we may consider its motive, end, purpose. If we now see it as badly motivated, we may well feel remorse and resolve to act in a different way in the future. If, however, we see it as wrong because unwise, we may feel regret but not remorse. We may feel responsible for such an action and blame ourself for not reflecting sufficiently about the situation.

We judge the actions of others primarily as right or wrong, or what the well-motivated person would or would not have done. If a person did what we take to be the right action, the typically good action, we may normally assume that it was well motivated and thus morally good. If a person does what we judge to be the wrong action, we do not, or rather should not, as a matter of course judge his action as morally bad. Only when we believe we know the agent's (bad) motive in doing a wrong action, or an accidentally right act, should we judge his action as morally bad, or correct our tacit assumption that his action was good.

In a moral situation the agent may be said to have two tasks: a theoretical one and a practical one. He should, on the one hand, attempt to find out to the best of his ability what the best action is and, on the other hand, do it or (in some cases) set out to do it.

Ross, it will be remembered, criticized motive theories on the ground that we cannot be obligated to act from certain motives because we cannot summon them up at will; and, furthermore, he might have added, we often do not know our "true motives." But it is evident that this criticism presupposes that consideration of our motives is part of our practical task. As I see it, a restricted motive theory considers motivation as relevant to understanding our theoretical task. Our theoretical task is to determine the right action, which may be understood, although not explicitly in every instance, as the good action. Our practical task is to do the right action, not to do it from certain motives.

In a particular situation love cannot be commanded, but one

may be obligated to do certain actions, those that the loving person would do. It may be true that we cannot simply by taking thought change or create certain desires or attitudes, but certainly we very often can stop ourself from acting upon certain desires and emotions. In a particular situation the central question is "What should I do?" "How should I look upon this action?" "Under what description should I conceive it?" and not "What are my real motives?" Yet, as Ross asserts, "Security of one's motives is a well known part of the technique of moral deliberation."[19] We have seen, however, that this is not our only technique; our main interest may center in the action itself if we are in a moral frame of mind.[20]

Our interest may center around actions in so far as certain types of actions are typically right or wrong. One may, with Ross, call these prima facie obligations or duties. But, against Ross, one can give normative reasons for prima facie dutifulness of these actions. Such actions are typical expressions of good or bad motives, are typically good or bad.

According to a restricted motive theory, then, a case of a conflict of duties is not first of all a conflict of prima facie obligations or a conflict of rules, but rather a conflict of the claim of ends of action. Some ends of action are typically good, others bad. To say that a certain end of action is good implies that we ought to have a pro-attitude toward it.[21] Normally, one should never do an action which is seen to have a bad end, to be the typical expression of bad pro-attitudes. One should never have a pro-attitude toward deceit, toward harming another person, or toward injustice. One should never act from these pro-attitudes.[22] This does not mean, however, that one should never tell a lie, commit an injustice, or harm someone. At times one may need to do one of these actions. But if so, one should do these actions from other motives and one should still have a con-attitude toward deceit, injustice, and harming. Such

---

19 *Foundations of Ethics*, p. 124.

20 Even when our interest centers in the action itself, we should be on guard against the all too common self-deception which permits us to ignore and misinterpret facts and also against the special pleading of our own interests.

21 I do not want to say that ends of action or pro-attitudes are principles, but perhaps the judgment that certain ends or pro-attitudes are either good or bad may be regarded as a principle. Yet, holding a moral principle involves in some sense having the relevant pro-attitude — being motivated to act on these principles.

22 This is not to say that one can readily excise all of one's bad feelings and emotions. Certainly at times it is best to "give vent" to them in some way. But of course one can vent them in radically different ways.

typically wrong actions can be justified only by motives that appear to be "better," more fittingly related to the particular situation. We may be justified in telling a lie to save a life (example 7), or to shield a person from a criminal or a madman, or from stormtroopers, but not for the purposes of getting a fee (example 6), or helping a friend get a position. Few deceitful or unjust acts can be justified by good motives: few pro-attitudes can override our con-attitudes toward deceit or injustice. Justifying typically bad actions is largely a matter of judgment; no exact rules can be given. However, I think one may say that, in general, certain ends, or alternatively pro-attitudes, are seen to be fitting in particular situations.

It may be recalled that one may with some plausibility give a utilitarian justification of examples 1 through 5. I suggest that the plausibility of this evaluation derives from the fact that in making it one takes a detached and hence artificial view of the whole situation. I would agree that in all five examples the action is wrong. But I believe that in terms of actual practice, it is more plausible to evaluate the actions in a different way.

Imagine oneself giving advice to a person contemplating the five actions. I suggest one might advise the person somewhat as follows: Example 1 is wrong because it is an unwise way of helping one's country — what good will it do? Think of the possible consequences. Is it not likely that the action will harm one's country? Example 2 is wrong because poorly motivated. One should never kill for reasons of vanity. If helping his country is the main motivation, then we might give the advice relevant to example 1. Example 3 is poorly motivated (quite like example 2). Example 4 is wrong because unwise (quite like example 1). Example 5 is wrong because it is either insensitive, unwise, or poorly motivated, depending upon the reason he thinks that the killing is the right thing to do.

V

I have spoken of certain ends of action and also pro-attitudes as being good and others as bad. I think that most people would agree that, for example, a pro-attitude to the well-being of others (benevolence, love), a pro-attitude toward truth and justice, and a con-attitude toward pain, suffering, and misery are good: a pro-attitude toward the ill-being of others (hatred, malevolence), a pro-attitude toward pain, suffering, and misery, and a pro-attitude toward deception and injustice are bad. Traditional utilitarianism would affirm that such pro-attitudes are instrumentally good or bad because they tend to lead to those actions which produce favorable or unfavorable consequences; Ross, on the other hand, asserts that they are intrinsically good or bad in the sense that they are or are not "worthy of admiration."

I do not doubt that good pro-attitudes are very useful, but I have doubts about saying that they are good merely because generally they have good consequences. But, in contrast to Ross, I believe that these pro-attitudes may be vindicated (as opposed to validated) by an appeal to the ideal form of life that we want to lead, which ideal, of course, includes what we regard as valuable. I suggest that many philosophers have this ideal in mind when they speak of benevolence or love as being the core of morality.[23]

I view the restricted motive theory as an attempt to understand rightness in terms of moral goodness. It should also be pointed out that it is an attempt to relate rightness to value by means of goodness. For there is a close relation between goodness and value. The ends and purposes that moral agents approve in a situation reflect what important value considerations are relevant to the situation. Typical motive words classify actions according to ends which make an implicit reference to intended consequences.

It is a mistake, I believe, to make a razor sharp distinction between the moral goodness of an action and the value of the consequences of the action. To judge the rightness of an action in terms of its moral goodness, or in terms of its intended consequences, or in terms of prima facie duties, I suggest, are not three completely different processes. Perhaps we may say that the three moral terms give us three different, but complementary, definition schema of rightness. The rightness of an action may be understood in terms of the value of its consequences, or its dutifulness, or its moral goodness. I think it likely that in actual practice people make use of all three schema. None of them is wrong.

In a loose and general way, we may characterize the three schema as follows: The duty schema represents the Old Testament commandment approach; the value schema represents the Greek Eudaemonism, the happiness approach; the goodness schema represents the New Testament spirit of love approach. In this light we might say that rule utilitarianism is the teleological, happiness ap-

---

23 It may be true, as some philosophers have suggested, that all peoples recognize an injunction to love one's neighbor but that they differ in regard to who is one's neighbor and also how one is to love him. If so, these differences appear mainly to be differences in sensitivity and wisdom.

proach which validates the Old Testament commandments and recognizes the utility of love; prima facie deontology is the Old Testament approach which recognizes a duty to seek valuable consequences and also a duty to try to inculcate the spirit of love; the restricted motive theory is the spirit of love approach which validates the Old Testament commandments and recognizes the wisdom inherent in the teleological approach.

The utilitarian might want to claim that his schema is fundamental and that the other two ar at best approximations that we need to use at times in practice. He may be right. Morality for perfect and omniscient agents might indeed be only a matter of prudence.

The deontologist might claim that his schema is fundamental and that the other two merely represent two prima facie duties that we have, namely, to seek valuable consequences and to try to improve oneself. He may be right. Indeed, children are taught by this duty approach.

The motive theorist might claim that his schema is fundamental and that the other two schema are tests for wisdom and sensitivity. He may be right. "It is impossible to conceive anything at all in the world, or even out of it, which can be taken as good without qualification, except a good will."

Which is the most fundamental? It depends upon which schema one takes as one's fundamental model — happiness, rules, or the good man. I suspect that which one a person accepts depends upon how he views this creature called man.

9

Love and Principle in Christian Ethics

WILLIAM K. FRANKENA, Professor of Philosophy, University of Michigan. A.B., Calvin College; A.M., University of Michigan; Ph.D., Harvard University. Author of *Ethics;* essays in *The Philosophy of G. E. Moore* (ed. P. A. Schlipp), *The Philosophy of C. D. Broad* (ed. P. A. Schlipp), *Philosophical Analysis* (ed. Max Black), *Religion and the State University* (ed. E. A. Walter), *Essays in Moral Philosophy* (ed. A. I. Melden), *Moral Philosophy and Moral Language* (ed. G. Nakhnikian and H. N. Castaneda), *Philosophy in the Mid-Century* (ed. R. Klibansky), *Dictionary of Morals* (ed. V. Ferm); articles in *The Philosophical Review, Mind, Philosophy, The Harvard Educational Review.*

Love and Principle in Christian Ethics

BY WILLIAM K. FRANKENA

I

A PHILOSOPHER READING ABOUT IN THE LITERATURE OF CHRISTIAN ETHICS, especially if he is steeped in that of recent philosophical ethics, is bound to be struck, not only by the topics discussed and the claims made, but by the relative absence of careful definition, clear statement, or cogent and rigorous argument, as these are judged by the standards with which he is familiar in his own field (even if he does not himself always conform to them). It seems all too seldom to occur to its writers that they should seriously try to expound and defend Christian ethics in terms of what Matthew Arnold called culture — "the best which has been thought and said in the world" — and in particular in terms of the best philosophical thinking of the time. As H. D. Lewis has put it,

> Much that is peculiarly instructive has been written about these matters by notable ethical thinkers of the present day, and the progress that has been made recently in ethics is one of the most distinctive and promising features of modern thought. But religious thinkers, in the main, have been curiously indifferent to these important advances in a field closely akin to their own.[1]

Indeed, they have not only been "curiously indifferent" to the work of the philosophers; many of them take the position, at least im-

---

[1] *Morals and Revelation* (New York, 1951), p. 14. In writing this Lewis had in mind the work of the intuitionists before World War II, but the remark holds equally well if one has in mind the work of the non-intuitionists after the war.

plicitly, that any recognition of its importance would be dangerous
— a sinful concession to the intellectual pride of the natural man
or the old Adam. At any rate, they reflect the same attitude and
manner of thought and expression that were castigated by ancient
Celsus, and by Arnold after him, as "the want of intellectual seriousness of the Christians." The issues they are dealing with are all too
rarely clearly formulated or rigorously reasoned about. It may be
that the philosopher who criticizes them can also be charged with
some kind of want of intellectual seriousness, or even with spiritual
pride, but his criticism may be correct nevertheless.

This essay represents an attempt, by a philosopher who feels
that its theological proponents may be selling Christian ethics short
by their manner of expounding and defending it, to do something
toward remedying the situation. In it I shall make only a beginning,
however, hoping that others who can speak with more authority will
follow suit. I shall only try to state what seem to me to be some
of the main issues and positions in Christian ethical theory, keeping
away from practical issues of the sort that theologians have been
writing about so much (more, I admit, than philosophers have).
And I shall limit myself to issues and positions in Christian normative ethics, leaving for another occasion the problems and points of
view of Christian meta-ethics, if there is such a thing.[2] As for answers — in stating the issues and positions I shall be indicating those
that are possible, but I shall not be doing much to settle on any of
them. To do so would involve my venturing farther into theology
than I can go with anything like the kind of intellectual seriousness
which I am advocating. Anyway, one can only try to throw a
certain amount of light at any given time.

In doing what I am doing I make an assumption — that the
function of reason and philosophy for the Christian is not simply
to serve as an instrument for refuting or otherwise disposing of
gentiles, pagans, and unbelievers, but also and especially to serve as
a colleague in helping him to understand and deepen the faith that
is in him. Some may say, on reading what follows, "Why should
we bother to think in such terms as these? What is good but to do
justly, and to love mercy, and to walk humbly with thy God? And
what is pure religion and undefiled but to visit the fatherless and

---

2 By "normative ethics" I mean the endeavor to propound and defend ethical
judgments, rules, or standards; by "meta-ethics" I mean a theory about the meaning or nature of such rules and principles or about the method and possibility
of justifying them.

the widows in their affliction, and to keep oneself unspotted from the world." But the writers on Christian ethics that I have in mind can themselves hardly make this reply, for they have already ventured out beyond the fold of such simple faith and duty into the forum of rational formulation and defense. My only complaint is that they have not been as careful as they should be if they are going to venture out in this way. As for those who would decry even such venturing into the forum, I can only remind them that the same Book that says,

"We are fools for Christ's sake. . . ."
also says,
"Buy . . . also wisdom, and instruction, and understanding,"
and
". . . whatsoever things are true, whatsoever things are honest, whatsoever things are just, whatsoever things are pure, whatsoever things are lovely, whatsoever things are of good report, . . . think on these things."

II

Actually, as I have indicated, there has been a good deal of thinking on these things by Christians. But we cannot consider it all here, and, in fact, I shall limit myself to one of its main themes. Much of this thinking has been about the role of moral rules and principles in Christian ethics. The ensuing debate is especially lively in Protestant circles, but Pope Pius XII and Dietrich von Hildebrand found it necessary not long ago to admonish young Catholics to beware of a "new morality" which they call "circumstance ethics" and which seeks to eliminate general principles from Christian morality, declaring "every moral decision to be based on a unique situation and to be the result of a confrontation of the 'I' of the person with the 'I' of God."[3] No doubt the debate is also present in Jewish ethics. At the one extreme are views variously referred to as antinomian, nominalist, existentialist, situationalist, or contextualist, which hold that each moral decision about what to do is to be a direct function of faith, love, or the experience of God together with a knowledge of the facts in the case, with no ethical principles coming into the matter. At the other, apparently, is the Thomist or near-Thomist view that many, if not all, moral decisions should involve,

---

[3] See von Hildebrand, *True Morality and its Counterfeits* (New York, 1955). The quotation is from p. 135.

at least in part, an appeal to certain moral principles whose validity does not depend on faith, love, revelation, or the knowledge of God. It is with the topic of this debate that I wish to deal here, first, because it seems to me to be most unclearly dealt with by theologians, and, second, because philosophers have been discussing somewhat similar subjects with a good deal more clarity and in terms which may, it seems to me, be of some use in the debate in question.

Before we begin, however, five preliminary remarks must be made. (1) A distinction is often made by philosophers and theologians alike between moral rules and ethical principles. A rule is relatively concrete and small, like "We ought to tell the truth," a principle relatively abstract and big, like "We ought to promote the general happiness." This distinction is important in certain contexts, but may here be kept in the background. Unless otherwise specified, then, I shall use "rule" and "principle" synonymously, to mean any general judgments about what is *morally* right, wrong, obligatory, or good, whether abstract or concrete, formal or material. (2) One may speak of love or "the law of love" as a rule or principle in the sense just indicated. Indeed, some of the debate has been on precisely the question whether this way of speaking of love is proper or not. But what interests me here is not so much the question whether love or the love-command is itself a rule or principle as the question whether there are *other* rules or principles which do not mention love, what their status is, and how they are related to the ethic of love (whether this is conceived as a principle or not). (3) The term "law" we may take here as meaning a rule or principle or a set of rules or principles, except perhaps when it is used in the phrase "the law of love." (4) I shall disregard the question whether the "law of love" enjoins or excludes love of self and the question how love of neighbor is related to love of God. It will be convenient to take it simply as enjoining love. We must also leave open the question whether the love enjoined is "an emotion or affection" or "primarily an active determination of the will,"[4] trying so to express what we say that it may be true either way. The main point is that, either way, love is aimed at an object and seeks it or its good. (5) Some may take faith or commitment to God as the basic virtue or posture of Christian ethics, rather than love, but even then most of what I shall say will hold with "faith" or "commitment to God" substituted where I say "love."

---

4 See C. H. Dodd, *Gospel and Law* (London, 1951), p. 42.

III

Our subject, then, is the theological debate about the relation of love and principles in Christian (and similar religious) ethics. To deal with it we must first look at the parallel debate which I indicated was going on among philosophers. Here the issue is not love versus principle or love versus natural law. Roughly speaking, where theologians talk about love, philosophers talk about beneficence or general utility. At any rate, among the latter, the main debate in normative ethics (as vs. meta-ethics) has been between the deontologists or formalists on one side, and the teleologists on the other. The latter hold that all rights and duties, particular or general, are to be determined directly or indirectly by looking to see what is conducive to the greatest balance of good over evil, and they are ethical egoists, nationalists, or universalists (utilitarians) depending on whose good they say is to be promoted, that of the agent, that of his nation, or that of the universe as a whole. The deontologists insist that there are rights and duties, general or particular, which hold independently of any conduciveness they may have to promote a balance of good over evil for agent, nation, or universe. Among the deontologists the main issues are whether beneficence or utility is a duty at all or not, whether all moral rules of right and duty fall under justice, and whether the basic judgments of right and duty are formal or material, general or particular. Most teleologists lately have been utilitarians of one sort or another, and here there has been a particularly lively debate between the extreme or act-utilitarians and the restricted or rule-utilitarians (also in another dimension, not directly relevant here, between the hedonistic and the "ideal" utilitarians). This needs a brief explanation here.

We may, in fact, distinguish three utilitarian positions for our purposes, according to the view taken about moral rules. (1) Pure act-utilitarianism is the view which has no place whatsoever for such rules, holding that one is to tell what is one's right or duty in a particular situation simply by an appeal to the principle of utility, that is, by looking to see what action will produce or probably produce the greatest general balance of good over evil, counting all of the consequences which it itself causes or will probably cause and no others, and in particular ignoring the consequences which might be brought about if the same thing were done in similar situations (i.e., if it were made a rule to do that act in such situations). (2) Pure rule-utilitarianism holds that one is to tell what is one's right or duty in a particular situation by appeal to some set of rules like

"Keep promises," "Tell the truth," etc., and not by appeal to the principle of utility. In this respect it is like extreme deontological theories. But, as against all deontological theories, it holds that we are to determine what rules should govern our lives by an appeal to the principle of utility, i.e., by looking to see what rules are such that always acting on them is for the greatest general good. That is, we are never to ask what act will have the best consequences in a particular situation, but either what the rules call for or what rule it is most useful always to follow in that kind of a situation. And it may be obligatory to follow the rule in a particular situation even if following it is known not to have the best possible consequences in this particular case. (3) Modified act-utilitarianism would allow us to formulate rules and to use them as guides, but they would be rules which say, not that always-acting in such and such a way in such and such a kind of situation is socially more useful than always-acting on any other rule would be, but that it is always or generally for the greatest good to act in a certain way in such situations. Take

"Keeping-promises-always is for the greatest general good"

and

"Keeping promises is always for the greatest general good."

The first is the rule-utilitarian's way of formulating his rules, the second that of the modified act-utilitarian. The main difference is that the latter cannot allow that a rule may ever be followed in a particular situation when following it is known not to have the best possible consequences in this particular case.

Of course, one may combine two of these forms of utilitarianism in one way or another; one might maintain, for instance, that in particular situations we are to appeal to rules justified by their utility in certain kinds of cases and directly to the principle of utility in certain other kinds of cases. I think it will also be clear that ethical egoism may take similar forms: pure act-egoism, modified act-egoism, pure rule-egoism, etc. What concerns me now, however, is to point out that a love-ethic, which I shall call agapism, may take parallel forms. Agapism is the view which assigns to the "law of love" the same position that utilitarianism assigns to the principle of utility; it allows no *basic* ethical principles other than or independent of the "law of love." It can take any of three main forms: pure act-agapism, modified act-agapism, and pure rule-agapism. These will be described more fully in the next section.

One might ask here whether there really is any difference between the ethics of love or agapism and utilitarianism. Theologians generally assume that there is, without discussing the point very carefully. Philosophers, on the other hand, seem to assume that there is no basic difference between them — see, for example, J. S. Mill or A. C. Garnett. This is an important question, and the answer is not very obvious, not at least until one has made some distinctions, and then it seems to me the answer is yes or no depending —.[5] But we must leave it to one side here, and rest with pointing out parallels. Even if the parallels turn out to be identities, however, all that we shall be saying about them will still be true.

But Christian "schemes of morality," as ethical systems were called in the eighteenth century before the word "scheme" came to mean something nefarious, need not be wholly agapistic. Just as a philosopher may hold that some or all rights and duties are independent of utility, so a theologian may hold that some or all rights and duties are independent of the "law of love," or, in other words, that love is not enough to give us all of morality even when taken together with all relevant factual belief or knowledge (empirical or theological).[6] If he does hold this, then his position is like those of the deontologists rather than like those of the utilitarians. In fact, there would be a position for him to take parallel to each of the various deontological positions. And here again we may distinguish three pure positions: pure act-deontologism, modified act-deontologism, and pure rule-deontologism. The first will say that every moral decision is somehow to be a function of a knowledge of the particular situation without any appeal to rules or to utility. The second would allow us to use rules, but would insist that the rules are mere inductions from particular cases and so may never contravene a clear direct verdict in any such case. What Henry Sidgwick called "perceptual intuitionism" might take either of these forms. Pure rule-deontologism would assert that we are always to tell what is right or wrong wholly by appeal to a set of rules or principles, insisting, of course, that these rules and principles are not mere problematic inductions, and that their validity does not depend on their utility. Both what Sidgwick called "dogmatic intuitionism" and what he called "philosophical intuitionism" would be forms of this view, differing only in the number and abstractness of the rules or principles regarded as basic. Again, of course, one might combine

---

5 There is, for instance, the question of the relation of the love of God to the love of neighbor and mankind (or to the promotion of the general welfare) .

6 When I say a theologian may hold a certain position, I mean that it is logically open to him, not that he can hold it and be orthodox.

two of these forms of deontologism; one might, for example, combine perceptual and dogmatic intuitionism as Sir David Ross does. These are all pure forms of deontologism, and, apart from questions of orthodoxy, positions of all these sorts are open to the theologian who is not being an agapist. If, however, one regards the principle of utility as one of the principles to be used in making moral decisions, though not the only basic one, then one is still a deontologist (not a teleologist) but an impure one. Similarly, if a theologian regards the "law of love" as one of the principles to be used, but not as the only basic one, then he is holding an impure or mixed view, only it will be more convenient in this case to call it an impure form of agapism or mixed agapism.

IV

Now, against this background and using my fragmentary knowledge of the literature of Judeo-Christian ethics, I can try to characterize various possible views about the place of principles and their relation to love — various "schemes" of Christian or religious ethics — and do something to relate them to positions actually taken in the literature. In fact, the following outline of positions will be my main contribution to the discussion I am trying to help along. For my conviction is that theologians would be much clearer and much more cogent if they were to state their issues and positions in such terms as these, and then make evident precisely why we should accept their answers. It may be that the Christian ethical thinker cannot be wholly content with the terms, methods, or conclusions of the mere "moral philosopher," as G. F. Thomas and many others before him have urged; but, even so, one may perhaps insist that his thinking ought at least to meet the standards which such a moral philosopher, at his best, sets himself.

It should be pointed out here that, whichever of the following schemes of morality a Christian thinker adopts (if any), there will be a question about just what he is claiming for it. (1) He might be claiming only that said scheme is *the* proper form for Christian or Judeo-Christian ethics to take, or at least that it is *a* proper form for it to take. (2) He may also be claiming, as H. Rashdall does in *Conscience and Christ*, that the Christian normative ethics, as he conceives it, is a satisfactory one in the eyes of the most enlightened moral consciousness and so is tenable by modern man. But if he makes only these claims, he may still be allowing that there are other valid schemes of morality (even of Christian morality) or part-schemes of morality, such as St. Paul seems to ascribe to the Gentiles. Hence a Christian may and often seems to make a stronger claim, namely, (3) that the normative ethics he subscribes to, or something very close to it, is the only adequate and tenable scheme of morality there is. This claim would be harder to defend, but theologians have been known to rush in where angels (not to mention philosophers) would be wary of treading. However this may be, let us get on with our outline. I merely wanted to point out that different claims may be made for the scheme adopted — and to add that theologians do not always make clear just what claim they are making or on what grounds they are making it, just as they do not always make clear precisely what the scheme is that they are adopting in the first place.

The first group of positions I shall call *pure agapism*. They all hold that the "law of love" is the sole basis of morality — that on it hang "the whole law and the prophets," i.e., that the rest of the moral law can and must be derived from love together with relevant non-ethical beliefs and knowledge, empirical, metaphysical, or theological. In Bertrand Russell's words, pure agapism holds that "the [morally] good life is a life inspired by love and guided by knowledge."[7] Its most extreme form is *pure act-agapism*. This admits no rules or principles other than the "law of love" itself, and it also does not allow that there are any "perceptual intuitions" about what is right or wrong in particular situations independently of the dictates of love. It insists that one is to discover or decide what one's right or duty in a particular situation is solely by confronting one's loving will with the facts about that situation, whether one is an individual or a group. Facts about other situations and ethical conclusions arrived at in other situations are, for this extreme view, simply irrelevant, if not misleading. It adopts with complete literalness, as the whole story, St. Augustine's dictum, "Love, and do as you please." Here belong at least the more drastic of the views sometimes referred to as anti-nomian, nominalist, existentialist, situationalist, simplistic, or contextualist. Thomas ascribes such a view to Emil Brunner, if I understand him, though he correctly points out that Brunner sometimes seems to hold one of the views to be described later.[8] Paul Ramsey, like Thomas and von Hildebrand, has been attacking

---

7 *What I Believe* (London, 1925), Ch. II.
8 G. F. Thomas, *Christian Ethics and Moral Philosophy* (New York, 1955), pp. 381-388.

such theories lately, but in *Basic Christian Ethics* he appeared to come very close to agreeing with them.

The other forms of pure agapism all take rules or principles to be necessary or at least helpful in guiding the loving Christian individual (or group) in the determination of his (its) rights and duties in particular cases. But, being forms of pure agapism, they regard all such rules or principles as somehow derivative from love. First of these forms is *modified act-agapism* or "summary rule" agapism.[9] This admits rules but regards them as summaries of past experience, useful, perhaps almost indispensable, but only as rules of thumb. It cannot allow that a rule may ever be followed in a situation when it is seen to conflict with what love dictates in that situation. For, if rules are to be followed only in so far as they are helpful as aids to love, they cannot constrain or constrict love in any way. But they may and perhaps should be used. I am not sure I know of any good cases of this modified act-agapism, but perhaps some of the so-called contextualists or "circumstance" moralists belong here; some of them at any rate do mention rules or principles on occasion without making clear just how they conceive of them, e.g., J. Sittler in *The Structure of Christian Ethics*.[10]

Pure rule-agapism is analogous to pure rule-utilitarianism; it maintains that we are always to tell what we are to do in particular situations by referring to a set of rules, and that what rules are to prevail and be followed is to be determined by seeing what rules (not what acts) best or most fully embody love. For modified act-agapism the proper way to state a rule is to say, for example,

"Keeping promises is always love-fulfilling."
For pure rule-agapism one must say, rather,

"Keeping-promises-always is love-fulfilling."
The difference is that on the latter view we may and sometimes must obey a rule in a particular situation even though the action it calls for is seen not to be what love itself would directly require. For

---

[9] Here and in connection with this entire section, see J. Rawls, "Two Concepts of Rules," *Philosophical Review*, 64 (1955), 3-32; J. D. Mabbott, "Moral Rules," *Proceedings of the British Academy*, XXXIX (1953), 97-118; J. J. C. Smart, "Extreme and Restricted Utilitarianism," *Philosophical Quarterly*, 6 (1956) ; R. B. Brandt, *Ethical Theory* (New York, 1959), Ch. 15.

[10] Baton Rouge, 1958. What Sittler means by "structure" here is hard to make out; as he represents it, Christian ethics has almost none. But he is both for and against principles, and this may mean that he is trying to be a modified act-agapist (or perhaps act-fideist, since he stresses faith rather than love). On the other hand, he may be trying, confusedly, to state one of the forms of rule agapism or even mixed agapism yet to be described.

pure rule-agapism, in other words, the rules may in a sense constrict the direct expression of love. For if love is, in fact, constrained to fulfill itself through acting according to rules, as Ramsey puts it in his more recent writings,[11] love must be "in-principled," or, as philosophers would now say, it must be "rule-governed."

If we ask here why love is thus constrained to express itself through rules or principles rather than by doing in each case the act which is most loving in that case,[12] the rule-agapist may answer in three apparently different ways which are usually not distinguished. (1) He may argue that love is constrained to cloak itself in principles, not by anything outside of itself, but by its own nature or "inner dialectic," as some might prefer to say. This is not an easy view to get clear — I am not even sure it can be made out — but it is suggested by 1 John 3:17,

> But whoso hath this world's good, and seeth his brother have need, and shutteth up his bowels of compassion from him, how dwelleth the love of God in him?

This suggests that it follows from the very nature of love that the rich should help the poor, and one might argue that all the rules of Christian morality can be derived from the nature of love in this direct way. Rashdall seems to try to follow this course in deducing the "corollaries and consequences" of the law of love: love to enemies, forgiveness, self-sacrifice, purity, repentance, etc.[13] In a somewhat similar way J. S. Mill reasoned (mistakenly, I think) that justice and equality are entailed by the principle of utility as such; a theologian might claim the same for love, possibly with more justice.[14]

(2) The second possibility is to claim, not that the rules are somehow contained in the very nature of love, but that love must act through rules because the world is so constituted that it can fulfill itself or attain its object more fully if it conforms its actions to rules than if it does not. On this view love is constrained to adopt rules, not by its own nature alone, but by its nature together with the facts about the world in which it is seeking to fulfill itself or reach its object. In a similar way a rule-utilitarian might contend that, although no rules are contained in the principle of utility, rules must be followed if the greatest general good is to be achieved, which

---

11 See *War and the Christian Conscience* (New York, 1961), p. 14.
12 A parallel question may be asked in the case of rule-utilitarianism.
13 *Op. cit.*, pp. 119-133.
14 *Utilitarianism*, near the end.

rules to follow being determined by a consideration of the relative utility of certain rules as against others.

(3) On the third view, the fact that love must adopt rules is due neither to its own nature nor to the nature of the world, but to the nature of reason or of morality. The argument would be that if love is to be the matrix of the *moral* life, then it must follow maxims which it wills to be universally acted on (i.e., embody itself in a set of "universal laws"), since this is a necessary condition of rationality, or of morality, or of both. The affinities of such a position with Kant's is obvious, for both insist that reason and morality require rules which are willed to be universal laws; the difference is in the method of determining which rules make up the moral law — for Kant the method is to see what rules we can will to be universal laws independently of whatever motives or ends we may have, but for the present view it is to see what rules we can or must will to be universal laws when our motivation is *love*. That it is to be rule-governed is required if it is to take the form of reason or morality, but what the rules shall be is still for it to say. They will still be determined as in (1) or (2).

Of these three views the third is suggested, to my mind at least, by some passages in Reinhold Niebuhr,[15] but, in general, they have not been distinguished by the more rule-agapistically minded writers. Presumably what Ramsey calls "in-principled love-ethics" falls under one of them, but I have not been able to tell which. I do not have labels for these three forms of rule-agapism. Enough is enough, and I am doing enough labelling here as it is. What matters is that the three views should not be confused by either friend or foe. I should point out, however, that it is only the second that is strictly analogous to what is usually called rule-utilitarianism, though rule-utilitarianism could also take forms analogous to (1) and (3).

The remaining forms of pure agapism are *combinations* of act-agapism and rule-agapism. Here would fall, for instance, the view that, while we may and should appeal to rules when we can in deciding what should be done in a particular case, as the rule-agapist holds, we may and should appeal to the "law of love" directly in cases for which there are no rules or in which the rules conflict, just as the act-agapist does. Such combinations may, in fact, be more plausible than either pure act-agapism or pure rule-agapism by themselves.

---

15 Especially, *An Interpretation of Christian Ethics* (New York, 1935), Ch. VII; *Moral Man and Immoral Society* (New York, 1932), Ch. II.

V

We may now look at what I shall call *pure non-agapistic theories*. These hold that *all* of the basic judgments of morality proper, whether these are particular or general, are independent of any "law of love" — that any such law of love, if it is valid at all, is neither necessary nor helpful in morality, and, in fact, does not belong to morality at all. These views are analogous to (or identical with) the forms of pure deontologism described in III, which do not recognize any moral obligation to be beneficent or to follow the principle of utility. There will be a purely non-agapistic theory corresponding to each of the purely deontological theories mentioned there. Speaking roughly, they all identify morality with justice and regard justice as determinable independently of either the principle of utility or the "law of love." It might seem that no such scheme of morality can be accepted by a Christian, since these schemes all regard the entire substance of morality as coming from some source other than love. But even Christians have "sought out many inventions," and there are at least two types of pure non-agapism which are approximated by what some of them have invented. One is a view which agrees that "love is the fulfilment of the [moral] law," but holds that the whole content of the law is discernible independently of love. In effect, it takes acting in accordance with an independently ascertainable moral code as the criterion or perhaps even as the definition of what love is. Thus it is only verbally and not in any substantive way agapistic.[16] It may therefore turn out to be a wolf in sheep's clothing, but at least some intuitionistic moralists of the past, Samuel Clarke, for example, have meant to be Christians while holding a view which can be described in some such terms as these. The other purely non-agapistic conception of morality to be mentioned here has a rather different character. It involves making a distinction between the moral life or "mere morality" and the religious way of life, adding that morality is to be conceived in a non-agapistic way, and then proposing that it should be supplanted by the religious way of life, this being conceived as a life of love and as transcending "mere morality." Like Nietzsche it goes "beyond good and evil" in the moral sense; unlike him it does so in the interest of religion. Its drift is agapistic, since it advocates a life of love (and its agapism may take any of the forms described

---

[16] One who holds this view may also be an agapist in the sense of holding that the *motive* for fulfilling the moral law is or should be love.

in IV), but its conception of morality is not. Something of this sort is suggested in different ways by at least some passages in Kierkegaard and Brunner.[17]

Very similar in substance is the *"two morality" theory* variously intimated or proposed by Henri Bergson, Lord Lindsay, and Eliseo Vivas. According to it there are two independent moralities, one the morality of love, the other that of social pressure, one's station and its duties, claims and counter-claims, or what have you. Each is complete and valid in its fashion, but the first is superior to and should supplant the second. This view thus combines a purely agapistic conception of one morality with a purely non-agapistic conception of the other. And, of course, it may conceive the former in any of the ways described in IV and the latter after the fashion of any of the forms of pure deontologism distinguished in III. Yet it is in a sense still a form of agapism since it proposes to replace the non-agapistic morality, where feasible, with that of love. Its ideal is the ethics of love. The only difference between it and the previous theory is that it speaks of two moralities where that theory speaks of two ways of life but calls one of them morality and the other religion.

VI

There are also, as I indicated earlier, mixed theories which I shall call *impure or mixed agapisms*. They are combinations of agapism and non-agapism but not along the lines of the "two morality" theory. For them there is only one morality by which we are to live but it has two parts. One of its parts is the "law of love," the other consists of judgments about right and wrong which are independent of the "law of love," judgments which may be either general (rules) or particular. It should be noted here that saying these judgments are independent of the "law of love" means only that they are not derivative from the "law of love" in any such way as agapists think they are (see IV); it does not mean that they are knowable apart from revelation, grace, or religion. Confusion here is easy and frequent, but the two points are distinct. The "law of love" may or may not be revealed, and the alleged independent ethical insights also may or may not be revealed. Whether they are or not is a question, not of normative ethics, but of meta-ethics or, if you will, of the epistemology of ethics.

---

17 See, e.g., Kierkegaard's *Three Stages on Life's Way;* Brunner as quoted by H. D. Lewis, *op. cit.,* p. 18. On Brunner see also N. H. G. Robinson, *Christ and Conscience* (New York, 1956), pp. 72ff.

Impure agapism is analogous to Ross' impure deontological theory. Ross holds that the principle of utility (non-hedonistically conceived) is one of the valid principles of ethics, but that there are others also whose validity is independent of the principle of utility. Substitute the law of love for the principle of utility here and you get impure or mixed agapism. But Sir David also holds (1) that the principle of utility and the other principles may conflict on occasion, (2) that in that case the former does not always take precedence over the others, and (3) that, partly for this reason, both are necessary for the guidance of our actions. Similarly, an impure agapist might take the position (1) that the "law of love" and the other principles of ethics may conflict, (2) that in such cases the former does not always take precedence, and (3) that, partly for this reason, both the "law of love" and the independent principles are necessary.[18] But he need not accept such an impure form of impure agapism. He may deny that the other principles can conflict with the law of love; or he may agree that they do conflict with it on occasion but contend that then it always takes precedence over them. In either case he would be maintaining that the other principles, while valid, are not necessary for the guidance of our conduct, though they may be helpful. Or he may argue that they are not even helpful — except to those who do not know the "law of love." If he takes any of these three lines, he remains pretty much an agapist in effect though not in strict theory. But he may — and some theologians do — go even farther. While admitting that there *are* ethical insights which are independent of the law of love, he may contend that, though they leave natural man "without excuse," they are so far from being helpful as to be positively misleading — that they are unclear, inaccurate, incomplete, corrupted, etc., and hence not standards of any "true virtue" at all and so not to be relied on by anyone who knows the law of love. For him then the ethics to work by is even more imperatively that of love, at least for those to whom it is available.

There are other, rather different, possible theories for which it is hard to find a label, but which must be mentioned because theologians do sometimes seem to subscribe to them. In all of the above theories, if the law of love is recognized at all (in a non-verbal way), it is regarded as a *basic* norm. But it is not necessary so to regard it if one recognizes it; one may consider it to be derived from some

18 See *The Right and the Good* (London, 1930). Ross is an intuitionist, but one need not take an intuitionist view of "independent principles."

other more basic principle which is in itself non-agapistic. Some thinkers, among them some theologians, take as the ultimate norm of our conduct the requirement of realizing ourselves, completing our natures, or fulfilling our beings, and then argue that the (or at least *a*) way to do this is through love. A. C. Garnett reasons thus in his little book *Can Ideals and Norms Be Justified?*

> . . . this discussion . . . has shown that utilitarianism (in its non-hedonistic form) [which he identifies with Christian agapism] has correctly pointed to the *end* at which ethically right conduct must aim, while the self-realization theory has correctly stated the *ground* or *reason* why conduct aiming at that end is ethically required.[19]

Similar lines of thought may be found in Tillich and in both Niebuhrs, though less clearly and explicitly expressed.[20] Here the ideal of love is derived in one way or another from what is basically a form of ethical egoism. But the outcome may still be a working agapism, depending on whether or not love is taken to be the only avenue to self-realization or fulfilment of being. If it is, then, of course, the resulting *derived pure agapism* may take any of the forms described in IV. If it is not, the outcome will be some kind of *derived impure agapism*.

There are, however, other schemes of morality in which the "law of love" is derivative and not basic. Suppose we hold, as some religious people do, that we have one and only one basic duty, namely, to obey God's commands. Then we might well go on to argue that God has summed up His will in the command to love, and thus again come out with a working agapism to live by (which again can take any of the forms described in IV). This line of thought appears in Reinhold Niebuhr's characterization of the ethics of Jesus. It is, he says, "oriented by only one vertical religious reference, to the will of God; and the will of God is defined in terms of all-inclusive love."[21] Here, too, agapism is deduced from a principle which in itself is non-agapistic. We might also, however, reason in one of the following ways, both familiar to Christians:

(a) We ought to imitate God ("Be ye perfect as I am perfect").
God loves us.
Therefore we ought to love one another.

[19] Pp. 91-92.
[20] See Tillich, *Love, Power, and Justice* (New York, 1954), pp. 76-77; Reinhold Niebuhr, *The Nature and Destiny of Man* (New York, 1941), Vol. I, Ch. X; H. R. Niebuhr, "The Center of Value," in *Moral Principles of Action*, edited by R. Anshen (New York, 1952).
[21] *An Interpretation of Christian Ethics*, p. 51.

(b) We ought to be grateful to our benefactors.
God has sent His Son into the world to save us, etc.
Therefore we ought to love Him.

If I remember correctly, Niebuhr suggests both of these lines of thought too.[22] In all such patterns of reasoning, however, the law of love is derivative from some principle which is independent of and basic to it. Whether the result is a working agapism or not depends again on whether one holds that there are other duties coordinate with or more basic than love (besides the one stated in the first premise). If one does not, one is a derived agapist of one of the kinds described in IV; if one does, one is some kind of a mixed agapist.

VII

Well, there in all its, I fear, boring but, I hope, clarifying detail is my outline of possible schemes of Christian ethics considered as bearing on the debate about love and principle. I am sure, to parody one of my favorite texts again, that some will say at this point, "God made man upright, but Frankena has sought out many inventions." Even so, I have no doubt missed some possibilities. No doubt also, in my quest for philosophical clarity, I have blurred some theological refinements and subtleties. Nevertheless, I do think that it would help greatly if theologians and religious thinkers were to use some such table of views as I have sketched, and some such terms as I have employed, in stating their issues, their positions, and their arguments for their positions — all without trying to preach to us at the same time (though there is a time for that too). Throughout, in the interest of relevance, I have sought to relate the positions described to positions actually taken or suggested in the literature, and now, before going on, I should like to add a little along this line. I have mentioned Ramsey, but am not clear just what his position is. It seems to be a form of pure agapism — or possibly of derived agapism — but it is not clear just what kind of pure agapism it is, and it may even be a kind of impure or mixed agapism. G. F. Thomas' position too is not entirely clear. In arguing against Brunner he is certainly rejecting act-agapism, but whether he is a pure rule-agapist or a mixed agapist of some sort I cannot tell for sure. It depends on what he means when he talks about "principles derived from an analysis of the various kinds of human needs and relationships and

22 For (a) see *ibid.*, pp. 46, 49.

the best methods of dealing with them"[23] and whether he takes the principle of love as one of the premises needed in deriving them. The position of St. Thomas, with its emphasis on natural law, is, on the other hand, pretty clearly what I have called a mixed theory, though it may involve a rule-utilitarian conception of "human law." Brunner's position I have referred to in one or two connections. It seems to me quite ambiguous; sometimes it looks like a form of act-agapism, but at others like a form of mixed agapism or even like a species of non-agapism. As for Reinhold Niebuhr, he appears to me to suggest, in one place or another, almost every one of the positions I have described; whether this spells richness or confusion of mind I shall leave for others to judge. As for me and my house, the most plausible position seems to me to be a certain kind of mixed theory — roughly, one which takes as basic in ethics (1) the "law of love" and (2) the "principles of justice" conceived as independently arrived at.

Here I must also notice the position of A. C. Garnett, one of the few philosophers who have taken part in the debate which is our topic. In the last chapter of *Religion and the Moral Life* he contends that Jesus did not conceive the agapistic point of view in ethics as "devoid of principles," for (1) He built "the principles of universality and impartiality" into the injunction to love — the former by interpreting "neighbor" to include enemies, and the latter by specifying that one is to love each neighbor *as oneself*. Garnett also argues (2) that Jesus "implies a place for principles of secondary generality," viz., "the moral laws that 'hang upon' the law of love" or which spell out "the implications of the law of love for certain specific human relations." Now, in our terms, which position is it that Garnett is thus ascribing to Jesus and accepting for himself? So far as (1) is concerned, it looks like a pure rule-agapism of the first sort distinguished in IV, for the two principles involved are represented as being contained in the injunction to love itself. And this does seem to be true for the principle of universality. But what about the principle of impartiality or justice? It is not clear whether it is being thought of as analytically entailed by the bare command to love our neighbors or as being added as a qualification of that command. It seems to me it must be the latter, and, in that case, the injunction to love really is equivalent to "Thou shalt love all men and thou shalt do so justly." And, then, it seems to me, the position is a form of impure or mixed agapism of the sort I myself

---

[23] *Op. cit.*, p. 387.

have just proposed. As for (2) — here, so far as "principles of secondary generality" go, the position seems to be a rule-agapism of the second kind described in IV, though it may still be simply a modified act-agapism. Incidentally, Garnett's proposed view shows, in any case, that one may hold one kind of theory for some ethical principles and another kind of theory for others — a point I did not make clear before.

I should also like to take this occasion to say a little about two well-known and relevant dicta of Christian and other religious moralists. The first is, "Love is the *fulfillment* of the law." I cannot try here to interpret St. John and St. Paul, both of whom use this formula. I wish, however, to point out that the formula can be interpreted in various ways, and may be accepted by all or almost all of the above views, even by non-agapistic ones. Thus, (1) the dictum may be taken to say that the moral law is simply to love, that the content of the moral law is wholly given by love. Agapists, pure or derived, accept it in this sense. (2) The dictum may also be understood as saying that the moral law is incomplete without the "law of love," that this law is necessary to make the moral standard complete. Impure, pure, and derived agapists may all understand it in this sense, though each will do so in his own way. (3) Again, the dictum may be conceived as meaning that loving is *formally* (in Descartes' sense) equivalent to fulfilling the law, i.e., not that the criterion of fulfilling the moral law is loving (agapism) but that the criterion or definition of loving is fulfilling the law. This view, which was introduced earlier, presupposes that the content of the moral law consists of principles and particular judgments which are arrived at independently of love, though not necessarily independently of Scripture or of special revelation. Only a non-agapist can interpret the formula in this sense. (4) But one may also interpret the formula as meaning that love or loving *eminently* (again in Descartes' sense) fulfills the law — that if one loves one fulfills the law and more, one does not fulfill it literally, one fulfills it or overfulfills it but at a higher level and in a different mode. Here again the content of the law itself is independent of the requirement to love, and a non-agapist therefore can accept the dictum in this sense, while an agapist cannot. But it is also implied that one may live by love alone and need not literally (formally) live by the law. In this sense this interpretation yields a working agapism; in fact, this interpretation yields the view, mentioned before, that there are two ways of life, the moral and the religious, the latter being the better in some way. It adds only that following the latter also "fulfills" the former. (5) Our first dictum may, however, also be construed as saying that love is to the law as Jesus Christ is to John the Baptist, as is suggested by Jesus' words, "I am not come to destroy [the law] but to fulfill [it]." But this is neither clear nor unambiguous. One might say this and hold that love is to *supplant* the law. Or one might say it and hold only that love fulfills the law in the sense of completing it [i.e., in sense (2)], or that it fulfills the law eminently in the sense just explained.

The second dictum I wish to say something about is, "Love is the *spirit* of the law." This is also vague and ambiguous, though in a different way. (1) It may mean that love is the motive with which one should obey the law. This does not make love the source of the content of the moral law, and hence non-agapists and mixed agapists can agree that love is the spirit of the law in this sense. (2) It may mean, however, that the rest of the moral law is or may be derived from the "law of love" and corrected in the light of it. In this sense it will, of course, be accepted by agapists (except perhaps derived agapists). If all that is claimed is only that "the whole law and the prophets" *can* be derived from the "law of love," then even mixed or non-agapists may agree (for them it may still be that some or all of "the law and the prophets" can also be independently derived). (3) Or it may mean that love fulfills the law eminently in the manner explained a moment ago. (4) Finally, it may mean that love is not a principle which can serve as a major premise for deriving the rest of morality, but a spirit of approaching questions about what to do which also somehow helps us to answer them though it cannot be encapsuled in any verbal formula — i.e., it is a conative and directive attitude or disposition. As indicated at the beginning, I have tried to avoid the issue about whether love is a principle or an attitude. I believe that with the proper distinctions, it can be both. All that needs to be said here, however, is that one can agree that love is the spirit of morality in this fourth sense on any of the views described above.

VIII

The end cometh, but it is not even yet. For we must still look, at least briefly, at the question how one is to decide which of the above schemes of Christian morality is the correct or most tenable one. How or by what method is the Christian thinker to tell whether he must admit principles in addition to love, how is he to conceive these principles, and which principles is he to admit, if any? By what means is the debate we have taken as our topic to be settled? This methodological matter the theologians have also been none too clear about, perhaps in part because they have not been very clear about the issues and possible positions involved. We must, therefore, consider it before we can close.

There are at least two questions here: (1) whether or not there are any ethical rules or principles (or any particular ethical judgments, for that matter) which do not merely repeat the "law of love" and which are authoritative, necessary, or helpful, (2) whether these ethical rules or principles (or particular judgments) are ascertainable independently of the "law of love" or not, and, in either case how they may be or are to be ascertained. In dealing with the first question, we must note that it is important to be clear just what one is claiming about the rules or principles (or particular judgments) in question. For they may be helpful without being necessary, and they may be authoritative or valid without being either necessary or helpful. But, whatever is being claimed, one method of settling the question at once suggests itself to the Christian thinker, namely, a direct appeal to Scripture, especially the teachings of Jesus and the Apostles. Thus Lindsay Dewar argues directly from the New Testament that Jesus did in fact "legislate certain rules or principles."[24] This sort of appeal seems to me to show only that there are some rules and principles other than the "law of love" (though perhaps not independent of it) which are authoritative or valid, not that they are necessary or helpful, unless it is assumed that Jesus would not have legislated them if they were not necessary or at least helpful (and the Bible does not tell us *this*). Indeed, it seems to me that such appeals do show, to the extent that they show said principles to be authoritative, that a Christian cannot be satisfied with pure act-agapism as a normative *theory* — in practice, however, unless the principles in question are necessary or at least helpful as well as authoritative, he may still proceed as a pure act-agapist would. But this seems to me the most that an appeal to revelation can show; in principle it can establish anything for a Christian, of course, but in fact it establishes only what is actually revealed, and Scripture does not actually tell us that the disputed rules or prin-

---

[24] See *A Short Introduction to Moral Theology* (London, 1956), Ch. I. Dewar does not go on to show just how they are related to the "law of love," but he seems to be holding a mixed theory, for he speaks of "natural law" as well as "divine law." C. H. Dodd in *Gospel and Law* also appeals directly to revelation to show that Christian ethics includes certain "ethical precepts."

ciples are necessary or helpful as well as authoritative (and this it tells only to one who accepts it as a divine revelation). To show (or refute) this, therefore, one must resort to "moral philosophy," for example, to a logico-empirical argument calculated to prove (or disprove) that the bare injunction to love, even taken together with relevant factual knowledge about particular situations, is insufficient to give us adequate guidance of a moral kind.

In connection with the second question, we must first observe that whether the alleged ethical rules and judgments are independent of the "law of love" or not, there are various possible alternative theories about how they may or are to be ascertained. If they are not independent of the "law of love," we must still try to decide between modified act-agapism and the various forms of rule-agapism; if they are independent we still have to decide between various possible kinds of mixed agapisms and non-agapisms — and here all sorts of theories are possible: natural law theories, intuitionism, revelationism, social approval theories, etc. In effect, the second question is how to decide between the various normative theories described above. And, again, a Christian theologian may seek to do so by appeal to Scripture; if Scripture were full enough in what it says, this would for him be decisive. But the texts are not full enough in a philosophical sense; some point one way, some another. Perhaps the most crucial is Romans 2:14-15, in which St. Paul says that the Gentiles, who presumably do not have the "law of love," yet have a moral law "written in their hearts." This appears to show that there is moral insight which is independent both of special revelation and the "law of love" — and so to establish the correctness of some kind of mixed or non-agapistic theory. Yet even this passage is hardly explicit and elaborate enough to settle such a theoretical point, and the same is still more true of all the other texts — they are not theoretical enough in their message to help the Christian to decide with any conclusiveness between the rival theories open to him, except perhaps to rule out pure agapism (*if* they can be claimed to do even this). Here again the theologian must resort to "moral philosophy" as well as to revelation, if he means to try to settle such points of theory at all on anything like intellectually sufficient grounds, as he seems to.[25]

If, however, the theologian does resort to moral philosophy, how is he to decide between rival normative schemes? Unfortunately,

---

25 I am not arguing here that moral philosophy is "omnicompetent" or even "sufficient."

contemporary moral philosophers are no more in agreement on this point than the theologians are. But I believe that at their best at any rate, they debate about it more clearly and more rigorously than theologians ever do, perhaps in part because they are not tempted to preach or to fall back on any scriptural or ecclesiastical revelation. In any case, the thinking theologian has no alternative but to become more adequately acquainted with "the best that has been thought and said in the world" of moral philosophy and then try to draw his own conclusions. In particular, he must make himself at home in the most rarified reaches of recent meta-ethical discussion, for his problem is not merely one within normative ethics; it includes the question how one scheme of normative ethics can be justified as against another, or if it can be justified at all. At this level I think theologians and Christian moralists have been much too unclear and much too unrigorous in their thinking. They almost invariably maintain that morality depends on religion or theology but they are rarely, if ever, very careful in their formulation of this claim or in their arguments in support of it. I myself doubt that it can be established, except perhaps in some greatly and carefully qualified sense, and believe that there are at least some "principles of justice" which are logically independent of the "law of love," of revelation, and of religion and theology. But that is another story which cannot be told now.[26]

It may be objected here that Jesus had no meta-ethics and hence that we need none. And it is, no doubt, true that the ethics of Jesus, and even of the Bible as a whole, is compatible with a variety of meta-ethical theories; the history of Judeo-Christian thought seems to show this. But, as I said at the outset, I am assuming that the theologians I have had in mind are right in feeling impelled to "think on [all] these things." If this is a mistake — and it too is a point which Christians have debated — then the mistake is as much theirs as mine.

[26] For parts of the story see my "Public Education and the Good Life," *Harvard Educational Review,* Fall Issue, 1961.